D0078255

153   Fab
FAB   D. TE DUE

Culture and
     consciousness

26852

2/86 $31.30

DATE			

® THE BAKER & TAYLOR CO.

CULTURE AND CONSCIOUSNESS

DISCARDED

CULTURE AND CONSCIOUSNESS
The Social Meaning of Altered Awareness

Faber, M. D. (Mel D.)
Culture and consciousness : the social mean-
ing of altered awareness
BF175 .F1515

RSN=00002045

M. D. Faber, Ph.D.
University of Victoria, British Columbia

26852

MID-PLAINS COMMUNITY COLLEGE
LEARNING RESOURCE CENTER

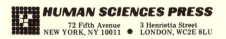

HUMAN SCIENCES PRESS
72 Fifth Avenue   3 Henrietta Street
NEW YORK, NY 10011 ● LONDON, WC2E 8LU

Copyright © 1981 by Human Sciences Press, Inc.
72 Fifth Avenue, New York, New York 10011

All rights reserved. No part of this work may be reproduced or utilized in any form or by any means, electronic or mechanical, including photocopying, microfilm and recording, or by any information storage and retrieval system without permission in writing from the publisher.

Printed in the United States of America
123456789   987654321

Library of Congress Cataloging in Publication Data
Faber, Mel D.
  Culture and consciousness.

  Includes bibliographical references and index.
  1. Psychoanalysis—Social aspects. 2. Awareness—Social aspects. I. Title.
BF175.F1515   153   LC 80–36683
ISBN 0–87705–505–X

For Elizabeth

Our two soules therefore, which are one,
Though I must goe, endure not yet
A breach, but an expansion,
Like gold to ayery thinnesse beate.

The psychologists who practise the description of phenomena are not normally aware of the philosophical implications of their method. They do not see that the return to perceptual experience, insofar as it is a consequential and radical reform, puts out of court all forms of realism, that is to say, all philosophies which leave consciousness and take as their datum one of its results—that the real sin of intellectualism lies precisely in having taken as its datum the determinate universe of science, that this reproach applies *a fortiori* to psychological thinking, since it places perceptual consciousness in the midst of a ready–made world. . . . A psychology is always brought face to face with the problem of the constitution of the world.

M. Merleau–Ponty,
The Phenomenology of Perception

CONTENTS

ACKNOWLEDGEMENTS

My ideas have been influenced by a number of individuals with whom I have enjoyed personal and intellectual interaction over the years: Dr. Kenneth Brown, University of Manchester; Dr. Robert Rogers, State University of New York, Buffalo; Drs. Leonard F. Manheim and Melvin Goldstein, University of Hartford; Dr. Horst Ruthrof, Murdoch University, Perth; Dr. Edwin S. Shneidman, University of California, Los Angeles; and Dr. Marie C. Nelson of *The Psychoanalytic Review,* New York. They, in addition to the thinkers with whom this book deals at length, Freud, Roheim, N. O. Brown, Herbert Marcuse, Gregory Bateson, and Ernest Becker, have helped me to sharpen and clarify my thoughts on psychological and philosophical matters.

Certain concepts developed in the first section of Part Two of this book were originally expressed in *Hartford Studies in Literature*. I want to thank the editors, Drs. Leonard F. Manheim and Melvin Goldstein for allowing me to draw on those concepts here. Again, certain paragraphs in the second section of Part Three were developed from material that originally appeared in the *Psychocultural Review*. I want to thank Dr. Roy Huss, and Mr. Stanley

Wolf of the Redgrave Publishing Co., for permission to use these materials.

The actual production of my manuscript was aided by the excellent secretarial work of Mrs. Jacqueline R. Crouch of the English Department of the University of Victoria, Victoria, British Columbia, Canada.

As for my children, Paul Faber, Ethan Faber, and Rebecca Faber, I offer thanks to them for constant support and inspiration. I am also indebted in many, many ways to my father, Paul A. Faber, and to the memory of my mother, Betty L. Faber. To the woman to whom this book is dedicated, Elizabeth Faber, my gratitude for endless concern and for considerable intellectual assistance.

MDF
Victoria, British Columbia,
January 1980.

PREFACE

My purpose in writing this book can be described as follows: I want to demonstrate the degree to which our ordinary, everyday awareness (to use William James' famous phrase) determines in a vital, even radical manner not only the nature and quality of our individual lives, but the nature and quality of our social institutions, including our economic, "capitalistic" ones. My psychoanalytic orientation, grounded firmly in the theory of object relations, shifts the critique of consciousness and society from the emotive to the perceptual sphere. Lest that dichotomy mislead anyone, however, I hasten to add that perceptual issues are in my analysis tied inextricably to emotive events. It is my thesis, in fact, that the way in which we perceive the world determines crucially the way in which we feel about it, and in it. Repression, the cornerstone of psychoanalysis, is ultimately a matter of what we refuse to admit to our "perceptual apparatus" as a whole. The devastations of repression are finally registered in the sorry human organism's partial, limited response to the perceptual challenges of life, the very wonder of being here, perceiving the world in the fullest mental and bodily sense.

But this is only one side of the problem. My examination of ordinary awareness, its defensive importance, its repressive significance, leads me to explore the nature of "the mystical" along psychoanalytic lines which have not been clearly laid down hitherto. Once again with my observations grounded in the theory of object relations, I strive to demonstrate the extent to which the alteration of awareness, achieved through an explicit, scientific methodology, offers a therapeutic instrument with revolutionary potentiality for social and individual change.

It is often suggested, of course, that if we, as a species, are to experience genuine contentment and well being, or even to survive, we must undergo a substantial modification of consciousness, a marked shift in our perception of ourselves and of our world. My purpose is to lend to that veracious suggestion a specific psychological dimension, a hard methodological dimension that provides it with immediate, tangible applicability, removes it from the realm of the old saw, and places it squarely in the tradition of the psychoanalytic critique of man and culture.

There are, needless to say, philosophical implications to all of this. My discussion is indebted to, even a continuation of, the phenomenological emphases in recent philosophical thought. It is my belief that psychoanalysis' tendency, particularly observable in Freud, to turn away from philosophy and consider "reality" as given rather than made, constitutes the Achilles' heel of psychoanalysis as a revolutionary instrument of change. To a large degree, this book serves the joint psychological and philosophical purpose of correcting that psychoanalytic error. Had Freud and his followers approached the problem of "civilization and its discontents" with "reality" in their minds as a manufactured and, hence, alterable "category," they would have reached conclusions far different from those they reached in their famous books. Permit me to stress the epistemological significance of my statements. When I declare that "reality" is made and not given, I do not declare it in a manner that aligns me with Herbert Marcuse in his contention that Freud's "reality principle" expresses the peculiar "reality" of a given mode of social and economic organization; or better, I do not declare it with that emphasis alone. Reality is made from the beginning of the individual's dynamic mental and physical development, in a hard epistemological sense which Marcuse simply ignores. The "reality principle" of *Eros and Civilization* is the culmination of a developmental process which must be grasped in perceptual, analytic terms if the critique of culture is to offer genuine hope to the future.

This attempt to move Freudian revisionism to the perceptual sphere, the sphere of altered as opposed to ordinary awareness, has evolutionary as well as philosophic implications. We are distinguished from the animals, after all, by the sophistication and flexibility of our brains, and by our capacity to extend and amplify genetic modifications of our "perceptual apparatus" through our own devices, our own practices. In regard specifically to our awareness of the universe, we are blessed with a kind of Lamarckian ability to inherit the inventions of the mind and wed them to our given physiological potential. Accordingly, I would demonstrate in the closing sections of this volume the degree to which the alteration of awareness bears on the advancement, not to mention the happiness of our species in concrete, evolutionary terms. With the discoveries of recent psychological and philosophical investigations focused upon human perception, there is no reason to view human existence as a futile, useless passion, and man as merely a sick animal trapped in the endless byways of his own neuroses. There is no reason to believe that our choice on this planet is the terrible one of illusion or despair. In this sense, my discussion is in sharp contrast with the work of an individual such as Ernest Becker to whose book, *The Denial of Death,* I devote my final paragraphs. I seek there not only to clarify that Becker's preoccupation with the denial of death is in actuality a denial of life, but more importantly, to show that the entire intellectual and spiritual tradition which stands behind Becker's book, the western existential tradition as informed by psychoanalysis, is no longer viable, no longer necessary, no longer useful to us as a species. The alteration of awareness opens onto new evolutionary realities, new evolutionary worlds—realities and worlds that may one day be quite unable to hear the old, glum sounds of our familiar doctrines. I offer this book, ultimately, as an argument of hope.

Part I

FREUD, HIS FOLLOWERS, AND THE DISCONTENTS OF CIVILIZATION

Chapter 1

THE MATERNAL OBJECT

1.

Psychoanalytic investigations of culture—the social, religious, and economic forces that surround us—have been hampered by their failure to "begin at the beginning," to address themselves to the problem of "civilization and its discontents" after having meticulously probed the manner in which our ordinary consciousness, awareness, and way of being in the world, develop. As a matter of fact, all the psychoanalytic investigations of culture conducted in the grand manner—and I am thinking here primarily upon the work of Freud, Reich, Marcuse, N. O. Brown, and Geza Roheim—are written as if our ordinary world of awareness were somehow "given," rather than constructed, "inherited," rather than made. Although the thinkers just mentioned are aware of the manner in which neurosis matures and expands toward the cultural situation that then comes to influence the individual born into it (let's not get involved in a chicken–egg debate, yet), they do not see that ordinary consciousness, the psychological world where neurosis comes to work, is, itself, a psychological problem, a condition of tension and stress engendering stress and tension in the "wider world."

Indeed, it is the contention of this book, extreme or radical as it appears, that no general, genuine, lasting amelioration of the *condition humaine* is possible until the majority of human beings achieve the capacity to alter their awareness, to break with the symbolical world of their ordinary mentation, their ordinary world of space and time, or what is usually taken to be consciousness itself. By altering awareness, the author does not mean a change in one's thinking or "attitude," such as a change that might occur after reading a moving pamphlet, undergoing group therapy, or joining a political party. He means an alteration of awareness in the classical sense, the state achieved through actual methods designed specifically to cause the suspension of what might be termed the "customary systems" of the mind, methods traditionally associated with mystical and religious schools.

To put the matter in another, perhaps more familiar guise, psychoanalytic investigations of culture are philosophically naive to the extent they assume ordinary consciousness is not itself a subject of analysis. Such investigations require a phenomenological emphasis, a willingness to go back to the very origins of awareness, to grasp the manner in which that awareness comes about, and then to go on to the manner in which specific libidinal inclinations (Freud's "libido," Marcuse's "Eros," Brown's "life") are shaped by the cultural forces the individual "inherits." As it turns out, the neglect of ordinary awareness as a preliminary study to the study of culture itself, has had the effect of leaving the worm undetected in the bud; for the essence of man's dilemma is inextricably tied to the development not of his "neurosis" as we usually conceive of it, but to the development of his "normal" mentation, the ground in which his neurosis takes root. Accordingly, the development of ordinary awareness and the psychological issues surrounding the alteration of consciousness have crucial evolutionary and revolutionary implications, implications that bear profoundly on the social and economic advancement of mankind.

Psychoanalytic investigations of culture have evinced another shortcoming that severely limits their contribution to the betterment of civilized society, namely their failure to *explore* the implications (including the economic ones) of the mother–infant relationship, particularly with reference to internalization and splitting. As will be demonstrated, ordinary awareness has a crucial defensive purpose: it provides the individual with a psychological avenue back to the mothering figure. The symbolic contents of the human mind, or the "stuff" of ordinary reality, "get there" basically through man's biological ability to internalize the world. And as the internalization of the maternal object is the chief defensive maneuver of the helpless, dependent, anxious human infant, the symbolic proclivity of human beings comes to be "automatically" associated with the need to retain, or hold on to, the mother. We do not merely perceive the world with our minds; we grip it. Man is not simply the "symbol–making animal" who lives in a world "apart from nature," as Cassirer and others have demonstrated. He is the animal who uses his symbols defensively to answer the crises of his interpersonal life, especially those crises surrounding his separation from the parent.

Accordingly, one would expect the world of culture, which is grounded in shared awareness and internalized attitudes and beliefs, to provide a similar psychological avenue back to the mothering figure, and a defensive purpose at the group level as opposed to individual life. Roheim gets at this truth in a general way when he writes,

> Culture . . . leads the libido into [acceptable] channels by the creation of substitute objects. The most important of these substitutions is a human being, the wife who replaces the mother. The basis of society is formed by these substitutions and therefore the psychology of growing up falls, in many respects, in line with the psychology of culture. Substitutes of another category—dolls, property, money, etc., in fact, material culture—are objects based on a withdrawal of libido from object love to a narcissistic position.

And again,

> Civilization originates in delayed infancy and its function is secur-
> ity. It is a huge network of more or less successful attempts to
> protect mankind against the danger of object–loss, the colossal
> efforts made by a baby who is afraid of being left alone in the dark.[1]

Yet, brilliant as Roheim's observation is, it is one that has
been largely ignored by "the Freudian left," to use Paul Robinson's
expression. The Freudian left (in spite of Roheim's central position in the psychoanalytic investigation of culture) focuses its
analyses in Freud. Freud's analyses, however, are conspicuous not
only for their failure to examine the development of ordinary
consciousness or probe the psychological implications of non–
ordinary awareness, "the occult", but also for their relegation of
the mother–infant interaction to a secondary or subordinate role.[2]
Even Roheim must be ultimately regarded as a figure in this
intellectual landscape. His conclusions were reached at the end of
a long career spent in the service of Freud's oedipal theory. They
are, therefore, streaked with the limitations of that theory. The
"substitute objects" of culture, he tells us, have in the last analysis,
a "libidinal," that is, a sexual purpose. The child who is left "alone
in the dark" wants ultimately to merge incestuously with the
parent.[3] In my view, and in the light of major developments in
psychoanalytic psychology, the nature of the infant's interaction
with the mother, and hence the purpose of "cultural objects," is
missed, or better *confused,* by such an emphasis. Unfortunately,
Roheim's conclusions were derived almost exclusively from his
observations of primitive peoples such as the Aranda and Kukata
of Central Australia and never applied in a rigorous way to his
own—and our—society. This is of the utmost significance and
brings me to one of my chief purposes, namely an exploration of
Roheim's insight for both its psychological and phenomenological
implications. I mean, to examine the *ways* in which culture,
including our own, develops out of the need to maintain the
mother–child relationship in both its libidinal and non-libidinal

aspects, to examine specific projections of the internalizing tendency onto the cultural ground, the basis of human time, space, relations, organizations, perceptions, is where psychoanalysis and phenomenology have the best chance of meeting, where depth psychology and philosophy can work a symbiosis so powerful as to hold out enormous hope for an acceptable, even desirable future. To clarify these matters we will turn now to an in-depth analysis of Freud and his followers.

2.

Perhaps the most remarkable passage in *Civilization and Its Discontents* (the fountainhead of analytic investigations of culture) is the one where Freud declares that "religious needs" are ultimately "derived" from the "infant's helplessness" and from the "longing for the father" "aroused" by such helplessness. To Freud, this causal scheme appears "incontrovertible," for he "cannot think of any need in childhood as strong as the need for a father's protection."[4] Where, one immediately inquires, is the mother in all of this, and where are those feelings tied to the child's interaction with the mother? Is not the need for symbiosis, union, or a close, protective relationship with the mothering figure as strong as the need for "a father's protection," and is not the problem of separation from the parents, and particularly from the mother, one of, if not the, key problems of childhood?[5] It is almost astonishing that Freud could so neglect this aspect of human development in his analysis of the origin of religious needs, and, ultimately, of the cultural configurations which arise therefrom.

But the matter does not end here. For immediately after writing that the origin of the religious attitude can be traced back to the infant's feeling of helplessness and to his longing for a father's protection, Freud declares, "there may be something further behind that, but for the present it is wrapped in obscurity" (*CD*, 9). It is as if he senses here precisely what Otto Rank was sensing during the course of his development, and what great numbers of Freud's

THE MATERNAL OBJECT   23

followers came to sense during the past four decades: behind the longing for the father's protection is the longing for union with the mothering figure and the anxiety which attends the separation from her. This author believes that Freud resisted analysis of the mother–infant relationship throughout the course of his career. Such resistance gave rise to psychoanalysis's most glaring theoretical weaknesses (this has been largely corrected, except in the area of "civilization and its discontents"). When Freud wrote, "something lying further behind" the helplessness of the infant and the concomitant need for the father's protection, the words arose from his conscience where he knew his analysis was incomplete. The significance of the mother–infant relationship and its role in religion and culture is wrapped in obscurity in Freud's work because he was unwilling to unwrap it and look in.

What is also remarkable about Freud's volume, however, is that the problem of "civilization and its discontents," as if in anticipation of our own age, is discussed in juxtaposition with an analysis of altered awareness, one of the few such analyses to appear in his work. This juxtaposition is a glimmer not only of the future, but of the liberation of consciousness itself. Its very appearance in Freud speaks for evolutionary forces pushing their way toward the light in a rudimentary fashion; yet, as it is handled, the juxtaposition leads nowhere, or better yet it leads to the intellectual deadend to which it must inevitably come in the halls of Freud's theoretical edifice.

Freud's view of mystical states, of what he termed "the oceanic feeling" (*CD*, 1), emerged in his correspondence with Romain Rolland. This correspondence resulted from the French author's reaction to Freud's earlier work, *The Future of an Illusion,* on the problem of religious feeling.

> He entirely agreed with my judgment upon religion [that it is a kind of illusion]," writes Freud, "but he was sorry I had not properly appreciated the true source of religious sentiments. This, he says, consists in a peculiar feeling, which he himself is never without, which he finds confirmed by many others, and which he may suppose is present in millions of people. It is a feeling which he

would like to call a sensation of 'eternity,' a feeling as of something
limitless, unbounded—as it were, 'oceanic.' This feeling, he adds,
is a purely subjective fact, not an article of faith; it brings with it no
assurance of personal immortality, but it is the source of religious
energy which is seized upon by the various churches and religious
systems . . . One may, he thinks, rightly call oneself religious on the
ground of this oceanic feeling alone, even if one rejects every belief
and every illusion" (CD, 1).

Confessing candidly that he has never been able to discover
such a sensation in himself, Freud doubts that the oceanic feeling is
"primary." Indeed, such a conception "fits in so badly with the
fabric of [his] psychology" (CD, 2) that Freud feels "justified" in
finding an explanation for it, an explanation suggesting such a
feeling is best described as a "regression," or a kind of psychic
return to a time in infantile life which occurred prior to the
differentiation of the self and the world. This time, when one's
narcissism was limitless, preceded the establishment of what
psychoanalysis would call ego boundaries (CD, 2–3). Freud then
writes, as an example of his theoretical postulation, the following:

An infant at the breast does not as yet distinguish his ego from the
external world as the source of the sensations flowing in upon him.
He gradually learns to do so, in response to various promptings. He
must be very strongly impressed by the fact that some sources of
excitation, which he will later recognize as his own bodily organs,
can provide him with sensations at any moment, whereas other
sources evade him from time to time—among them what he desires
most of all, his mother's breast (CD, 3–4).

The oceanic feeling, then, may be traced back to an early
phase of development, but that it is to be regarded as the source of
religious needs, or even a source, Freud explicitly denies. At this
point in his discussion, the reader is forcefully directed to the
influence of the father, and the need for the father's protection
(CD, 5). Incredibly, Freud spies no need in the "oceanic feeling,"
not recognizing, or admitting, that such a feeling might well be
prompted by a need to rejoin the nurturing figure of one's infancy,

by a need for the security and satisfaction of the breast, that religion, or one aspect of it, or one brand of it, might well constitute the projection of the infantile need for symbiotic union with the maternal object onto the external world. Freud's opening chapter concludes with the author declining to discuss "mysticism" any further, particularly as it relates to specific bodily functions.

Rolland has "assured" Freud that "through the practices of Yoga, by withdrawing from the world, by fixing attention on bodily functions and by peculiar methods of breathing, one can . . . evoke new sensations and . . . regressions to primordial states of mind which [are] a physiological basis . . . of much of the wisdom of mysticism" (CD, 9). Tempted momentarily "to find connections here with a number of obscure modifications of mental life" (remember, "obscurity" was the word employed with reference to what might "lie behind the infant's helplessness"), Freud, a psychologist, is ultimately "moved to exclaim in the words of Schiller's diver: 'Let him rejoice who breathes up here in the roseate light' " (CD, 10). Freud, in other words, prefers Apollo, the sun; reason, heaven; he has come close enough in his initial discussions to the mother–obscurity, to the maternal depths, to the "oceanic feeling," to the hated "occult." Schiller's diver indeed!

The limitations that Freud's view of these matters place on his analysis of "civilization" are enormous. That religion and culture are closely connected is obvious; that religion is, in large measure, a function of mankind's symbolic capacity is also obvious; that mankind's symbolic capacity is a feature of his internalizing tendencies is obvious, too; and what one also knows well at this time is that the internalizing tendency in human beings develops in inextricable association with the maternal figure. It is in large measure used to defensively answer the problem of separation from the mother. We are, of course, back to Roheim's general view of the cultural project, the precise significance of which will subsequently emerge as we "update" his findings to bring them into line with recent investigations.

3.

The thesis of *Civilization and Its Discontents,* a thesis that must be made clear as it profoundly influences the work of all succeeding writers on the subject, is that culture, or civilization, demands the repression, and renunciation of, much of our instinctual inclination, and life. Such repression breeds suffering and hostility; mankind relieves its suffering or expresses its hostility through a variety of "sublimations," including art, religion, and aggressive "games," such as war. The "neurotic" is one who "cannot tolerate the amount of frustration which society imposes upon him" (*CD,* 24). As for war, it breaks out when collective frustration and guilt reach intolerable levels that demand, as it were, a kind of easement. "Men are proud" of the "achievements" of science and culture, Freud writes, "but they seem to have observed that this newly–won power over space and time, this subjugation of the forces of nature, . . . has not increased the amount of pleasurable satisfaction which they may expect from life and has not made them feel happier" (*CD,* 24–25). Civilization brings advantages but it also breeds discontent, a "sacrifice of instinct" (*CD,* 32). This can mean any number of "restrictive measures" (*CD,* 41), particularly in the area of sexual fulfillment. And it is men themselves, in their very natures, who contribute to the dilemma, Freud says, and not just "civilization," for men

> are not gentle creatures who want to be loved . . . ; they are, on the contrary, creatures among whose instinctual endowments is to be reckoned a powerful share of aggressiveness. As a result, their neighbor is for them not only a potential helper or sexual object, but also someone who tempts them to satisfy their aggressiveness on him, to exploit his capacity for work without compensation, to use him sexually without his consent, to seize his possessions (*CD,* 48).

Thus, the ills of civilization include—we must be careful to note here—the ills of economic injustice.

So great are the tensions of civilized society, tensions surrounding the repression of instinctual urges, the burden of guilt arising from "transgression," and the primitive, unruly nature of men themselves, that the very survival of mankind as a species became for Freud a problematical issue. "The evolution of civilization may . . . be simply described as the struggle for life of the human species" (CD, 59). Mankind, he wrote in one of his most controversial passages, appears to have not only an instinct for life but an instinct for death as well. Profoundly ambivalent about his situation in culture, he stands between Eros and Thanatos, between the forces of life and death, and the outcome of the "eternal struggle" of these "adversaries" is by no means certain. "If civilization is a necessary course of development from the family to humanity as a whole, then—as a result of the inborn conflict arising from ambivalence, of the external struggle between the trends of love and death—there is inextricably bound up with it an increase of the sense of guilt" (CD, 70). It is precisely this sense of guilt that Freud came to finally regard as the "most important problem in the development of civilization" (CD, 71).

These observations of Freud will be examined in a later section in an effort to demonstrate their integral connection to the development of human mentation, generally. Now, an earlier work of Freud that touches on the problem of culture and that helps us to understand not only the direction from which arose the conclusions of *Civilization and Its Discontents*, but also the direction from which arose the revolutionary interests of Freud's followers will be explored. As for the philosophical limitations that Freud imposed on his analyses, particularly with regard to the role of ordinary consciousness in the evolution of society, they, too, will emerge from the discussion.

4.

Let us notice, first, Freud's keen perception of social injustice, indeed of class conflict and economic exploitation, a perception which establishes an ideational link between his work and the work of Karl Marx. The "laws" and the "institutions" of culture, writes Freud, "aim not only at establishing a certain distribution of property, but also at maintaining it."⁶ In fact, "one gets the impression that culture is something which was imposed on a resisting majority by a minority that understood how to possess itself of the means of power and coercion" (*FI*, 4), a state of affairs that is not necessarily "inherent" in culture, itself, but in the "imperfections of the cultural forms that have so far been developed" (*FI*, 5). A utopian note is faintly struck here, but, as is always the case with Freud, nothing comes of it. Indeed, it is vain to anticipate a "golden age" in that "every culture must be built up on coercion and instinctual renunciation" (*FI*, 5). The "critical issue" thus becomes "whether and to what extent can one succeed, first, in diminishing the burden of the instinctual sacrifice imposed on men; secondly, in reconciling them to those that must necessarily remain; and thirdly, in compensating them for these" (*FI*, 6). Since "all modern cultures" evince class favoritism and class conflict, a social and economic organization in which "the satisfaction of one group of its members necessarily involves the suppression of another," it is foolish to expect the "suppressed classes" to internalize the values of the exploitative society to the degree to which the favored classes do (*FI*, 16–17). Hence, the neglected classes are usually on the verge of breaking out. It is only a "narcissistic satisfaction" provided by a "cultural ideal" that, along with the conservative and, ultimately, restrictive influence of religion, prevents hostility from disrupting the prevailing order (*FI*, 16). Such an ideal can be shared "not only by the favoured classes, which enjoy the benefits of this culture, but also by the suppressed, since the right to despise those that are outside it compensates them for the wrongs they suffer in their own group. True, one is a miserable plebian . . . , but withal one is a Roman citizen" (*FI*, 18). To this extent, the suppressed "identify" with the "governing class" (*FI*, 18).

Such passages make it abundantly clear that Freud's writings provide the political theorist, the social reformer, the prober of power structures and economic "setups" with plenty of material with which to commence an analysis. Not only the actual observations but the tone of these passages calls Marx immediately to mind, with the notable qualification that in Marx such ruminations inevitably beget the disgust and concern of the revolutionist. In Freud, they invariably beget a speculative curiosity as to their psychological meaning and, ultimately, a kind of stoical resignation or acceptance. Freud's final word on the dilemma of culture is his brief hope, expressed at the close of *Civilization and Its Discontents,* that love, in the end, may conquer death.

   The Future of an Illusion evinces the same belief in the all–pervasive father–power as does *Civilization and Its Discontents.* Once again, the mother seems to have no role at all in holding civilization together. The explanatory scheme is essentially the same. Religion compensates men for the miseries of the imperfect world and, at the same time, enjoins them to submit to authority and behave themselves. In addition, it provides a measure of security in an indifferent and, indeed, dangerous universe. In this regard, it reflects the purpose of culture generally which is to provide the human animal with safety through social organization. The absence of the mother, matriarchal influence, and the problems of infancy, including separation, becomes astonishing as one reads the actual writing: "Man makes the forces of nature not simply in the image of men with whom he can associate as his equals—that would not do justice to the overpowering impression they make on him—but he gives them the characteristics of the father, makes them into gods, thereby following not only an infantile, but also . . . a phylogenetic prototype" (*FI,* 26–27). Where are the goddesses? They have suddenly disappeared from the face of civilization and history. Freud goes on: "In the course of time the first observations of law and order in natural phenomena are made, and therewith the forces of nature lose their human traits. But men's helplessness remains, and with it their father–longing and the gods" (*FI,* 27). How "mother–loving" did not in some manner, in some degree, find its way into all of this can only be explained, as suggested earlier, by postulating a curious resistance, or blind spot, in this man of genius.

   Later, almost as if he is insisting upon the mother's insignificance and denying that our minds retain influences from all the levels of psychosexual development—something that Freud affirmed again and again in his writings—he wrote:

> The mother, who satisfies hunger, becomes the first love–object, and certainly also the first protection against all the undefined and threatening dangers of the outer world; becomes, if we may so express it, the first protection against anxiety. In this function the mother is soon replaced by the stronger father, and this situation persists from now on over the whole of childhood.

And,

> when the child grows up and finds that he is destined to remain a child for ever, and that he can never do without protection against unknown and mighty powers, he invests these with the traits of the father–figure; he creates the gods, of whom he is afraid, whom he seeks to propitiate, and to whom he nevertheless entrusts the task of protecting him (*FI*, 39–40).

Religion, the "universal obsessional neurosis" (*FI*, 77) of mankind, originates in the Oedipus complex, "*the relation to the father*" (*FI*, 78, my emphasis). It is remarkable, in the face of these statements, that Roheim, who devoted his life and work to exemplifying and substantiating the conclusions of Freud, was able to shift the emphasis to the mother at all.

Finally, *The Future of an Illusion* begets from Freud observations of a philosophical nature on what one may call phenomenological issues. These are observations that make it perfectly clear Freud was prone to accept ordinary reality as if it were *there*, that he was *not* prone to see any *unconscious significance* in the way our "normal" sense of reality developed through the give–and–take of interpersonal relations, and, most of all, that he was unable to discover a connection between the evolution of ordinary awareness and society. As a matter of record, in one or two places Freud calls to mind, with his postulation of "reality," Piaget's observation that children "gradually construct" the "universe" around them and then go on to "experience" that universe as "external to themselves," as something that is actually there, thus making it difficult for themselves as adults to realize their entire "psychological evolution" was determined by the nature of this early development, the construction of the world of space and time, or what Kant called mental "categories."[7] Religion, Freud writes in one section, "consists of certain dogmas, assertions about facts and conditions of external (and internal) reality" (*FI*, 41). In another section, he declares that "scientific work" and "scientific observation" are the best possible foundation for examining "external reality" (*FI*, 59). The assumption, of course, is that such a "reality" is there and is analyzable only in its "thereness." How it came to be there in the first place is *not* pertinent to "examining" it as there. Such an assumption is philosophically unacceptable and should be psychologically unacceptable, too. "Our normal personal consciousness," writes Ornstein, "is not a complete, passive registration of the external environment, but a highly-evolved, selective, personal construction . . . We learn to select a socially acceptable personal consciousness," to fashion a "relatively stable world."[8]

But the truly crucial passage occurs near the end of Freud's work where he writes of our "mental apparatus" as follows:

> Firstly, . . . it has been developed actually in the attempt to explore the outer world, and therefore it must have realized in its structure a certain measure of appropriateness; secondly, it itself is a constituent part of that world which we investigate, and readily admits of such investigation; thirdly, the task of science is fully circumscribed if we confine it to showing how the world must appear to us in consequence of the particular character of our organization (*FI*, 101).

The development of ordinary awareness, then, is of little interest to psychoanalysis. Our ordinary consciousness, our ordinary perception, our "organization," must be more or less as "nature" intended it to be or else we would have encountered difficulty in "exploring" the world. The fact that such "exploration" culminated ultimately in the grievous situation of mankind in culture, the dilemma of man and his many "illusions," his obsessional

neuroses, and his exploitation of his fellows, is apparently forgotten for the moment. Indeed, had Freud concluded that our "organization" in its development and application seemed suspect in
terms of what we have become as a species, had he suggested that
the sick animal's sickness might have something to do with his
ordinary way of perceiving the universe, he would have reached a
conclusion more in keeping with the context of *The Future of an
Illusion* and the substance of the later work, *Civilization and Its
Discontents*. There is surely very little "appropriateness" in the
picture of man that emerges from these books.

Freud is correct and reasonable in stating that our minds are
part of the world, and therefore, open to investigation, but again,
his presentation of the matter is Kantian. The mind he would
investigate comes after the moulding to ordinary awareness.
Although Freud was eager to explore what was in the mind, and
while he did this magnificently, he believed the container itself
was somehow developmentally given in terms of its apprehension
of "reality." He just could not see that what was in the container
was linked inextricably to the particular circumstances surrounding its growth as a container, that the frame and what it held were
connected. To think for a moment on the degree to which the time
sense, a biological "given" and a Kantian "category," is tied
developmentally to the coming and going of the mother, a psychological "variable," is enough to clarify the overwhelmingness of
the point. Precisely because he turned away from such issues,[9]
Freud could not fully describe for us "how the world must appear."
And because of this, he could not fully "circumscribe" the "task of
his science" in its relation *both* to the individual and to the culture
which surrounds him.

5.

"Freud, with his genius and his humanity," writes Norman O.
Brown, "tried to keep in the field of psychoanalytical consciousness not only the problems of the neurotic patient, but also the

problems of mankind as a whole."[10] But Freud "never faced fully" the "existential and theoretical consequences" of taking on the problem of mankind's "general neurosis." He was "unable to make the shift to an anthropological point of view." What is needed—and my point here is that Brown fails to include philosophy, and particularly the philosophy of consciousness, in the list—is a "synthesis of psychoanalysis, anthropology, and history" (*LAD*, xiii). What is really notable regarding Brown's volume, however, is this: After singling out Roheim's work as the great pioneering effort in the attempt to disclose mankind's neurosis, "second only to Freud's," Brown, in his own analysis, chooses not to explore Roheim's conclusion, the upshot of everything Roheim wrote. It is *not* the mother–child situation that is investigated in Brown, but the vicissitudes of anality, and *this* along the lines of Freud's classical libido theory. We shall return to this issue momentarily.

The philosophical limitations of Brown's discussion emerge early when he writes that "the crux of Freud's discovery is that neurotic symptoms, as well as the dreams and errors of everyday life, do have meaning, and that the meaning of 'meaning' has to be radically revised because they have meaning. Since the purport of these purposive expressions is generally unknown to the person whose purpose they express, Freud is driven to embrace the paradox that there are in a human being purposes of which he knows nothing, involuntary purposes, or, . . . 'unconscious ideas' " (*LAD*, 4). What needs to be stressed here is that ordinary consciousness, our ordinary way of perceiving and being in the world, is, itself, one of these "unconscious ideas." It is an "involuntary" response to the pressures and anxieties of experience, a defensive gripping of "reality" begun at the time of the mother–infant interaction and used defensively as a tie to the parental, and particularly to the maternal, figure. Writes Gruen,

> The child's experience of himself and the world is mediated through the tactual, visual, and kinesthetic contact with the mother. His initial intake of the world comes through her and with her. Erikson put it poetically, saying that a mother teaches man 'to touch

the world with his searching mouth and his probing senses.' This 'passive–receptiveness' . . . is 'the very oldest and . . . the most neglected mode of our experiencing.' . . . The child's perception is the mother's perception.[11]

Surely, Freud's monumental discovery that, as Brown expresses it, "neurosis is not an occasional aberration; it is in us, and in us all the time" (*LAD*, 6) must, just on the face of it, bear a crucial relation to the origins of our ordinary consciousness, the consciousness that constitutes quite as much a part of "people's" mental life as do their dreams and slips of the tongue. It is the whole mind that is neglected in the analysis, and it is "normal waking consciousness," apart from its slips, that escapes investigation precisely because it seems so "normal," "natural," and "appropriate" in Freud's expression, to those who are in it.

Brown writes, "if we take 'desire' as the most suitable abstract of [psychoanalytic] terms, it is a Freudian axiom that the essence of man consists, not, as Descartes maintained, in thinking, but in desiring" (*LAD*, 7). But the very maintenance of ordinary awareness is an act of desire; the very continuation of our daily thoughts is an act of desire; indeed, the inception of these mental phenomena is tied to an act of desire—the desire to internalize the parental figure and, thereby, remain in emotional contact with it. This same desire, at a later stage, spills over into our very impetus to use language, speak, and think in symbolic forms, as well as image the world. For imaging, a key feature of ordinary awareness, is the way the child comes to hold the mother in her absence.[12] From this perspective, the ordinary consciousness we exist in as "given" may, itself, have been the greatest desire, the greatest desiring, of men, and not the oedipal desire as described in the work of Freud. If the child's perception *is* the mother's perception, then perceiving and mothering may be connected at the deepest level of need. Consequently, ordinary awareness may contain an unconscious purpose of security that ultimately dictates the nature not only of our "private lives" but of our religious and economic institutions as well.

At one point Brown declares in the most forceful way that an analysis of the maternal influence is crucial to our understanding of mankind's neurosis. He even goes on to suggest that Freud's emphasis on the father is an impediment to our progress because it prevents us from reaching the matriarchal level that lies beneath the patriarchal scheme of things.

> The proper starting point for a Freudian anthropology is the pre–Oedipal mother. What is given by nature, in the family, is the dependence of the child on the mother. Male domination must be grasped as a secondary formation, the product of the child's revolt against the primal mother, bequeathed to adulthood and culture by the castration complex. Freudian anthropology must therefore turn from Freud's preoccupation with patriarchal monotheism; it must take out of the hands of Jungian Schwärmerei the exploitation of Bachofen's great discovery of the religion of the Great Mother, a substratum underlying the religion of the Father—the anthropological analogue to Freud's discovery of the Oedipal mother underlying the Oedipal father, and comparable, like Freud's, to the discovery of Minoan–Mycenaean civilization underlying Greek civilization. (*LAD*, 126)

The accuracy of these remarks seems incontestable; yet, in the face of them, one is deeply struck by Brown's subsequent position. That is, at the heart of his discussion of economic institutions that express the sickness of man and virtually consign those born into them to a certain degree of psychological stress, in other words *our* economic institutions, he states that "identification with the father" is only a way of "denying dependence on the mother." He also adds that "as long as psychoanalytical theory of the pre–Oedipal mother remains backward," the "individualism" of the Protestant era, and ultimately of our time, as well as the significance of the entire shift in western social organization from matriarchy to patriarchy, will "remain psychologically obscure" (*LAD*, 280). What Brown is confessing here is this: just as Freud was not "fully equipped" to "make the shift" to an "anthropological point of view" that would have allowed him to find a cure for mankind's "general neurosis," he (Brown) in his reliance on a "backward" psychoanalytical theory, is also not fully equipped to analyze the problem. For as Brown, himself, states, it is the mother–infant interaction that demands exploration. Unfortunately, it is precisely that interaction which Brown doesn't explore, beyond suggesting that the problems of ambivalence and guilt, for Brown the central problems in the development of culture, have as much to do with the mother as with the father (*LAD,* 290). In the main, Brown is content with discussing the incompleteness of the psychoanalytical theory, an incompleteness that derives from the reliance on the father as the starting point of the analysis. Moreover, Brown does not get very far beyond Roheim, not simply with regard to a general recognition of the mother's key role, but even with regard to his analyses of anality, wealth, repression, the unconscious, and the death drive.

Exploration must begin precisely where Brown says it must, and one regrets that he, with his large following, did not choose to begin it there. By 1959, the year when his book appeared, writers such as Spitz, Jacobson, Winnicott, Mahler, Klein, and Fairbairn were shedding considerable and valuable light on precisely those problems which he sees as crucial—the psychoanalytical nature of the first years of life, the tensions of maternal separation, and the ambivalence inherent in the mother–infant relationship. Brown's work is literally void of reference to these writers. His theory is grounded in Freud, and Freud's followers who subscribed to the libido theory, such as Sandor Ferenczi and Karl Abraham. Edmund Glover on Melanie Klein is about as close as Brown comes to the whole area, and even later, in *Love's Body,* Brown seems to have thoroughly studied only Klein. The point is, the psychoanalytical theory to which Brown is referring is not nearly as "backward" as he suggests. Indeed, it is there, waiting to be applied. What is particularly fascinating about the entire issue is this: as it becomes evident that the problem of civilization and its discontents cannot be grasped apart from an analysis of the manner in which our institutions reflect the mother–infant situation, it also becomes evident that the development of ordinary consciousness calls for a similar analysis itself. The conclusion emerges: just as there appears to be an inextricable connection between the development of awareness and culture, so there may be an inextricable connection between the alteration of awareness and culture.

6.

Eros and Civilization is also without reference to the authors just cited. Interested in questioning the "origin and legitimacy" of the environment in which we discover ourselves, Marcuse stresses Freud's philosophical importance. As those who stood in the great traditions of philosophy, Freud strove to fashion a "theory of man," and a "psycho–logy" in the "strict sense."[13] The emphasis on philosophy is crucial to our purpose and valuable in focusing the integral connection between philosophical and psychological investigation. Yet Marcuse, for all his familiarity with phenomenological issues as they emerged from the work of both Hegel and Marx, has nothing to say about the development of ordinary awareness, as "strict" an aspect of "man" as one could wish. Like Freud, and his followers, Marcuse writes of the "reality principle" as if *that* were not an area of psychological and *philosophical* analysis. One paragraph begins, "with the establishment of the reality principle," and goes on to declare that "under the reality principle, the human being develops the function of reason: it learns to 'test' the reality" (*EC*, 13). Yet, it is precisely what is happening to, and with, the individual as this "reality" enters the picture which comprises the basis of the understanding of what happens to the individual after the "reality" has "established" itself. Unless the mother–infant bond is meticulously examined in exactly this regard, the development of "reality" will remain obscure.

Although Marcuse, as Brown, differentiates himself from Freud by according to the matriarchal, and the maternal, a fundamental significance in the development of western society,[14] at no point does he *analyze* the mother–infant interaction as relevant to the nature of those social forces that coerce the individual in the form of "institutions." Not only is the discussion of these "matriarchal matters" too general to be genuinely innovative, it is also reflective of Freud's classical approach. The mother in *Eros and Civilization* is chiefly the "Oedipal object" of the child's sexuality, (*EC,* 69), the one from whom he is separated by the father (*EC,* 72), and, thus, a kind of "aim inhibiter." The "strongest of all childhood wishes" derives from "the Oedipus situation" (*EC,* 186), not from anything pre–oedipal. It is this "situation" to which Marcuse addresses himself as he searches for solutions to the Freudian–capitalist dilemma, solutions that take the form of "non–repressive sublimations" rooted in "the release of libidinal forces" (*EC,* 198–199).

Indeed, from a theoretical viewpoint, Marcuse's emphasis is overwhelmingly Freudian, and his analysis of "civilization" is primarily a philosophical and sociological deepening of Freud's doctrine of repression. For Marcuse, the "death instinct" or the "Nirvana principle" becomes the tendency of the individual to withdraw from a repressive society, to detach himself from an "order" that frustrates his instinctual life. Only in the context of which it manifests itself socially can the "drive" for death, the "drive" for quiescence, be correctly understood. The human being in our present environment is sick from "domination," economic and ideational domination that prevents him from playing with the universe around him, playing in the deepest aesthetic, philosophical, and psychological sense. He will remain sick until he is permitted, in his mind and in his body, to play again.

7.

Ernest Becker wrote of Freud's *Group Psychology and the Analysis of the Ego,* "this great work, a book of fewer than 100 pages, is in my opinion probably the single most potentially liberating tract that has ever been fashioned by man."[15] As it turns out, there is considerable truth in this view. Nor is it without interest that a "cure" for "mankind's neurosis" should begin to emerge from Freud's book on group psychology rather than from those works of his which were devoted exclusively to an examination of the general malaise of culture, namely *The Future of an Illusion* and *Civilization and Its Discontents*.

After writing that group psychology is "concerned with the individual man as a member of a race, of a nation, of a caste, of a profession, of an institution, or as a component part of a crowd of people who have been organized into a group at some particular time for some definite purpose,"[16] Freud, always cognizant of and willing to learn from the work of his predecessors, undertakes to examine Le Bon's "deservedly famous" *Psychologie Des Foules* (1895). This is generally regarded by the savants of the 1890s as the "last word" on the subject. Freud is content, indeed impressed, with much of what he finds there.

Take, for example, his general summation of Le Bon's lengthy descriptive analyses:

> A group is impulsive, changeable and irritable. It is led almost exclusively by the unconscious. The impulses which a group obeys may according to circumstances be generous or cruel. . . . Nothing about it is premeditated. Though it may desire things passionately, yet this is never so for long, for it is incapable of perseverance. . . . A group is extraordinarily credulous and open to influence, it has no critical faculty. . . . It thinks in images, which call one another up by association. . . . and whose agreement with reality is never checked by any reasonable agency. The feelings of a group are always very simple and exaggerated. . . . So that a group knows neither doubt nor uncertainty (*GP*, 77–78).

For Freud, this is an accurate and valuable account. Moreover, he agrees with Le Bon that in a group the importance of individual differences is apt to vanish; the most heterogeneous types, who could not possibly have "stomached" one another around the vegetable cart or across the billiard table, are suddenly, as St. Peter put it, "of one mind, united in feeling." It is the emergence of a kind of "collective mentality," finally, that holds the dissimilar mass together. But Freud also points out a difficulty here, and, criticizing Le Bon for not passing beyond the level of descriptive analysis, presents it this way:

> If individuals in the group are combined into a unity, there must surely be something to unite them, and this bond might be precisely the thing that is characteristic of a group. But Le Bon does not answer this question; he goes on to consider the alteration which the individual undergoes when in a group and describes it in terms which harmonize well with the fundamental postulates of our own depth–psychology (*GP,* 73).

That is to say, "what the individual undergoes" Le Bon, like Freud, explains in terms of the unconscious. For Le Bon, however, this unconscious is not individual but ethnic, an "archaic heritage" that stays in the darker recesses of the simian brain and is apt to emerge when the members of the "herd," ordinarily independent and groomed and civilized, reconvene under stress–filled conditions. And this is, of course, a second difficulty. Writes Freud:

> For us it [is] enough to say that in a group the individual is brought under conditions which allow him to throw off the repressions of his unconscious instinctual impulses. The apparently new characteristics which he then displays are in fact the manifestations of this unconscious, in which all that is evil in the human mind is contained as a predisposition. We can find no difficulty in understanding the disappearance of conscience or a sense of responsibility in these circumstances. It has long been our contention that 'social anxiety' is the essence of what is called conscience (*GP,* 74–75).

Thus, group behavior does not, according to Freud, include the emergence of "archaic human traits"—a dead–end idea from an experimental standpoint; it entails, rather, the emergence of "unconscious instinctual impulses" that have been freed from the claims of the ordinarily vigilant superego.

Again, Le Bon maintains, and correctly according to Freud, that individuals in a group often behave as though hypnotized, lending themselves to the purposes of another and transacting dutifully whatever they have been told to transact. But once again, Freud criticizes Le Bon for depositing the reader somewhat short of the mark; for in spite of the latter's insightful analogy, the question remains: who is the hypnotizer? As Freud expresses it:

> We cannot avoid being struck with a sense of deficiency when we notice that one of the chief elements of the comparison, namely the person who is to replace the hypnotist in the case of the group, is not mentioned in Le Bon's exposition (*GP*, 76–77).

It is at this point in his discussion that Freud leaves the graphic descriptions of Le Bon behind and makes a full-fledged attempt to clarify the reader's understanding of the inner dynamics of group behavior. He does this by dwelling at length, and in depth, on the significance of the leader and demonstrating that the group's attachment to the leader, as well as the attachment of the individual members to each other, is ultimately libidinal in nature. Taking up the second point first, he writes:

> We will [begin], then, with the supposition that love relationships (or, to use a more neutral expression, emotional ties) . . . constitute the essence of the group mind. . . . Our hypothesis finds support in the first instance from two passing thoughts. First, that a group is clearly held together by a power of some kind: and to what power could this feat be better ascribed than to Eros, which holds together everything in the world? Secondly, that if an individual gives up his distinctiveness in a group and lets its other members influence him by suggestion, it gives one the impression that he does it because he feels the need of being in harmony with them rather than in opposition to them—so that perhaps after all he does it "ihnen zu Liebe." (*GP*, 91–92).

Using the Church and the army as his primary examples, Freud continues:

> In a Church . . . as well as in an army . . . the same illusion holds good of there being a head . . . who loves all the individuals in the group with an equal love. Everything depends upon this illusion; if it were to be dropped, then both Church and army would dissolve,

so far as the external force permitted them to. This equal love was expressly enunciated by Christ: "Inasmuch as ye have done it unto one of the least of these my brethren, ye have done it unto me." He stands to the individual members of the group of believers in the relation of a kind elder brother; he is their substitute father. All the demands that are made upon the individual are derived from this love of Christ's. A democratic strain runs through the Church, for the very reason that before Christ everyone is equal, and that everyone has an equal share in his love. It is not without a deep reason that the similarity between the Christian community and a family is invoked, and that believers call themselves brothers in Christ. . . . (*GP*, 93–94).

Freud underscores his thesis by mildly reproaching "earlier writers" for not "having sufficiently appreciated the importance of the leader in the psychology of the group" (*GP*, 95).

Now, it is precisely this "importance of the leader" that, in Freud's view, explains the phenomenon of group panic:

The typical occasion of the outbreak of a panic is very much as it is represented in Nestroy's parody of Hebbel's play about Judith and Holofernes. A soldier cries out: 'The general has lost his head!' and thereupon all the Assyrians take to flight. The loss of the leader in some sense or other, the birth of misgivings about him, brings on the outbreake of panic, though the danger remains the same. . . . (*GP*, 97).

Essentially then, the panic in the mob arises from a threat to, or indeed (as in this case, if you will allow the pun), a severance of what might be called a collective dependence on the substitute father. Because the relationship of the group to the leader is ultimately regressive, because it is rooted in the infantile dependency needs which human beings, in spite of their "adulthood," never manage to entirely outgrow, there is always the possibility that the group's members will experience an abandonment similar emotionally to the one the child experiences when he finds himself alone in the house at night. Thus, the group needs its leader, which clarifies, of course, why the latter often has such an easy time imposing his will on the former.

Clarified in the final pages of the discussion is the erotic nature of the invisible bond (identification) that holds the group together initially. What Freud maintains essentially is this: the leader must possess qualities and characteristics capable of eliciting from the group a "desexualized" version of the "libido" which ordinarily charges the individual's attachment to the parent, or better, to the intrapsychic conception of the parent. This, Freud calls the "ego–ideal." The leader, in short, must conduct him/herself in such a way as to get the crowd to idealize him/her. When this happens, the leader becomes the "group ideal" and hence, the depository of right and wrong—as the parent, or ego–ideal, formerly was. But as such the leader must not falter, must not shatter the illusion so rewarding to the group, must not show himself to be less than the embodiment of the ideal father. Thus, the first prerequisite to his/her success is that he/she treat the members of the flock equally and impartially. Says Freud:

> The first demand made by this reaction–formation is for equal justice, for equal treatment for all. We all know how loudly and implacably this claim is put forward at school. If one cannot be the favorite oneself, at all events nobody else shall be the favorite (*GP*, 120).

This brings us to the following concluding point. Since the relationship of the group to the leader is rooted in those impulses that originally determined the parent–child relationship, one can expect it, in the last analysis, to be more, or less, ambivalent in nature. That is to say, one can expect it to contain not only desexualized libido (though this, Freud would insist, is its main "ingredient") but fear and hostility as well. In no sense does one have here a betrayal of earlier conclusions; instead, one has simply a recognition on Freud's part that fathers are feared as well as loved, that dependent or regressive emotional ties are bound with hostility, and that opposed or "contradictory" feelings often exist within the same individual at the same time. And this explains, of course, why groups sometimes turn so savagely and suddenly on the "man of the hour," or why the death of the chief is apt to bring relief as well as sorrow. Summarizing succinctly the essence of his stand, Freud concludes with this assertion:

> The leader of the group is still the dreaded primal father; the group still wishes to be governed by unrestricted force; it has an extreme passion for authority; in Le Bon's phrase, it has a thirst for obedience. The primal father is the group ideal, which governs the ego in the place of the ego ideal. Hypnosis has a good claim to being described as a group of two. There remains as a definition for suggestion: a conviction which is not based upon perception and reasoning but upon an erotic tie (GP, 127–128).

8.

Freud's conclusions are, of course, presented in the shape of a general framework or model with which the student could approach the entire issue. The exact clinical nature of each group, the psychodynamics of its peculiar development and interaction, is left open to the analyses, and the particular extrapolations of each investigator.[17] The model developed in the pages to follow should be taken in an identical sense. The author will get at the issue of the individual's participation in "civilization" in a broad, extensive way, recognizing that specific cases and participations will have their unique shape and will correspond only more or less to the model he is creating. Questions immediately arise regarding this model. Is it accurate? Does it actually break ground? Does it present the problem of "civilization and its discontents" from a challenging, and promising, perspective? The answers to these questions will, of course, be left to the reader.

What must be stressed at once, however, is that the bond that holds the group together in Freud's analysis, namely identification, is ultimately grounded in an overwhelmingly significant feature of psychological development—the internalization of the external world, and particularly of the parental figures who inhabit it. In this way, Freud's assertions regarding the group may be applied to "civilization" as a whole, for civilization is also grounded in the psychological fact of internalization and from a psychoanalytic perspective, is quite as much a version of the familial situation as is the "group" to which he addresses his analysis. But to probe specific issues swirling about the psychodynamics of internalization is to recognize that the individual's tie to his culture is inextricably associated with his tie to his mother, indeed with his tie to ordinary awareness which functions largely as an avenue back to the mothering figure. Internalization is, among other things, a defensive solution to separation anxiety, separation anxiety which is emotively linked not simply to the paternal figure, as Freud's analysis would suggest, but to the "maternal object" herself. Specifically with reference to the mother–infant interaction, to the development of ordinary awareness, and to the psychoanalytic implications of altered states of mind, let us examine briefly what happens to the human animal during the course of his early development, during the period which might be called, in Eliade's expression, "the early time."

Part II

THE DEVELOPMENT OF
ORDINARY CONSCIOUSNESS

Chapter 2

TRAUMATIC ANXIETY AND THE
SENSUAL UNIVERSE

1.

The separation anxiety that Roheim regarded as a conspicuous feature of human development and a powerful inducement to
the creation of culture begins with the very hour of our birth and
contributes to what we can call the process of conversion. Each of
us undergoes this during the course of our infancy and childhood.
To go at once to the heart of the thesis, the writer regards ordinary
awareness itself as a conversion symptom, as a mode or "system"
of consciousness which serves a defensive and psychological
purpose as well as the obvious biological one of protecting the
organism from overstimulation. As is invariably the case with the
species *Homo sapiens,* biology and psychology are interdependent.

The term "conversion" is, of course, Freud's, and he intro-
duced it at the very inception of his monumental discoveries. For
example, in one of his earliest papers, "The Defence Neuro–
Psychoses," he writes of an "unbearable idea" being "rendered

innocuous" when the "quantity of excitation attached to it" is "transmuted into some bodily form of expression, a process for which I should like to propose the name of conversion".[18] Freud continues,

> The conversion may be either total or partial, and it proceeds along the line of the motor or sensory innervation that is more or less intimately related to the traumatic experience. Thus the ego succeeds in resolving the incompatibility within itself; but instead it has burdened itself with a memory–symbol, which dwells in consciousness, like a sort of parasite, either in the form of a persistent motor innervation or else as a constantly recurring hallucinatory sensation, and remains until a reversion takes place in the opposite direction.[19]

In an even earlier paper he states that the "paralyses" of hysteria frequently involve additional "sensory disturbances."[20] Although Freud's interests eventually led him away from strict concentration on the bodily registration of emotive disorders, and although he maintained in one place that phobias and obsessions were not "transmuted into some bodily form of expression,"[21] a number of his followers pursued the problem vigorously. What they concluded has been generally accepted by the psychological community and can be briefly summarized as follows.

There are no purely organic processes in human life, even from the beginning. At every stage of his development, the human being is a "psycho–physical entity" in which "bodily and emotional processes" are "fused."[22] To speak of the body apart from the mind is as incorrect as to speak of the mind apart from the body. This means that mental stress, whatever its origin, will leave its mark on the body and be registered there. Freud's "conversion process" is a universal aspect of human development because human development always involves emotional stress and because it always receives physiological expression. It is not only the neurotic symptom of the disturbed individual that one must regard as a "compromise formation,"[23] or as a method of warding off anxiety, or coping with psychological tension. The behavior of each and every human being reveals "compromise formations" and bears witness to his/her having answered the anxieties and tensions of his/her own life through the conversion process. Neurosis is simply an exaggerated version of what one regards as "normal" behavior. Now, when one considers that perception is as much a behavior as maintaining a certain posture, eating, or making love, when one returns, in short, to the basic premise that the human organism is a "psycho-physical entity," one squarely confronts the realization set forth at the inception of this section: man's ordinary consciousness, and way of perceiving the world, may well evince features of the conversion process, or be itself a kind of "compromise formation."

2.

As was suggested earlier, the trauma of birth is integrally related with these matters. This does not imply simply that conversion symptoms can be linked to "severe birth trauma," as Otto Rank demonstrates,[24] or that birth symbolism, and even the pangs of birth, turn up with arresting regularity among individuals who discover themselves in the midst of intensive drug therapy and hence altered states of awareness;[25] it implies that the traumatic experience of birth, by profoundly influencing the body–mind of the human animal, bears directly upon the manner in which we "normally" perceive the world. Leboyer's work gets at this most effectively.

First of all, there is "the intensity, the boundless scope and variety of the experience, its suffocating richness. People say—and believe—that a newborn baby feels nothing. He feels everything. Everything—utterly, without choice or filter or discrimination. Birth is a tidal wave of sensation, surpassing anything we can imagine. A sensory experience so vast we can barely conceive of it."[26]

Again,

> if seeing is perceiving light, then yes, the infant does see. Vividly.
> The baby has the same love, the same thirst, for the light that plants

and flowers have. The baby is mad for this light . . . So much so that
we should take infinite precautions; we should offer it infinitely
slowly. In fact, the baby is so sensitive to light that he or she
perceives it while still in the mother's womb . . . And now this little
creature, so sensitive to light, is thrust suddenly out of its dark
cavern.[27]

As for hearing, the child is no more deaf than blind.

While they are still in the womb, the noises of their mothers' bodies
reach them: joints cracking, intestinal rumblings. And giving the
rhythm to it all is the strong drumbeat of the mother's heart. And
then—her voice. The mother's voice, which sets its stamp on the
child forever . . . Sounds, muted until now, suddenly strike the
young arrival with all their force . . . The young ears are suddenly
vulnerable. Nothing protects them any longer from the world's
uproars. The infant is born into a thunderous explosion. It con-
vulses. Should we be surprised? The world cries out. The child
gives an answering cry.[28]

The baby's response to the very process of expulsion cannot
be overlooked.

Midway through the pregnancy, everything changes. The infant
continues to grow and to develop rapidly. But the egg that contains
him grows only slightly by comparison. His tribulations begin. The
baby begins to feel closed in; slowly the universe is contracting.
What was once unbounded space becomes more confining each
day. Gone is the limitless ocean of earlier—and happier—days . . .
and one day the baby finds itself . . . a prisoner. And in such a
prison! The cell is so small that the prisoner's body touches the
walls—all of them—at once. Walls that draw nearer all the time . . .
One day, these contractions are no longer a game. They crush, they
stifle, they assault. One day labor starts. The delivery has begun . . .
The prison has gone berserk . . . The walls close in still further. The
cell becomes a passageway; the passageway, a tunnel. With its heart
bursting, the infant sinks into this hell. Its fear is without limit . . .
Yet all this force, this monstrous unremitting pressure that is
crushing the baby, pushing it out toward the world—and this blind
wall, which is holding it back, confining it—these things are all one:
the mother![29]

The terrors of birth can, of course, be mitigated by a radical departure from certain "rough," ingrained procedures. Darkness, gentleness, silence, gradual severing of the umbilicus, immediate, naked reunion with the mother, immersion in warm fluids, calm, and unaggressive attendants, can be used to change the current situation. Still, no matter how much methods are improved, there will be "good" and "bad" stimulation from the start. The womb will contract, crush, expel; the first breath will shock; the inevitable imperfections of early handling and feeding will appear to go on forever. In the words of Leboyer, although newborn babies usually "adapt" to their world, they do so only by "withdrawing into themselves," by "deadening their senses."[30] Profound emotive stress, as well as psychological and physical trauma, register themselves in the organism at birth and cause the human being to hold himself in a certain posture, a posture of defence, a posture that will influence his subsequent perception of the world. Being born is not only the first altered state of awareness; it is an experience that will invariably set the process of conversion into motion, trigger the "alarm system" and posture of defensive anticipation which derive from it. A degree of sensory alienation and pain, a kind of "fall from paradise," is simply an aspect of man's origins. One learns from birth to use "compromise formations." Free, full, direct perceptual contact with the environment has already come to mean annihilation. The ability to convert, to freeze the sensorial bent of the organism in a protective gesture, has already been "utilized" by the new arrival.

3.

The traumatic features of what we have chosen to call the conversion process do not cease with the accomplishment of birth. On the contrary, they only begin there. Let us concentrate now on three major areas of human development, namely internalization, symbol formation, and the use of language, in an effort to characterize fully the manner in which they 1) further the establishment of "compromise formations," 2) lead to the impoverishment of our relationship with the world, and 3) culminate in what we can best describe as the Converted Self, an entity that must be relinquished if the "discontents" of "civilization" are to be substantially reduced.

By the time a three– or four–year–old has been left for the first time at nursery school, he/she has achieved the ability to "still have" or "still be with" his/her mother after she has gone. This is true since he/she has achieved the ability to internalize her, or have her "there" within him/her even though she is absent. Freud writes,

> A portion of the external world has, at least partially, been abandoned as an object and has instead, by identification, been taken into the ego and thus become an integral part of the internal world. This new psychical agency continues to carry on the functions which have hitherto been performed by people in the external world.[31]

What is clear from recent psychological studies, however, is that crucial internalizing or "taking in" tendencies are occurring in the child long before Freud believed they were. As Rheingold puts it, the *object,* specifically the mother, "enters" the infant's "dawning psyche" as the "deep introjection" of the earliest phase of development, and she persists there as a "presence," only later to become an "image," during the symbolic phase. This early interplay between mother and infant is directly involved in the "structuring" of the infant's "personality."[32] Again, according to Rheingold, "intuitive or feeling perception" begins with "maximal intensity" at birth when the infant becomes immediately subject "in a structuring way" to the maternal attitude, and this is attested to by "Deutsch, H. S. Sullivan, Spitz, Benedek, Fries, Mahler, and Sperling."[33] By the time the human being reaches adulthood he carries within him an "inner world," a kind of psychic universe, which is "peopled" with the "objects" that have entered him, or more properly, the objects he has taken into himself, during both the very early stages of infancy and the later stages of childhood (we retain the tendency to internalize people and things throughout the course of our lives). In this way, man lives from the beginning in two worlds, and his mental and emotional life must be regarded as a function of the interaction of these worlds which continually impinge upon one another. Our mental make–up is significantly determined by those with whom we entered into "object-relationships" during the early phases of our development. Our earliest "objects" become dynamic parts of our personality structure and continue to exist within us and to influence us in all that we do long after the actual objects who were the aim of our internalizing tendency have ceased to exist in actuality.

Early development of the self (the self that undergoes conversion) comes largely through the mother. In a strict sense, it is incorrect to stress the separateness of the self toward the beginning. Infant and mother form a single psychological unit; their relationship comprises a symbiosis. What must be emphasized is this: just as the experience of birth invariably involves trauma and conversion, so does the early object–relationship with the mother. For no matter how solicitous she is, the infant is fated to undergo tension, frustration, discomfort, and even a certain amount of pain. These experiences, these negative experiences, mobilize anxiety in the child simply because he "interprets" the loss of the object (loss meaning any imperfection in the relationship) as a negation of his desires.

> Sullivan states that anxiety is first manifested early in infancy. Very young infants show grossly identical patterns of behavior when they are subjected to frightening situations and when they are in contact with the person who mothers them and that person is anxious, angry, or otherwise disquieted. The complement of . . . 'people' which each of us carries within him and lives with reaches back in every instance to the first pair of our personifications: the good mother and the bad evil mother. The next link in the inevitable developmental chain is the triple personifications of Good Me, Bad Me, and the always rather shadowy, but dreadful, Not Me.[34]

It is in this dichotomous creation of Good Mother–Bad Mother that inner divisiveness or lack of integration begins. When we split the mother, we split ourselves; we convert the integrated animal into the split person, and this conversion is felt in the body. What this means, of course, is that every adult carries within him, to one degree or another, "bad objects," a kind of unconscious ego that has been forged defensively in the disappointments of early infancy and childhood. Hence, unpleasant experiences in the "now" of life, bad hallucinogenic trips, for example, will involve the interaction of internal elements which have taken on a dynamic, unconscious life of their own in the personality, and external elements which are fated to be colored by the internal ones. Traumatic experiences always evince the reactivation of early events at the center of which stands the bad object.

The archetype of the terrible mother derives from the actual experiences of human beings who have undergone maternal ambivalence. To some degree, it may be suggested, all mothers are ambivalent, are capable of engendering the bad mother image. Birth is painful, the infant is bothersome, the mother is tired and beset, the relationship with the husband may be strained, but most of all, the mother's own unconscious inclination predicated by the existence of the bad mother within her own personality can influence her treatment of the infant. Searles, writing about disturbed mothers in a passage that to some extent applies to all mothers, captures this projective tendency:

> In one mother–child relationship after another, the mother's view of the child as a genuinely new individual is obscured, persistently and with few if any breaks, by a peculiar combination of unconscious perceptions which the mother has of this particular child. She perceives him, on the one hand, as the embodiment of a galaxy of repressed concepts of herself: to her he represents her lonely, isolated self, or her hopelessly hostile, rejectable self, or her appalingly animal–like, lustful self, and so on. On the other hand, as I have found with astonishment, she reacts to this same child as an omnipotent mother–figure whose acceptance she (the actual mother) recurrently seeks, in a self–abasing fashion . . . The more I have thought about this . . . the more it appears to me to point to the mother's having reconstituted, with her young child, a symbiotic relatedness such as had existed . . . in the mother's own childhood, between herself and her own mother.[35]

The point is, somewhere along the line the mother will communicate, usually unconsciously, a negative attitude toward the child whose overwhelming sensitivity to such communication will result in anxiety and contribute to the creation of the bad mother image who harbors the threat of annihilation: not simply loss, but destruction. It is the internalizing of this "bad object" that explains our emotional fear of death. "What is impressed is not death as the adult conceives it but a threat of a quality and magnitude beyond the adult's imagination. We get a glimpse of it in panic states and the momentary probe into infancy that some persons experience during therapy. The struggle between the forces of life and death inherent in the biologically precarious infantile condition becomes involved in the reactions to the satis-fying–protective mother and the deprivative–destructive moth-er."[36] Our fear of death, then, is a fear that derives from the internalized object whom we have "taken inside."

The early, "archetypal" images of the good and bad mother persist in our unconscious minds throughout the course of our lives. They are ubiquitous, mythic, cross–cultural, inevitable, an aspect of our human condition. Erich Neumann in *The Great Mother* puts the matter this way:

> The symbolism of the Terrible Mother draws its images predomi-nantly from the 'inside'; that is to say, the negative elementary character of the feminine expresses itself in fantastic and chimerical images that do not originate in the outside world . . . The dark side of the Terrible Mother takes the form of monsters, whether in Egypt or India, Mexico or Etruria, Bali or Rome. In the myths and tales of all peoples, ages, and countries—and even in the nightmares of our own nights—witches and vampires, ghouls and specters, assail us, all terrifyingly alike.[37]

Clearly then, just as the traumas of birth prompt a withdraw-al, a deadening of the senses, a conversion that is ultimately defensive in nature, so do the traumas of early infancy prompt a psychological splitting that is also defensive in nature. The child declares, in effect, "Mother is not bad. There just happens to be this bad mother who appears once in a while. She and mother are not really the same person, for mother is always good and will never hurt and disappoint." It is only later, when the child matures, that he/she will be able to accept "goodness" and "badness" in the same individual.

That such early splitting, such early divisiveness, is ultimately felt in the individual's body, in his very chemical make–up, and that it determines importantly the nature of his sensorial participation in life, can no longer be disputed. Just as the trauma of birth calls an "alarm system" into play and prompts a withdrawal, or shrinking, so does the emergence of the bad object within us, the felt apprehension of that danger, prompt a similar withdrawal, shrinking, and posture of defense which erodes our ability to relax, to just be. The evidence for this, striking and unforgettable in itself, provides a key to the understanding of ordinary consciousness as well as the struggle to transcend it.

Here is the heart of the matter. "Because specific sensory stimuli become tied to objects and evoke, in condensed form, the history of specific object–relationships" we are obliged to recognize that "internal reactions to sensory stimuli do not follow exclusively physiological laws."[22] The "regulation of bodily functions" in which "sensory organs are used" is determined by the degree to which and the way in which the object and the senses have come to be associated.[22]

Sean O'Casey, in his sixth autobiographical volume, *Sunset and Evening Star,* gives a remarkable example of a massive response to specific sensory stimuli in an account of a visit by him one winter to the University of Cambridge for a talk with students. At a relatively early hour at night the lights were switched off, . . . and the students stayed to carry on their discussions with O'Casey by flashlight. The conversations ended when the last flashlight failed, and the students made their way to their rooms in pitch–black darkness. For a man who since childhood had had greatly impaired vision and who had compensated for it by developing an intense capacity for visual imagery, on the surface O'Casey appeared to mildly react by musing on the spiritlessness of the students for their passive acceptance of such college regulations. But this scorn indicated a deeper

arousal than O'Casey was aware of. . . . It is . . . when he is brought
to the sleeping quarters assigned to him in the dormitory that he
begins to react. For him alone a dim naked light has been left on and
immediately he is shaken by the dreariness of the room. 'A slum
room without a slum room's brightness . . . the floor bare, dirty, no
fireplace . . . the one window unclad even with the symbol of a rag.'
But it is the bone–chilling cold of the . . . room and virtually
blanketless bed that finally undoes him and overwhelms him. All
this evoked in capsule form the whole history of his past with its
terrible privations beginning in childhood with the death of his
father. . . . [38]

O'Casey spent the night sleepless and acutely agitated. He
regained his equanimity the next morning when he was entertained
at breakfast by one of the students. He was moved by the fact that
the student, though himself impoverished, had provided a brightly
burning fire and a large breakfast for O'Casey, while he ate very
little himself. Tactfully, O'Casey, as his mother had often done for
him, persuaded the student to share a large portion of his breakfast
and proceeded to offer the student encouragement. Loss of light
(darkness) and loss of warmth (cold and bleakness of room) had
combined to disrupt the unconscious bonds of O'Casey to his
mother, and triggered a long delayed grief reaction to her death.
Warmth, concrete and symbolic, and 'warm' light restored these
bonds.[38]

Another example further demonstrates the psychological–
physiological link between sensory stimuli and key objects. A
young, female patient describes

how she grew up in a warm climate in another country. Her parents
made a practice of having the entire family sleep at night on the
same screen porch through a good part of the year. She scarcely
slept at night, trying to stay awake, scarcely breathing, trying to see
in the dark, and especially listening to her parents. Their sexual
activity both terrified and excited her, especially her mother's
remarks on different occasions, 'Don't; stop; you're hurting me'.
She also recalled how all the family raised their voices and shouted
in anger. Her mother would yell at her and, on one occasion, took a
knife and threatened to cut off her braids. The trauma of constant
exposure to such sensory stimulation had a profound effect on her
personality. . . . She lived in a continual state of sexual excitement,

and fear of violence between mother and father, between men and women; she was absorbed in sexual fantasies in which she played both the role of mother and father, man and woman. This excitement and her fantasy life were now sustained by the feeling that all sounds, especially speech, were sexualized and evoked the recollection of these experiences with her father and mother. *Vision and sound maintained her bonds to her mother and father and to objects in a sexualized form.*[39]

In this way,

> sensory modalities can be manipulated unconsciously and used defensively, one against the other, in their symbolic representations and expressed through a change in the line of associations. . . . Unconscious fantasy activity provides the 'mental set' in which sensory stimuli are perceived and integrated. External events, on the other hand, stimulate and organize the re–emergence of unconscious fantasies.[40]

Moreover, during the course of early development and throughout life,

> fusion of sensory perceptions takes place and there occurs a symbolic interchangeability of all sensory modalities. Visual perception, for example, can take over the symbolic representation of other modalities. In this way vision not only involves physiological reception of visual stimuli but may subserve symbolically the function of other modalities such as touch and hearing.[41]

As for the body image, it is formed by

> the deposit of images and symbols of key external figures, internalized by stimuli from without, fusing with sensory perceptions from within. . . . People treat their bodies and themselves much as they react to meaningful persons in ther lives.[42]

The conclusions are inescapable. The internalized object of infancy and childhood is internalized into our very organs, into our very senses. Our bodies do not function only in accordance with physiological laws; they also function in accordance with psychological requirements, requirements which are inextricably tied to the presence of the bad object within. The conversion process that commences at birth is sharpened and deepened through internalization and splitting. In a massive defensive response to the exigencies of the early period, the child is learning not to receive the world with his senses, but to grip the world with his senses, for to hold on to the object through internalization is to allow that object to influence the manner in which the senses will be employed to perceive the world. The concept of retaining one's "grip on reality" or of "losing one's grip on reality" has its origins here, in the psychodynamics of internalization. Because the influence of the object within never ceases, ordinary consciousness turns out to be, in large measure, a matter of pre–determined gripping. The restoration of full, free, sensorial interaction with the universe depends on undoing the fusion of perceptual behavior with internalized object, an undoing which depends in its turn on resolving the conflict, the psycho-physiological tension, that exists between the individual and the key figures of his inner world. Only through such a resolution can the channels and modes of perception be liberated.

4.

The processes thus far described are, by and large, pre-verbal, pre-symbolic ones. We will now discuss the nature of the conversion process as it develops through the symbolic phase, the phase in which internalization meets and combines with the individual's ability to think in symbolic terms. By the time this developmental phase has concluded, the individual has set up, within himself, an entire world of symbols, mental pictures, and ideas that discovers its full, human expression in the employment of the sounds called "language." In order to grasp the connection between early splitting and withdrawal and later development of symbolic mentation, we will concentrate briefly upon another aspect of the mother–child relationship, an aspect that sheds important light upon the manner in which the human animal comes to associate the mother with the whole process of bodily and emotive stimulation.

The function of mothering is, to a significant degree, protective. Not only does the mothering figure avoid and ward off dangers and attacks from the external world, but she also attempts to protect the infant from sheer overstimulation. Indeed, the management of stimulation is, by and large, what mothering is. This does not mean that mother simply avoids loud sounds and bright lights, adjusts the knob controls as it were; for the matter goes deeper than this and bears on the whole question of the child's growth and development. "An essential feature of mothering," writes Gruen, "would seems to entail the mother's capacity to screen stimuli impinging on her child in such a way as to make it possible for connections to form between relevant stimuli and her child's inner readiness to respond to them. . . . Good mothering is that which through relevant screening of the stimulus field furthers appropriate learning. . . . This is why overstimulation prevents the young organism from integrating itself."[43]

When Piaget writes that stimuli are meaningful only when they fit the schema of inner processes, he reminds us that interference with the formation of connections impedes development and forces the child to continue his dependence upon the mother. In this way, if mother fails to protect her child from overstimulation,

> The child becomes handicapped in learning to differentiate and to link outer and inner schemas. Furthermore, being subjected to an undifferentiated stimulus makes stimulation itself appear threatening. . . . On the other hand, through her absence the neglecting mother at least does not add to overstimulation. However, this may also create for the child a situation in which the environment becomes disturbing.[44]

The point is, "whichever way this development occurs, the child's experience of himself and the world is mediated through the tactual, visual, and kinesthetic contact with the mother."[45]

What is the upshot? Emphatically that the mothering figure is going to be integrally, inextricably, inevitably tied with the human being's reception of stimuli and, hence, with his perception of the world around him. "The child's perception is the mother's perception."[46] Accordingly, to alter one's awareness is to alter one's relationship with the deeply–internalized mothering figure and with the "habitual" or "customary" self that arose out of that relationship. The problem of altered awareness is, among other things, a problem of separation.

5.

Man's biological ability to create symbols distinguishes him from other animals. It makes him uniquely human. Modern psychology and philosophy, through the work of Cassirer, Langer, Husserl, Jung, and many others, has been telling us this for decades. As grown–ups, as "adults," we symbolify virtually everything. Time becomes not simply the awareness of duration but an old, wrinkled man carrying an hour–glass. Evil becomes a snake; goodness an angel; jealousy a green–eyed monster; spring a beautiful maiden; the earth, a fertile mother. Every detail of our lives, every object we encounter, begets its verbal counterpart and comes to receive an "abstract" expression in our minds. We carry around in our heads the idea of foot, mountain, horse, highway, beef steak, soldier, woman, atom, hair, ocean, sex.

As we know from the great religious and philosophical literature of the world, there is an irony in this. For our ability to make symbols and to live mentally within a world of symbols leads not only to the accomplishments of culture in the widest sense, the wondrous productions of sculpture, painting, music, poetry, law, and government; it leads, as well, to an alienation from the world, an existence in which we are more in touch with words and ideas than with concrete objects, or a life where words are continually substituted for things. In this way, enlightenment or transcendence comes to equal in most religious disciplines the cessation of symbolic or verbal "seeing" and the institution of direct or immediate "sight." Underscored here, however, is that man's ability to create symbols and to live in, or even behind, a world of symbols is not only an ability; it is a proclivity as well. One mustn't, in this area any more than in any other, think dualistically. One must remember that man is a psycho–physical organism and that all his characteristic features develop in a human, emotive context as well as in a physiological one. One substitutes the word for the thing, the symbol for the object, because to do so is to be safe and secure. The problems of maternal care and maternal separation cannot be disassociated from the problems of symbol formation and the use of language.

By the time the human animal is experiencing his ability to retain the image of the object in his mind and to attach to it a verbal equivalent, by the time his brain has developed to that point, the more "primitive" process of internalization has already been at work for many months. At the level of feeling, at the level of emotive, pre–verbal awareness, the child has actualized his need to take the mother in, and even to split or divide her in an effort to cope with the anxiety that arises from her "bad" or discomfiting behaviors. As has been stressed, a considerable amount of tension and a posture of anticipation result from the child harboring the "bad object" within himself. It is not an "image" or a "picture" of the mothering figure, however, which enters the child during the early time; *relationships,* not pictures, are internalized. And even later, when the ability to retain pictures is there, the internalization of relationships predominates. Indeed, the mental image of the significant other, the other who has been internalized, is always a projective version of the primary, relational attitude. Thus, by the age of 2½, the child has experienced and learned to cope with a series of traumatic separations. He has separated from his mother at birth; he has been weaned; and he has been confronted on a daily basis with the mother's coming and going and with the anxiety that this can engender. From one perspective, the whole task of infancy and childhood is getting separate, getting independent, getting autonomous. As is generally known, the majority of human beings struggle and stumble toward that condition throughout the course of their lives. Indeed, the inclination to alter one's ordinary awareness, to achieve another kind of consciousness, is largely an inclination to go beyond the early time and beyond the individuals who made up that time. At the deepest level, it is the inclination to have oneself.

But the crises of separation do not diminish after birth and weaning; on the contrary, they only intensify. More and more, the child must learn to survive without the mother; increasingly he learns that mother must eventually be relinquished. What is the result? The early inclination to cope with separation through the process of internalization is reinforced or buttressed by the ability to create an entire symbolical world and to have it "inside," in a "space" that the child psychologist D. W. Winnicott calls "transitional." He writes,

> In favorable circumstances, [and by that he means in more or less "normal" circumstances where "mothering" is "good enough" to prompt "ordinary" development] the potential space becomes filled with the products of the baby's own creative imagination. . . . Given the change, the baby begins to live creatively, and to use actual objects to be creative into. If the baby is not given this change then there is no area in which the baby may have play, or may have cultural experience; then there is no link with the cultural inheritance, and there will be no contribution to the cultural pool.[47]

On the one hand, then, our ability to use our powerful brains, to make symbols, to imagine, to create, is an innate ability that is nourished into production by "good enough" maternal care. On the other hand, however, that ability is goaded into action by the very real problem of maternal separation. In the development of symbolic mentation, and in the perceptual behaviors which arise therefrom, there is an element of conversion.

After insisting that cognitive and affective development cannot be disassociated, Bleich reminds us that symbol formation arises from the infant's sharing experience with the mother.

> The common act of referential pointing starts with the invitation by the mother, but soon eventuates in the child inviting the mother to

contemplate some object together. This represents the beginning of
intellectual stereoscopy, the start of the schemata of objectification
as being dependent upon social interaction. The child develops a
schema of naming things to someone. . . . The love and attention he
gets becomes the motive for his naming further things. . . . The
mother's love and attention to the naming procedure helps deposit
the schemata of mutuality to be later incorporated in the important
step of conceptualizing the whole idea of two–ness and separateness.[48]

Thus, the presence and absence of the mother, and of important physical objects or "things" in the child's world, play motivational roles in the development of representational thought.
Indeed,

the cognitive component of the ability to recognize mother—conceptualizing her—is, at the onset of representational thought and
language, goaded into existence by the need to cope with . . .
affective loss. The feeling of affective loss is the motive for acquiring the capacity to represent absent objects, or, the capacity to
represent objects regardless of their presence or absence. . . . By
naming the absent object, the infant predicates it on its previous
presence: 'Mommy gone.' The same act predicates subsequent
presence on current absence. The schema 'gone' and the schema
'Mommy' are independently linked and placed in relation to one
another. Chomsky's major insight . . . is his discovery that all
languages, regardless of culture, are built on transformations of a
simple basic act of predication.[49]

Again, and this, too, is vital,

when the child links up 'Mommy' and 'gone' he creates a dependent
relationship between two ideas which substitutes for each idea's
dependency on real experience. This action if identical to what
Piaget calls 'reciprocal assimilation' with which he describes the
child's ability to invent new means to cope with a new problem in
the sixth sensorimotor stage. . . . Because the new representational
capability allows the child new power to re–call—both in the sense
of memory and action—mother at will, it represents to the child a
way back to the missing libidinal object.[50]

Gruen expresses the problem somewhat differently:

> The child's sense of cohesion, of meaning, of order . . . is
> threatened by [mother's] disappearance or emotional withdrawal. .
> . . The first discontinuity in the development of the self is the
> transition from a self that is the other's—from a state wherein the
> order of things is attained through the other's order—through a
> frightening state of chaos and aloneness to an order of one's own.[51]

It is, of course, the symbolical world, the world of one's own
representations, the world developed in Winnicott's "transitional
space," that comes to comprise one's own "order."

The implications of these findings are crucial, and strikingly
clear. To give up one's ordinary world of symbols in an effort to
achieve a direct apprehension of objects is to lose one's way back
to the mother. Because the verbal representation of the thing is the
culmination of the symbolic process, the word is the magical tie
that reunites us with the all–important figure(s) of infancy and
childhood. There is a "close reciprocal relationship between language and affect development."[52] Our symbolic seeing is charged
with the emotive energy, the power, that went into our life and
death struggle to maintain our connection with mother at the same
time we were giving her up. Through the terrors of birth, and
through the early imperfections of mothering, we learn to grip the
world with our bodies, with our tense anticipation, as we have
seen. Through the crises of separation which continue to transpire
after the early time, we learn to grip the world with our minds, with
our symbols, with our words. To a significant extent, "reality" as
we know it *is* the parental figure.

One can appreciate from this perspective the accuracy and
profundity of Roheim's contention that culture itself, at the
deepest psychological level, is a means back to the mother, a
symbolic connection with the early time—a creative manifestation
through which separation is overcome and security maintained,
however precariously. "We suggest," writes Roheim, "that thinking, which at its apex is very much an ego activity, is deeply rooted
in the libido, and that between the two we must place the mental

image as magic. It means both 'away from the object' and (by means of the image) 'back to the object'."[53] And again, "It would seem that the function of the word as a cultural object is to link the internal to the external world—in other words, to summon the mother when the child is hungry."[54] The "word" as a "cultural object," then, has the same psychodynamic significance as the "stimulus" generally.

6.

"Time and space," as well as "cause and effect," the so-called categories of Kantian philosophy, are aspects of human mentation that cannot be thoroughly grasped apart from their connection with the problems of birth and separation. As we have already seen, the use of language develops within an emotive context, a context of "object–relations" in which the growing person struggles to achieve his separateness, and differentiation from the other. The symbolic world, and the word that is its culmination, magically permits the human being to give up the mother yet retain her at the same time.

In a similar way,

> spatial representations are an integral part of the individual's attempt to understand and organize reality and to achieve individuation and differentiation. The development of object–relations and advances in object constancy occur with progress in the separation of the self from objects and with increased differentiation and articulation of the self and of objects. These advances in the differentiation of self and objects can be evaluated by the cognitive development of spatial representations. Complex and developmentally advanced spatial representations indicate greater self and object differentiation and more mature object relations.[55]

The self, as one usually conceives of it, needs someplace to live. When we speak of the "breathing room" that individuals require to maintain their existence in the world, we recapitulate unconsciously the whole struggle of the human being to escape the womb which crushes and expels him, to cope with the appearance of the "bad" maternal object whose imperfect care makes him choke with rage, and to survive the loss of the "good" maternal figure who breathes his very life into his lips.

We have cited those defensive strategies, those compromise formations, that bear witness, one and all, to the anxiety of the early period of life. They include the deadening of the senses that follows upon birth; the posture of withdrawal, tension and anticipation that follows upon the appearance of the bad maternal object; the development of a symbolic universe that provides the human being with a way back to the mother. The point is: these defensive strategies are formed within levels of spatial representation. Indeed, spatial representation is the cognitive matrix from which defensive strategies arise. When we withdraw, we withdraw to someplace, a psychic place, that allows us to be there. We split the maternal figure off to another place which permits us to split it off. We reduce the world to a space in which we dwell securely, our substitute womb of enumerated types. The concept of separateness implies exclusion, boundaries that establish the "end" of one individual and the "beginning" of another. When Bachelard writes that "all really inhabited space bears the essence of the notion of home"[56] he describes the inextricable connection between spatial representation and the problems of separation and mothering: all notions of home bear the essence of the notion of mother.

7.

According to James, "awareness of change is . . . the condition on which our perception of time flow depends."[57] Since awareness of change begins with maximal intensity at birth, one would assume the existence of some rudimentary time sense from the inception of post–natal life. For Piaget, however, the perception of space precedes that of time. The child confuses temporal intervals with points traversed in movement; hence, time percep-

tion develops "secondarily" through the concept of "velocity."[58]
Clearly then, the perception of space and time develop very closely
and apprehension of time is, like the apprehension of space,
integrally tied with the problems of separation and mothering.

From what could be regarded as the most basic or rudimentary perspective on the subject, the sense of time, or the sense
of its passage or happening, bespeaks a relation between the
registrator of stimuli and the environment in which he exists. The
"present," which separates "past" from "future," indicates the
instant in which the "undetermined" happens and, thereby, becomes "fixed in time" as the "determined." If our experience
transpires in the "present," every time we perform a thinking act
we create a point of reference in time. Freud maintained that our
concept of time begins with our primitive body perception, or
auto–perception of the unconscious energy that enables our perceptual apparatus to register stimuli. This energy, when placed and
withdrawn rhythmically from the unconscious on to the perceptual
apparatus, creates a link between our own biological time rhythms
and those of nature generally.[59] As for thoughts, they do not exist
as such during the period of early infancy; they exist as "very
primitive sensory and emotional experiences which have the quality of proto–thoughts."[60] What is crucial to keep in mind here is the
close connection between time and energy.

The personal strength required to alter awareness in a positive
way can be gained only through constructive alteration of our time
sense into the maintenance of which is channelled an enormous
amount of psychic energy. Also important to note is the close
connection between the alarm system created during the crises of
birth, posture of anticipation engendered in infancy, and the
awareness of time. The agreement on this among depth psychologists and experts in child development is remarkable.[61] Just as
affect or emotion—specifically the need to internalize—goads the
symbolic capacity into life, so does affect or emotion goad the
sense of duration into life. It is this sense of duration that gives our
ordinary or "rational" perceptions their meaning. But we have still
to tie in the problem of time with the problem of maternal care.

The infant attempts to protect himself from traumatic experiences of frustration by anticipating the fulfillment of his needs. Here is a typical "sequence" as developed in the work of Hartocollis:

> As tension rises and the mother is not yet there the 'good' object image or representation emerges protectively in fantasy and unites with the self-image in a need–fulfilling hallucinatory experience; but if the mother's arrival is further delayed, it begins to fade away rapidly. As the infant tries to hold onto it and unpleasure increases, the uncertain 'good' object image begins to turn into a 'bad' one. It is the effort to hold onto the 'good' object and to expel the 'bad' one that . . . creates the ability to anticipate the future; and, while tension is still tolerable, the situation is experienced as anxiety. As tension continues to rise, however, the 'bad' object image tends to prevail over the 'good' one; anxiety gives way to fear, and, as Erikson put it, "impotent rage . . . in which anticipation (and with it, future) is obliterated." If the mother's arrival is delayed further, the infant becomes flooded with excitation, his mental state regressing to the level of an undifferentiated 'bad' self–object image—an experience of catastrophic dimensions. Such an experience would be timeless.[62]

Eventually, however, what Hartocollis calls "object constancy" develops in the maturing child; the early hallucinatory process is replaced by the ability to anticipate the fulfilment of need. As the fused "good" and "bad" maternal figures are internalized or set up within as the scaffolding for normal character development, a relatively trustful tendency to believe in good outcomes is projected onto the environment which begins to be experienced as continuous, as possessing the attribute of duration. At the same time, the rather tense, anxious proclivity to believe in the good outcome is attached to the child's growing representation of himself, a representation that he projects beyond the confines of his immediate environment. Time becomes *perspective;* the "future" is born. Thus, for the infant to experience time, as such, it is necessary that he go through a motivational process in which he experiences mother as need–fulfilling *and* as frustrating.

Clearly, the "good enough" mothering that stands behind the development of symbolic thought also stands behind the development of percept generally; for if percept depends on duration for its existence, and if duration depends upon motivational processes involving the mother, then time and the mother, time and the internalized object, are inextricably connected at the deepest levels of our being. As one psychologist puts it, "the young child has intuitions not only of speed and distance but also of duration. He sees the latter in the elementary form of an interval which stands between him and the fulfillment of his desires." As long as he is able "to maintain a trustful expectancy of mother's presence (in her absence) time is experienced as duration."[63] With this in mind, we can understand more fully the meaning of the following statement that appears in a psychological case history and that is representative of thousands of such statements both written and spoken: "Time subjectively had stopped for her when her mother developed cancer and died."[64]

We can also appreciate the origin and significance of something that relates in an absolutely crucial way to the problem of altered awareness, namely, the existence of "good time" and "bad time." The myths and metaphors of mankind everywhere present us with versions of these entities. Good time, derivative of the good mothering figure, is endless happy days, long life, summer, eternity, heavenly bliss, the joyous bells of morning, the chimes at midnight. Bad time is the wrinkled, toothless hag, the companion of death, the ragged grave, the hourglass held in the bony hand, the bell that tolls the departed; it is prison, solitary confinement, the endless torments of hell, bad eternity. Altered states of awareness are integrally tied to the interplay of these "times," as well as with the interplay of what we can regard as the phenomenological cousins of good and bad time, namely, good and bad space.

Finally, with the connection between symbolic thought, good enough mothering, and the sense of duration in mind, we can understand more fully the manner in which the symbolical world serves as an avenue back to the mothering figure and, therefore, provides us with our ordinary emotive security. While memory is located in time and space, it is first experienced as anticipation, as future satisfaction or frustration. Heidegger puts it this way: "The future presupposes the past, but only the sense of past if there is a future."[65]

But what is it that we "remember" at all times? What is is that stands at the foundation of any memory that we are capable of having? Obviously, our ordinary world of symbols, ordinary consciousness, the ground of our mentation. This is what we "remember" at all times; this is what makes the "future" possible; this, in short, is what eases the perpetual anticipation of the unknown that we confront every instant of our lives. Our symbolical mode is also basic to our ordinary way of existing. That is, we are chemically, energically, bodily tensed for our experiences in "life" because we are always faced with maintaining the symbolical universe which ostensibly guarantees our safety in the world. However, since our ordinary emotive security derives from a symbolical universe that is integrally connected with the sense of time as duration, and since the sense of time as duration is forged in the infant's experience of the mothering figure as both good and bad, the security with which we are provided by maintaining our inner world of symbols is phylogenetically fated to be imperfect, to be "bad" as well as "good," tension–producing as well as tension–removing. Therefore, our tie to the symbolical world is ultimately an infirm basis of being, a compromise formation molded in the anxiety of infancy. It represents the security of a "converted" organism.

8.

The problem of causality must also be seen in the light of our early experience. The concept of cause and effect cannot be grasped apart from its temporal and spatial parameters, as well as its inextricable connection with language, itself a process originating in the early period. As the child comes to develop a sense of duration, as he grows toward the conviction that relief with the "good" mother will soon come, he begins to "intend" the future, to actively expect gratification. This volitional "magic" becomes the foundation of our confidence in living. If we do not as children develop a belief in our "magical power" to alter the environment, or if such basic, healthy narcissism is eroded through punishment, loss, neglect, or rejection, we live with a sense of impotence and defeat, and a sense of impairment. According to Piaget and others, the concept of causality develops directly from the child's anticipation of the environment, his expectation, his growing "intentionality." Indeed, the concept of causality and space (encompassing succession, simultaneity, and velocity) are, in Piaget's view, necessary psycho–physical determinants of the time sense which, as we have seen, is firmly connected with the problem of maternal care.[66] Although the concept of "cause" may be, in the Kantian sense, a necessary dimension of human consciousness, just as space and time are, the manner in which we come to that idea, as well as the particular version of that idea which we have, cannot be accurately understood apart from its emotive, affective roots, its psychodynamic meaning.[67] Altered states of awareness involve altered conceptions of causality because one's ordinary idea of causality is connected with the internalized object, the central figures of the early time, upon whom one's "normal" consciousness rests. Kant's "categories"—time, space, and causality—are, as one experiences them, components of our mental gripping of the world, basic units of the psychological umbilical cord that we attach to creation and that we are tensed in our bodies to protect at all costs.

Certain periods of history unconsciously reveal this with startling precision, the "great chain of being" of the Middle Ages, for example, or the great anxiety engendered by Galileo's alteration of our basic conceptions of the universe, of time, of space, of cause and effect. But studies in the field of cultural anthropology also reveal the phenomenology of our concept of causality and its close relation to the problems of birth and separation. "The assumption," writes Lee, "is not that reality itself is relative; rather that it is differently punctuated and categorized, or that different aspects of it are noticed by, or presented to the participants of different cultures."[68] Among the Trobrianders of New Guinea, Doctor Lee notes,

> there is neither a temporal connection made—or, according to our own premises, perceived—between events; in fact, temporality is meaningless. There are no tenses, no linguistic distinction between past or present. There is no arrangement of activity into means and ends, no causal or teleologic relationships. . . . The taytu [yam] always remains itself; it does not become over–ripe; over–ripeness is an ingredient of another, a different being. At some point, the taytu turns into a yowana, which contains over–ripeness.[69]

These considerations prompted the anthropologist to investigate the concept of the line in human thought and its relation to the idea of cause.

> When we see a line of trees, or a circle of stones, we assume the presence of a connecting line which is not actually visible. And we assume it metaphorically when we follow a line of thought, a course of action, or the direction of an argument; . . . our performance tests and even our tests for sanity often assume that the line is present in nature. . . . But is the line present in reality? Malinowski, writing for members of our culture, . . . described the Trobriand village as follows: 'Concentrically with the circular row of yam houses there runs a ring of dwelling huts.' . . . But . . . the Trobrianders at no time mention circles or rings or even rows when they refer to their villages. . . . They . . . refer to a village . . . as [an] aggregate of bumps. . . . The Trobrianders do not describe their activity lineally; they do no dynamic relating of acts; they do not even use so innocuous a connective as *and*.[70]

The implications of this are striking indeed.

> We arrange events and objects in a sequence which is climactic, in size and intensity, in emotional meaning, or according to some other principle. We often arrange events from earlier to later, not because we are interested in historical causation, but because the present is the climax of our history. But when the Trobriander

relates happenings, there is no developmental arrangement, no building up of emotional tone. . . . To the Trobriander, climax in history is abominable, the denial of all good; . . . to him value lies in sameness, in repeated pattern, in the incorporation of all time within the same point. . . . As we see our history climactically, so do we plan future experiences climactically, leading up to future satisfaction or meaning. Who but a young child would think of starting a meal with strawberry short cake and ending it with spinach? We have come to identify the end of the meal with the height of satisfaction, and we identify semantically the words dessert and reward. . . . The Trobriand meal has no dessert, no line, no climax. The special bit, the relish, is eaten *with* the staple food; it is not something to 'look forward to,' while disposing of a meaningless staple.[71]

At this point in her discussion, the author turns to the questions of pregnancy and childbirth. Her writing here indicates the significance that linear thinking may have in the rearing of children, in the shaping of adults:

In our culture, childbearing is climactic. Pregnancy is represented by the usual obstetrician as an uncomfortable means to a dramatic end. . . . The approach of birth . . . is a period of mounting tension, and drama is supplied by the intensive social recognition of the event. . . . A pregnancy is not formally announced since, if it does not eventuate in birth, it has failed to achieve its end; and failure to reach the climax brings shame. . . . Among the Tobrianders, pregnancy has meaning in itself, as a state of being. At a first pregnancy, there is a long ceremonial involving preparatory work on the part of many people, which merely celebrates the pregnancy. It does not anchor the baby, it does not have as its purpose a more comfortable time during the pregnancy, it does not lead to an easier birth. . . . It makes the woman's skin white, and makes her be at her most beautiful; yet this leads to nothing, since she must not attract men, not even her own husband.[72]

And then,

Failure is devastating in our culture, because it is not failure of the undertaking alone; it is the moving, becoming, lineally conceived self which has failed.[73]

It would appear that our concept of lineal causality not only becomes an aspect of our ordinary consciousness but an aspect that engenders within our minds and bodies an enormous amount of tension and anxiety as well. Here, as elsewhere, the self we take to be normal, customary, or "fine," is in actuality a tense, converted self forged in the pressures of our peculiar infancy and childhood.

Chapter 3

THE ALTERATION OF AWARENESS
A New Psychoanalytic Approach to "The Mystical"

1.

Thus far, we have been exploring the process of conversion, the process by which our early experience in the world goads us into living at half pressure, alienated from our full potential as sensorial beings, and shut up in a condition we have chosen to describe as "ordinary awareness." In particular, we have concentrated on those psychological factors that make altered or non–ordinary awareness difficult to achieve. We have attempted to trace with some meticulousness specific areas of conflict which cause our "normal" state to appear an acceptable "place" to exist, better, surely, than the terror and strangeness of "new worlds." Paradoxically, however, the condition of ordinary awareness frequently drives the individual to attempt an alteration, drives him to escape the dynamic conflicts of his inner world and the sense of suffocation and stagnation which past experience has bred in him. As has been demonstrated elsewhere,[74] the "bad" alteration of awareness, the "bad trip" of drug abuse or "mental illness," invariably confronts the afflicted individual with "bad" materials from infancy and childhood, bad object, bad time, bad space, an interminable agony of abandonment, isolation, rejection, and failure.

In the material that follows "the break," the "happy" or "positive" alteration of consciousness achieved through a number of methods including meditation, physical exercise, psychotherapy, and drugs will be discussed. In every instance, the "happiness" of the achievement will derive from escaping an aspect of the conversion process. Two points must be firmly established from the outset. First, the achievement of a break may be partial or total, superficial or profound, joyous or mildly gratifying. One may discover himself in an entirely "new" condition, in an entirely new relationship to creation, in an entirely new universe, or one may simply have a glimmer of such things. In addition to this, the achievement of a break may be false or true, lasting or only very temporary. It can be based in genuine change; it may indicate genuine confrontation with, and overcoming of, the legacy of conversion, the ogres of the inner world. Or it may be falsely grounded in stiffening defenses, radical denial of internal conflict, a deepened alienation and withdrawal that passes for sublime detachment. Contact with the unconscious by no means predicates emotional and spiritual advancement.

The second point is this. Understanding of the break cannot be complete apart from an understanding of the method employed to achieve it. What one does in accomplishing the break is often what one is in the realization of it. The method is the end one seeks. The significance of this last point will emerge as the discussion proceeds.

It is frequently suggested in the psychological literature that the "good" alteration of awareness, the "mystical experience," or "peak," is a kind of "transitional phenomenon" that comprises, ultimately, the rediscovery of the "good object."[75] Such a view not only presents us with the danger of reductionism, it also presents us with the danger of analytical misemphasis, an even more serious error. Although a "good trip" will invariably involve some fresh contact with the good presences within, fresh contact which implies redistribution of internal boundaries, the reascendancy of positive internalizations and the diminution of negative ones, that contact may actually be minimal in any given instance. Indeed, the quality of a break is frequently determined not by the degree to which the individual reparticipates in the good object, finds his way to the benign internalizations, but by the degree to which he breaks free of all internalized objects, good ones as well as bad ones. Thus, the questions may arise: How can this be? If the individual breaks the tie to all internalized objects, what is the source of his positive emotion? What is it that he recontacts? Surely his good feelings must originate somewhere; they do not come from the void. But in a very real sense, that is precisely from where they come. They are the result of the individual recontacting what is traditionally called his "original nature," his "being," his "existence" as it is given to him by those natural forces that created him. In this way, there is an aspect of the break which is not derived from the world of the internalized object but which goes beyond or behind that world to the realm of essence, the realm in which vibrating atoms evolve along an infinite continuum of structural possibilities.

One may say, then, that the break will invariably constitute a kind of amalgamation of the individual's good objects and his true or original self. The relative presence, or the relative absence, of the good object in any given break will be determined, above all, by the extent to which the individual who is "having the trip" experiences the cessation or disappearance of time and space as we usually conceive of them, and the cessation or disappearance of symbols, or symbolical thoughts, as we usually conceive of them. (In the bad trip, of course, there is neither the absence of time and space nor the presence of good time and space; there is only bad time and space. Likewise, there is neither the absence of symbols nor the presence of good symbols; there is only the bad object.)

One of James's subjects, for example, speaks of her "mystical interlude" in this way:

> I was alone upon the seashore as all these thoughts flowed over me, liberating and reconciling; and now again, as once before in distant days in the Alps, . . . I was impelled to kneel down, this time before

> the illimitable ocean, symbol of the Infinite. . . . Earth, heaven, and
> sea resounded as in one vast world–encircling harmony. It was as if
> the chorus of all great men who have ever lived were about me. I felt
> myself one with them.[76]

It is the conspicuous presence of the ocean as symbol that indicates the relative presence of the "good object" in this "trip." The tie to the benign internalization is rediscovered, strengthened, renewed. The boundaries of the inner landscape shift in a positive way. Another "mystical experience" in James is presented as follows:

> There is no feeling of I, and yet the mind works, desireless, free
> from restlessness, objectless, bodiless. . . . The transport rises from
> the perception of forms and figures to a degree which escapes all
> expression.[77]

And again,

> The soul finds no terms, no means, no comparison, whereby to
> render the sublimity. . . . We receive this mystical knowledge . . .
> clothed in none of the kinds of images, in none of the sensible
> representations, which our mind makes use of in other cir-
> cumstances.[78]

Here, one has the relative absence of the good object. The ties to the inner world are radically severed. Such an experience, at first glance, could appear to resemble psychosis. But psychosis involves not the severing or loss of all ties to the inner world, as is often thought to be the case; it involves, rather, the severing or the loss of, only the good ties. The bad ones remain, as they do for Symonds whose "pathological trance" is thus described: "It consisted in a gradual but swiftly progressive obliteration of space, time, sensation, and the multitudinous factors of experience. . . . And what then? The apprehension of a coming dissolution, . . . the sense that I had followed the last thread of being to the verge of the abyss."[79]

To put it somewhat differently, psychosis does not occur when the individual truncates his connection with "reality," and, therefore, loses his way back to the "ordinary universe." It occurs when the individual becomes absorbed into the bad object, when nothing remains but an inimical, persecuting presence. The yoga who sits contentedly in a deep, meditative trance may resemble the psychotic in that he has detached himself from the "ordinary universe." But he is different from the psychotic in that his detachment grows out of a willful renunciation of all ties to the inner world, rather than out of a tragic, hopeless sense of rejection. The yoga knows that "the world" is forged in the conversion process and, therefore, contributes to his suffering; he has survived the conversion process and wants to renounce the "ordinary reality" which is its result. The psychotic is still struggling to gain "the world"; he has not survived the conversion process. As for the "mystical interlude," it consists in the intuitive or bodily expression of what the yoga has raised to the level of philosophical practice. Our job at the present moment is to grasp, first, *why* the disappearance of the symbol, of time, and of space should produce the good feelings which are present during the break, and second, *how* the disappearance of these items is triggered in the human organism.

2.

Relied upon here is the most vivid and influential account of a "break" precipitated through the use of an hallucinogen, namely Huxley's *Doors of Perception*. First, Huxley's report is, in respect of its key phenomenological features, identical with other vivid, influential accounts by such writers as Havelock Ellis and Christopher Mayhew.[80] Second, Huxley's pages look forward, once again in respect of key phenomenological items, to philosophical and religious utterances that stand at the center of the "mystical" tradition. Below are crucial passages:

> I took my pill at eleven. An hour and a half later I was sitting in my study, looking intently at a small glass vase. The vase contained only three flowers—a full-blown Belle of Portugal rose, shell pink

with a hint at every petal's base of a hotter, flamier hue; a large magenta and cream-coloured carnation; and, pale purple at the end of its broken stalk, the bold heraldic blossom of an iris. Fortuitous and provisional, the little nosegay broke all the rules of traditional good taste. At breakfast that morning I had been struck by the lively dissonance of its colours. But that was no longer the point. I was not looking now at an unusual flower arrangement. I was seeing what Adam had seen on the morning of his creation—the miracle, moment by moment, of naked existence.[81]

Huxley goes on,

I continued to look at the flowers, and in their living light I seemed to detect the qualitative equivalent of breathing—but of a breathing without returns to a starting–point, with no recurrent ebbs but only a repeated flow from beauty to heightened beauty, from deeper to ever deeper meaning. Words like Grace and Transfiguration came to my mind, and this of course was what, among other things, they stood for. . . . The really important facts were that spatial relationships had ceased to matter very much and that my mind was perceiving the world in terms of other than spatial categories. At ordinary times the eye concerns itself with such problems as *Where?—How far?—How situated in relation to what?* In the mescalin experience the implied questions to which the eye responds are of another order. Place and distance cease to be of much interest. The mind does its perceiving in terms of intensity of existence, profundity of significance, relationships within a pattern. I saw the books, but was not at all concerned with their positions in space. What I noticed, what impressed itself upon my mind was the fact that all of them glowed with living light.[82]

And again,

From the books the investigator directed my attention to the furniture. . . . The legs, for example, of that chair—how miraculous their tubularity, how supernatural their polished smoothness! I spent several minutes—or was it several centuries?—not merely gazing at those bamboo legs, but actually *being* them—or rather being myself in them; or, to be still more accurate (for 'I' was not involved in the case, nor in a certain sense were 'they') being my Not–self in the Not–self which was the chair.[83]

From his experience Huxley concludes,

> The chair Van Gogh had seen was obviously the same in essence as the chair I had seen. But, though incomparably more real than the chair of ordinary perception, the chair in his picture remained no more than an unusually expressive symbol of the fact. The fact had been manifested Suchness; this was only an emblem. Such emblems are sources of true knowledge about the Nature of Things, and this true knowledge may serve to prepare the mind which accepts it for immediate insights on its own account. But that is all. However expressive, symbols can never be the things they stand for. . . . Art, I suppose, is only for beginners, or else for those resolute dead–enders, who have made up their minds to be content with the *ersatz* of Suchness, with symbols rather than with what they signify.[84]

Under the influence of mescaline,

> Visual impressions are greatly intensified and the eye recovers some of the perceptual innocence of childhood, when the sensum was not immediately and automatically subordinated to the concept. Interest in space is diminished and interest in time falls almost to zero.[85]

The "equation" of the break, then, is clear: out of time and space, out of symbolified thinking, the organism is suddenly filled with feelings of knowingness, wonder, and bliss, feelings that arise from what can be termed a new or altered mode of perception. What is it, then, that underlies this process?

Because symbolical sight depends on a translation of the particular "thing" into an instance of the class of things to which it belongs in ordinary perception, symbolical sight of necessity requires duration. There can be no translation without time. Note, for example, this characterization of "cerebral activity" in "healthy adults" that appears in Kleitman's classic paper on dreaming:

> Responding to the impulses that stream in from the various receptor organs of the sensory system, the cortex first subjects them to analysis. It refers the present moment of experience to its memory of the past and present into the future, weighing the consequences of action not yet taken. A decision is reached, and the cortex generates

an integrated response. This is manifested in the action of the
effector organs (mostly muscles) or in the deliberate inhibition of
action.[86]

Neisser, in *The Processes of Vision,* puts it even more succinctly: "Perceiving involves a memory that is not representational
but schematic."[87] The implications are evident. The cessation of
time that occurs in the break—and by time is meant linear time as
we usually comprehend it—precludes or inhibits the formation of
symbols. The "thing" that comes into the ken of the perceiver is
apprehended directly rather than "schematically." A chair, vase,
flower, or mountain is not subconsciously translated, in an instan-
taneous quantum burst of cerebral energy, into an example of the
species "chair," "vase," "flower," or "mountain"; it becomes
instead the "creature" that it simply is. Thus, without categories
within which to fit items, the world is suddenly there, fresh, new,
pristine, with each perception of it. The alienation that stems from
one's habitual or ordinary awareness ceases suddenly; one *has* his
world as he "has never had it before." Says Don Juan to Castaneda
(and this author italicizes the words that underscore the thesis),
" '[The world] appeared to be an alien world to you, because your
perception had not been trimmed yet to fit the desired mold.' . . .
'Was that the way I really saw the world?' I asked. 'Certainly,' he
said. *'That was your memory.'* "[88]
    Again, because symbols "live" or exist in time, the time that
permits the translation to occur, the apprehension of timelessness,
or the feeling of eternity, will ordinarily increase with the cessation
of symbolical sight. What is being described is a kind of pulsation,
or reinforcing give and take between the cessation of linear time
and the direct perception of the world. As the "items" that comprise the "external universe" are born anew, over and over again,
or "forever," eternity becomes as real to the perceiver as his own
being—the organismic "unit" through which his perception transpires. "Believe it or not," declares Huxley, "eternity is real; it is as
real as shit."[89]

3.

If symbolical sight depends upon linear time for its existence, however, linear time, in turn, depends for its existence on the continuous generation of cerebral or perceptual energy. "Perceptions are in quanta," writes James; "the concept of time as duration develops out of incessant impulses of voluntary reinforcement in maintaining attention with effort." Hence, "experience comes in quanta," and it is the "intellect only" that "makes it continuous."[90]

Freud's conclusions are virtually identical with James's: "The attention which we bestow on objects is due to rapid but successive cathexes which might be regarded in a sense as quanta issuing from the ego. Our inner perceptual activity would only later make a continuity of it, and it is here that we find, projected into the outside world, the prototype of time."[91] Clearly then, the translation of "thing" into "member of class of things," a translation that is grounded in linear time and constitutes the essence of ordinary awareness, is a particular kind of behavior or action, a specialized mental and emotive performance on the part of the human organism. As that behavior subsides, or action ceases, as that performance ends, the organism is suddenly charged, infused or flooded with the energy, power, and quanta that formerly went into the translation, into the making and maintaining of the temporal world and its symbolified inhabitants, the "items" of "ordinary awareness." When Freud writes of "the attention" we "bestow" on "objects," and when James writes of the "experience" we undergo daily, each fails to specify that it is our ordinary attention, or ordinary experience, that is at issue. "The ubiquitous use of light as a metaphor for mystic experience . . . may not be just a metaphor," suggests Deikman. " 'Illumination' may be derived from an actual sensory experience" involving the "liberation of energy."[92] With the energic connection between time and symbol firmly established in our minds, we are able to perceive the source of this "liberation."

This author is not implying, of course, that the entire store of

the organism's energy is consumed in the moment of "illumination." Obviously, a portion of that power is involved in the individual's positive sensorial experiences. Reminding us that "entrancing displays of imagery of great beauty and clarity can be
experienced by ordinary people under the influence of hallucinogenic drugs such as mescaline," Eccles declares that "the cortex
under these conditions tends to develop ever more complex and
effectively interlocked patterns of neuronal activity involving
large fractions of its neuronal population."[93] It is precisely those
"large fractions" of the "neuronal population" customarily devoted
to the preservation of ordinary reality that are freed to create such
"entrancing displays." In the words of Jacobson, "the cathexes of
the self–representations, though gaining such powerful contribu-
tions from the object–libidinous sources, are certainly founded on
the original stock of undifferentiated psychic energy with which
the whole self, including the organs that are the kernels of the
future . . . ego, had been primarily vested."[94] In the "break," where
such "self–representations" (self–symbols in time and space)
cease, the "stock" of such "energy" is considerably restored.

To stress the liberation of neurons, the redistribution of quan-
tified impulses emanating from the cerebral cortex, is to stress
what could be termed the physiological side of the problem. To
stress the manner in which such phenomena bear on the conversion
process is to stress what might be termed the psychological side.
Once again, James and Freud point the way. For when James
writes that time as duration develops out of "incessant impulses" of
"voluntary reinforcement," and when Freud writes of the "successive cathexes" which we "bestow upon objects," each helps to
remind us that ordinary awareness fulfils a need within the individual. This need cannot be understood apart from its connection
to the whole development of the person as a psycho–physical
organism.

The voluntary maintenance of time as duration is rooted in the
individual's need to translate the thing into the symbol, and hence,
to retain the tie to the internalized object, to keep open the percep-

tual, psychological avenue that leads back to the inhabitants of the inner world. Because we answer the separation crises of infancy by internalizing the individuals we have to give up, and because the capacity for language and symbolic thought is the culmination of the internalizing process (a developmental feature that is actually goaded into operation by the anxiety surrounding separation) we cling to the symbolified mode of perception that arises from the early time and that provides us with the familiar, "ordinary" world. But the translation of the "thing" into the symbol can only occur in time. Internalization, in other words, can only occur in time. Hence, time as duration is voluntarily maintained by the individual because time as duration permits the "translation" upon which his ordinary emotive security rests. We keep on making our temporal, symbolical world over and over again because just beneath it, we believe, lies the void, separation, isolation, starvation, oblivion. What Roheim calls "dual–unity," the ability to be separate from the object of infancy and yet, at the same time, to maintain contact, is grounded in the ability and will to keep time going. For as long as time is kept going, internalization and the ordinary world which is its product, can also be kept going.

What one experiences in the break is the astounding, earth–shaking realization that his well–being does not necessarily depend on the tie to the internalized object. The world that serves as a "transitional phenomenon," as a substitute for the relinquished parent, *can* be given up, and one *can* still be all right. To be out of linear time, ordinary space, or without one's habitual symbolic associations, one's "language," does not mean disaster, isolation, oblivion. On the contrary, to truncate the tie to the internalized object (the good object as well as the bad object) is to appreciate that one has a self that is one's own, that is not derived from the existence of the other, and that is not dependent upon the old, internalized relationship. The love of the self, or the delight in the self, as we ordinarily experience and conceive it, is derived from the mother's affection and care. It is her love onto us that we transfer onto ourselves through internalization. What we ordinarily take to be love of the self is, in actuality, love of the made self, the symbolical self, the self we can analyze and think about, the self that leads to the self–image, in a word, the ego.

4.

One is able to grasp from this perspective the true significance of the "empty mind." This state is the highest achievement of eastern religion and philosophy, the culmination of one's struggle toward "enlightenment." Writes Suzuki,

> When you have something in your consciousness you do not have perfect composure. The best way toward perfect composure is to forget everything. Then your mind is calm, and it is wide and clear enough to see and feel things as they are without any effort. . . . Actually, emptiness of mind is not even a state of mind, but the original essence of mind which Buddha and the Sixth Patriarch experienced.[95]

To the degree that one truncates his tie to the internalized object, he empties his mind. For as we have seen, the world of "ordinary awareness," of ordinary time and space, of ordinary symbolified thinking, was achieved in the effort to retain that tie. The very running on of our thoughts becomes our habitual way of preserving our security. That is why it is so difficult to stop the running on. When Freud writes that we project our sense of duration onto an external world which we create out of that very sense,[96] he unwittingly describes the inception of ordinary awareness. This is, in actuality, the filling of our minds with our own projections.

"Reality" is our fantasy version of the parent. When the tie to the internalized object is broken, we are able to see the variety and freshness of the universe because we no longer need to see only that, or primarily that, which re–establishes and reconfirms our safety, our bond with the object within. It is precisely when, in Horton's terms, we are able to make external occurrences into internal events that we have escaped, if only for a moment, our "normal," habitual proclivity to make internal events into external occurrences.[97] As Huxley puts it, we no longer come to the world with an "emotionally charged ego";[98] we come, rather, with a renewed, liberated self whose truest inclination is to be in a kind of interlocking relationship with the given, and, thereby, to fulfil its sensorial capacity for living. Those "entrancing displays" of the hallucinogenic journey are registered on the "empty mind" of the "subject," the mind that is no longer afraid to break its ancient perceptual connection with the other, the mind that no longer has separation on its mind. With the tie to the object of infancy broken, one is free to play with creation, to allow the external world to be precisely what it "wishes" to be, to enjoy to the full one's remarkable, registering brain, that wonder of evolution which had been long curtailed by the press of one's dependent, emotional needs. The withdrawal from the world, the deadening of the senses that began with the violence of birth and that led to the splitting of the maternal figure, to "analysis," all of this has ceased. One is *in* the universe again, and one is there with one's "original nature," one's pure subjectivity, one's "empty mind."

Attempting to characterize the heart of Buddhist philosophy, Huxley writes,

> Appearances are discriminated by the sense organs, then reified by naming, so that words are taken for things and symbols are used as the measure for reality. According to this view, language is a main source of the sense of separateness and the blasphemous idea of individual self–sufficiency, with their inevitable corollaries of greed, envy, lust for power, anger and cruelty.[99]

But the human being's innate capacity for symbolical thinking is inextricably tied to the conversion process; it is used defensively to answer the anxieties of birth and separation. Hence, we become alienated from ourselves through the very powerfulness of our brain, and that brain's highest analytical functions come to be associated in our emotions with the terrors and discomforts of the early time. One is able to understand from this perspective why "naming" becomes so important, why "words" are eventually taken for things, and why it feels so good to relinquish this "ordinary awareness," to "blindly behold," to contemplate the universe freely and directly without the intervention of a "language" that is fixed in an emotive requirement. But we have still to enlarge upon the issue of *how* such contemplation comes about.

5.

As was earlier stressed, the human being is a "psycho–physical entity". His "bodily processes" and his "emotional processes" are, from the beginning, "fused."[100] The child's experience of himself and of his world "is mediated through the tactual, visual, and kinesthetic contact with the mother. His initial intake of the world comes through her and with her."[101]

> The precursors of the abstract concept of mother are the inner perceptions represented by the fusion of sensations arising from touch, smell, taste, hearing, vision, and movement of the object, with all the sensory perceptions arising from changes in bodily sensations, bodily activity, and movement within the body induced by these external stimuli. . . . Internal reactions to sensory stimuli do not follow exclusively physiological laws. . . . Specific sensory stimuli become tied to objects and evoke in condensed form the history of specific object relationships.[102]

In this way, the "sensorial perceptions" of the individual (stimuli) can be linked with his "symbolifications." The upshot is clear: our ordinary awareness, the durational, spatial, and symbolical manner in which we ordinarily perceive the world is related directly to the manner in which we "handle" the physical stimulus. "Ordinary awareness" does not constitute simply a "mental" tie to the object. It constitutes a chemical and/or physical tie as well. A perception is a physical action. As such, it has physical consequences. These are registered in our bodies, organs, and chemistry. The way we "hold" ourselves "mentally" (the way in which we receive stimulation) is the way in which we hold ourselves chemically. In other words, it is the way in which we control or govern the physiological condition of our bodies. Since the stimulus and the mother are linked from the beginning, to depart our "ordinary chemistry," our "ordinary physiology," is to sever our deepest unconscious bond with the internalized object, i.e. the mother, upon whom our survival and well–being depended during the crises of birth and separation. Hence, to alter the manner in which we ordinarily receive the stimulus is to alter the manner in which we ordinarily hold onto the object. To alter the manner in which we ordinarily hold onto the object is to alter the manner in which we ordinarily perceive the world, for the manner in which we ordinarily perceive the world is itself the manner in which we ordinarily hold onto the object.

Writing of concentrative meditation, one of the most important methods of altering awareness, Ornstein points out that

> continuous repetition of the same stimulus may be considered the equivalent of no stimulation at all. . . . Concentrative meditation is a practical technique which uses an experiential knowledge of the structure of our nervous system to 'turn off' awareness of the external world. . . . The techniques of concentrative meditation are not deliberately mysterious or exotic but are simply a matter of practical applied psychology.[103]

Similarly, Deikman contends that the "deautomatization of response" on which the "alteration of awareness" depends, can only be induced by "renunciation," specifically the renunciation of sensorial input or stimuli.[104] But unless such explanations include the human, emotive dimension they become mechanical, alienating, and ultimately meaningless. To restrict, or "renounce" one's reception of stimuli is to sever the tie to the internalized object with which those stimuli are "fused" and on which the perception of the world is based. One cannot have "vision" until one has freedom; one cannot "expand his awareness" until he is emotionally free to do so. The struggle to see is inseparable from the struggle to gain one's self. And the attainment of selfhood is largely a matter of truncating the dependent bond within. No wonder that individual subjects who are deprived of sensory stimuli during the course of psychological experiments become irritable, childish, depressed, hallucinatory, and "eager for stimulation."[105] They feel bad in their bodies because they have been deprived of their psycho-physical nourishment, the stimulation that hooks them up with the significant others of the inner world, that permits ordinary awareness to transpire, and that re–establishes thereby the old, habitual security.

To suggest that the internalized object of infancy is rooted in one's chemistry, musculature, and body, and that the alteration of one's physiological processes can change one's emotive existence by changing one's perceptual mode, may appear somewhat strange. The results of certain psychological investigations, such as Dicara's recent work in the area of "autonomic" response, change that view, however. Guarding against the "contamination" of results, Dicara administered curare to each of his experimental animals (rats). Although the drug "paralyzes" the "subject's skeletal muscles" it "does not interfere with consciousness or with the transmitters that mediate autonomic responses."[106] Dicara's experiment "showed that the instrumental learning of two visceral responses can occur independently of each other and that what is learned is specifically the rewarded response."[107] Such findings "have profound significance for theories of learning." They "should lead to better understanding of the cause and cure of psychosomatic disorders and of the mechanisms whereby the body maintains homeostasis, or a stable internal environment."[108] The autonomic nervous system, then, is not so "autonomic" after all. "Visceral responses" can be "modified" by "learning."

Similar results were obtained by Kohler who concentrated his efforts on the functioning of the eye. Having "saddled" his human subjects with a certain kind of goggle that "distorted" what one may term their "normal" vision, Kohler discovered the extent to which the "organ" of sight is able to "abandon" its "established habits" and "to respond" in a manner that is genuinely "new."[109] He writes,

> When we make the system break down and learn a new way of functioning, we do not believe we are forcing the system to function

artificially or abnormally. We assume, rather, that a single mechanism is at work at all times. The mechanism that removes or minimizes an artificially created disturbance is the same one that brings about a normal functioning.

He goes on in what one must regard as a crucial passage, "organs are not rigid machines but living and variable systems, the functioning of which is itself subject to variation. If a sensory system is exposed to a new and prolonged stimulus situation that departs from the one normally experienced, the system can be expected to undergo a fundamental change in its normal mode of operation".[110]

Bertalanffy "raises" this concept to the level of biological principle:

> Separation between a pre–established structure and processes occurring in this structure does not apply to the living organism. For the organism is the expression of an everlasting orderly process, though, on the other hand, this process is sustained by underlying structures and organized forms. What is described in morphology as organic forms and structures is, in reality, a momentary cross–section through a spatio-temporal pattern. What are called structures are slow processes of long duration; functions are quick processes of short duration. If we say that a function, such as the contraction of a muscle, is performed by a structure, it means that a quick and short process wave is superimposed on a long–lasting and slowly running wave.[111]

The psychodynamic implications of this material are striking. What the infant experiences during birth and separation will be "learned" in his body, organs, and in his chemistry (the conversion process).

Because function is structure and structure function, because we cannot separate the two, what one does is what he is. To internalize the maternal figure in response to specific infantile traumata is to internalize her into the body–ego where she will continue to dwell until a change occurs. As we have seen, the ordinary chemical condition of our bodies controls our ordinary perception of the world because it controls the manner in which we receive the external stimulus. What this means emotionally is that our ordinary perception of the world is controlled by the object within, the object whose imprint is stamped upon our muscles, and whose dwelling is up and down our veins. Thus, the break can only derive from the alteration of chemical "posture." This means the undoing of the conversion process in psychodynamic terms. One cannot experience the world anew until one *feels* anew inside. And to feel anew inside one must change one's "composition." One's physiology, one's *body,* must become one's own. Unlike the child who "belongs" to the mother, one must belong, finally, to oneself.

There are, needless to say, numerous procedures for altering one's physiological processes in such a way as to loosen the deep, chemical bond to the "other" within. Ellis, Mayhew, and Huxley ingest mescaline, as do the members of the Native American Church described in Slotkin's well known account.[112] The Dervishes, Shah writes, chant and sway:

> We enter a dimly lighted room where a number of men are gathered. As we do so a signal is given by a man who appears to be the leader of the assembly, and the doors are shut. There is a hush as twelve men form into two parallel lines in the center of the room. The glimmer of a solitary hurricane lamp falls on dark faces in which only the eyes seem to live. The rest of us fall back to the sides of the room. The Dhikr is about to begin. With a startline clap of the hands the leader starts swaying from right to left. Very slowly he begins, and the men fall into the rhythm of his swaying. Every time they sway to the left they call 'Hu!' in chorus, 'Hu . . . Hu . . . Hu . . .'.[113]

The Sufis, who also chant and sway, tell "teaching stories" as well, stories that presumably have a profound effect on the listener, awakening within him a kind of "ah ha!" sensation marking a sudden shift of his bodily processes. This, consequently, induces a modified perception of the world. Don Juan, the mentor of Carlos Castaneda, goes for long, arduous walks in the desert. The student of Zen Buddhism concentrates on his "koan." The transcendental meditator concentrates on his "mantrum." The Jewish mystic fasts, a procedure that asserts independence by breaking the oral tie to the parent in a relatively obvious way, and which also reaches down to the "mother within" by radically disrupting the normal bodily state.

The author does not want to create the impression that he is thinking in terms of rigorous cause and effect. The break may begin at the top or at the bottom. It may be triggered primarily by a mental content that affects the chemistry or primarily by a chemical change that affects the mental content. In every instance, however, the break will attest to the interdependence of body and brain. It will feel good partly because it will announce the fact that the subject is ultimately an integrated organism, that his "mental" side is inextricably related to his "physical" side, and his physical side to his mental. Always, the break will be a transaction between body and brain. Never will its cause be exclusive.

As had been pointed out, the break induced by any or all of the procedures just described may last for a moment or for a day; it may be relatively mild or relatively intense; it may be forgotten immediately at its conclusion, or it may have a profound and lasting influence on the individual. We cannot, of course, discuss all of the procedures in detail here. Not only does each of them merit a thorough analysis along psychological lines, but the topic of the hallucinogens is so entirely embedded in controversy that an exploration of it alone would require a separate volume. Still, we must discuss briefly an aspect of the break that commonly accompanies all of the procedures mentioned, and that also accompanies the "spontaneous alteration," the break that occurs apart from the employment of any procedures at all: relaxation.

6.

Let us recall that in virtually every instance the "mystical interludes" that James reports in his *Varieties of Religious Experience* are accompanied by a degree of mental and muscular relaxation. Dr. Burke's "enlightenment" transpires as he sits calmly in his hansom driving home after a strenuous evening of philosophical discussion. Mr. Trine's "mystical policeman" invariably undergoes his alteration when he has just gone "off duty" and is "on his way home in the evening." The "loveliness of the morning" comes over Mr. Trevor when he is no longer experiencing the unpleasant obligation to attend a church service in the company of his "wife and boys." To "go down there to the chapel, would be for the time an act of spiritual suicide." Kingsley's "mystical consciousness" is awakened as he "walks in the fields" without purpose or aim.[114]

Everywhere in the religious and meditative literature one discovers similar clues. "There is a state of mind, known to religious men, but to no others," writes James,

> in which the will to assert ourselves and hold our own has been displaced by a willingness to close our mouths and be as nothing in the floods and waterspouts of God. In this state of mind, what we most dreaded has become the habitation of our safety, and the hour of our moral death has turned into our spiritual birthday. The time for tension in our soul is over and that of happy relaxation, of calm, deep breathing, of an eternal present, with no discordant future to be anxious about, has arrived.[115]

According to the Chinese text, *The Awakening of Faith*, the individual who proposes to "stop" his ordinary thoughts and to achieve thereby another kind of awareness must "retire to some quiet place and there, sitting erect, earnestly seek to tranquillize and concentrate the mind."[116] "All our actions must be devoted, in the last analysis," writes Huxley, "to making ourselves passive in relation to the activity and the being of divine Reality."[117] "Zazen practice for the student," writes Kapleau, "begins with his counting the inhalations and exhalations of his breath while he is in the motionless zazen posture. This is the first step in the process of stilling the bodily functions."[118] According to the Lama Govinda, "From this state of perfect mental and physical equilibrium and its resulting inner harmony grows that serenity and happiness which fills the whole body with a feeling of supreme bliss."[119] "Good and bad is not the point," writes the Zen master, Shunryu Suzuki, "whether or not you make yourself peaceful is the point, and whether or not you persist to do so."[120] And indeed, the majority of meditative schools strive to induce in the "subject" a "happy" or "positive" change of awareness by helping him/her achieve a state of relaxation, a state of "composure" and "peace." It would appear, in fact, that an altered state of consciousness can arise quite naturally from a relaxed condition. Why should this be so?

The process of conversion is a bodily process, one that leaves its mark upon the body. We have seen the newborn infant tense himself, brace himself, indeed struggle to withdraw himself during the violent moments of his birth. We have recognized that his earliest "ego," his earliest "self," is a body ego, a body self, and that his discomfort is registered there. We have also recognized that internalization is not simply a psychological but a psycho–physical process. The infant and young child who takes in the object experiences that object in his body, in his anxious respiration, in his posture of avoidance, in his stiff, contracted frustration and rage. The splitting and divisiveness of the early time transpire within the cells of the organism, only later to be "elevated" to the level of symbolical representation. But even when anxiety, tension, and divisiveness are "raised" to the symbolic level, they still retain their hold upon the body; they still exist, as persistently and as powerfully as ever, in the individual's "length of blood and bone."

Indeed, here is the very essence of the notion of integration. Mental contents cannot be separated from bodily contents. To empty or to "tranquillize" the mind is to empty or to "tranquillize" the body precisely. The symbol, with its time and space, is rooted in the body, grows out of the body, is but a "higher" development of bodily awareness. One grasps from this perspective the psychodynamic significance of recent experiments with individuals in the midst of meditative trances, experiments that establish not only a significant rise in "skin resistance," a sign of diminishing anxiety, but also a significant drop in lactate production and consequently in the blood–lactate level. Wallace and Benson suggest that meditation

> generates an integrated response, or reflex, that is mediated by the central nervous system. A well–known reflex of such a nature was described many years ago by the noted Harvard physiologist Walter B. Cannon; it is called the 'fight or flight' or 'defense alarm' reaction. The aroused sympathetic nervous system mobilizes a set of physiological responses marked by increases in the blood pressure, heart rate, blood flow to the muscles and oxygen consumption. The hypometabolic state produced by meditation is of course opposite to this in almost all respects. . . . During man's early history the defense–alarm reaction may well have had high survival value.[121]

But what these authors miss is that each man's "early history" begins with his birth and infancy. The "defense–alarm" in question is triggered when the helpless, breathless infant undergoes the process of violent birth, when his lungs are traumatized, when he respires anaerobically, thus producing lactate, in an effort to keep himself alive. It is also triggered, to one degree or another, throughout the course of infancy, throughout the time in which the terrors of separation beset the child, throughout the time in which frustration and rage are upon him, throughout the time in which he defensively internalizes the object, throughout the time in which the entire conversion process transpires. In this way, the peaceful body one attains during the process of meditation is the somatic equivalent of the empty mind. To relax is to stop one's "bodily thoughts," to sever the connection with the early period at the unconscious, bodily level, the level of physiological processes. That such relaxation should go hand–in–hand with an alteration of mental awareness is perfectly natural when we recall once again that ordinary consciousness, consciousness in time and space and symbol, is the outgrowth of our chemical and physical processes and the means of retaining the tie to the object within.

It is not only for innate, biological reasons that "normal mentation" acts as a "reducing valve," or a filter to screen out "useless and irrelevant information"; it is for defensive, psychological reasons as well. In Horton's psychoanalytic terms, it is not only the "mystical experience" which may be regarded as a "transitional phenomenon."[122] Ordinary awareness is itself such a phenomenon, a "compromise formation" that provides emotive security at the enormous price of bodily tension and sensorial alienation from the universe. When we relax we not only reduce that tension by decreasing the contact with the object within, the internalized other who is integrally bound up with our defensive posture and ever–present anticipation, we also regain our natural inclination to participate sensorially in a world that is no longer threatening. Confident enough to let our senses ingather the enormous treasures they are able to receive, we confront a creation of inexhaustible variety, beauty, and delight. Again, it is hardly a coincidence that meditation and religion are closely aligned in the literature and in the practice of all nations. Although it may sound a bit odd to put it this way, religion is intended in large measure to relax us, ease us out of the old relation to the internalized object, alter our bodies in which the object dwells, and, thereby, make us more secure in our lives. The "creature" which we are, writes St. Bernard, "has need of a body, without which it could nowise attain that knowledge which it obtains as the only approach to those things, by knowledge of which it is made blessed."[123] In the words of Eliade, one experiences "the nostalgia for a lost paradise, the longing to know Divinity," with "our very senses."[124] The "peace" that "passeth understainding" is, by definition, the conscious and unconscious peace that obtains when the tie to the old inner world is severed at both the mental and bodily levels. Hence, we are "saved" when we are relaxed; we are saved when we are safe from the terrors and rigors of the conversion process, from its legacy of tension and paranoid fear. To maintain, as does Freud, that religion is regression in that it provides an avenue back to the parental figure within, and consists primarily in the unconscious placation of the forces of the superego, is to characterize only one side of the problem. In its most profound, ideal functioning religion's purpose in both the east and west is to provide us with an escape from the

parental figures, from the customary, daily regression that ordinary or "profane" awareness constitutes, from the miseries, mental
and bodily, of a world that is forged in the first, terrible psycho–
physical conversion of the infant man. It is when the religious
meaning of the term conversion combines at the level of understanding and practice with the psychoanalytical meaning that the
enormous benefits to be derived from the "mystical," benefits with
both individual and cultural significance, begin to emerge.

7.

The individual is tied to his culture by the very same psychological forces that tie him to the objects of his inner world and
hence to his ordinary consciousness. Alteration of awareness is not
simply a method of disrupting the so–called intrapsychic bonds;
rather, it is a method of disrupting the social bonds as well. The
institutions of culture are, in large measure, defensive replies to
the imperfections that attend the establishment of ordinary reality,
replies to the problems of conversion, separation, rejection, and
loss. At the same time, such institutions foster cultural orders in
which inequalities of wealth, inequalities of power, characterize
the collective life of the people. The discontents of civilization
ultimately arise whence the discontents of the converted individual
arise, namely the dynamics of internalization and the tensions of
the inner world that are "worked out" at the level of "ordinary"
social relations. In this way, the alteration of awareness is a
potential revolutionary instrument which can be employed in con-
junction with other techniques, such as sociopsychoanalysis,[125] to
loosen the tie to the internalized object in which institutional
mentality is grounded and hence raise the consciousness of those in
society who harbor the power to create change. The tie to the
internalized object of infancy, ordinary reality, and hence to culture is, as we have seen, an energic and power tie. In a specific
sense, it is a work tie. To truncate these connections through
altered awareness, or what we have come to regard as a "break," is

to divert one's power from institutional, cultural, and transitional aims that link the individual to the inner world as well as language and the symbolic realm. That power can then be redirected toward the goal of liberation. This would mean, of course, that a measure of one's power would no longer be available to what can be termed "the establishment." Reich's concept that ideologies are internalized into the body through familial and specifically patriarchal influence is important here.[126] But Reich, lacking awareness of the mother–infant relationship, the dynamics of internalization, and the analytical significance of ordinary consciousness, was unable to suggest in any realizable way a direction from which genuine change might occur.

Concentrating on the extent to which the early object of infancy is internalized into the body, and the degree to which that object is rooted in the senses, we can spy a fresh perspective from which to regard the work of Marcuse and Brown. Both, remember, insist that the tyranny of culture and the sickness of civilization exert their deepest influences through the suppression of the individual's body.

As the parent is internalized into the body, and as the tie to the parent begets the tie to the group (Freud), the alteration of awareness betokens a return of the individual's body to himself. The underlying significance of Freud's suggestion that repression and guilt constitute the cornerstones of "civilization" is apparent. Repression allows the body to remain in its converted condition, tied to the object, doomed to discontent, and taken over by the institutional forces of society that derive *their* power through a psychophysical extension of the parental bond. One's guilt derives from the betrayal of oneself and from rebellious inclinations that lie repressed at the very foundation of one's personality. These inclinations are not to murder the father, but to *separate* from the mother, and from the father as her successor, in a word, to alter the nature of one's participation in the world, to perceive things differently, and to be sensorially, perceptually, bodily free.

That this conclusion holds crucial economic implications, indeed, allows the reader to grasp more fully the nature of our economic institutions, or the psychoanalytic significance of capitalism, will emerge as another model develops, one that indicates the manner in which Roheim's observation that culture maintains the dual–unity situation, re-establishes the unconscious bond with the parent, may be worked out in relation to the western economies. For that is what has been lacking, the working out of Roheim's idea. After having developed the economic model we can return to Freud, and Marcuse, and Brown in an effort to meticulously analyze their work from the perspective of the mother–infant interaction, the establishment of ordinary awareness, the alteration of consciousness, and the social, religious, and economic implications of these items. When *that* is done, the ecological, evolutionary, and spiritual implications of the entire analysis will be in view. It is ironic that religion or "the occult," something Freud warred on throughout the course of his life, should hold a key to the problem he presented with such ardor on several occasions. This is, of course, the problem of "civilization and its discontents." One cannot help wondering, what would he say!

Part III

THE ECONOMIC WORLD

Chapter 4

MONEY, SACRIFICE, AND OBJECT
RELATIONS

1.

Gesell declares in his classic study *The Natural Economic
Order* that "goods, not money, are the real foundation of economic
life."[127] He then asserts: "Money is an instrument of exchange and
nothing else."[128] These are crucial assertions that can, when care-
fully explored from a psychoanalytic angle, help us to understand
what might be termed the transitional mode of economic organization, and even the transitional mode of cultural organization generally.

We have seen the term "transitional" before, specifically in
relation to the "mystical" experience. One analytical view of it
holds that the experiencer contacts his "good objects" during the
course of his "peak" and, thus, discovers, or better, rediscovers,
psychological "entities" that are unavailable to him in ordinary
consciousness.[129] The term "transitional" also figures importantly
in Winnicott's work where "good enough mothering" permits the
growing child to participate in the "objects" of his "cultural experi-

ence" and, hence, to find a method of separating from the parental figure while, paradoxically, maintaining the connection to that figure, all in the same psychological moment.[130] More will be said regarding Winnicott's views later.

Of the transitional object itself Greenacre writes,

> [It] represents not only the mother's breast and body but the total maternal environment as it is experienced in combination with sensations from the infant's body. It serves as a support and 'convoy' during that period of rapid growth which necessitates increasing separation from the mother. The infantile fetish, although related to the transitional object, is the product of marked disturbance in infancy and is a defensive measure in response to great need stemming from early inadequate object relationships. The fetish is more concretized in its form and use, and tends to be permanently incorporated into the individual's life, constricting further development of object relationships. The transitional object which arises at about the same time (the end of the first year and early in the second year of life) is chosen and created by the child as a 'faithful protective escort.' Its softness and pliability are useful at a time when the infant's perceptions and physical relationships with the outer world are changing and when speech is in the process of formation. Thus it lends itself to symbolic representation. The transitional object plays a role in promoting illusion formation. By relating new experiences back to earlier ones, it lends illusory support to new experiences and helps the infant to investigate and widen his interests. The fetish represents a replacement of breast and penis and may gain anal–genital significance. By its solidity and durability of form, it may consolidate the illusion of maternal supplementation to the body in children whose early relationship to the mother has been 'not good enough.' The transitional object aids growth.[131]

What should be immediately emphasized is this: the creation and "exploitation" of the transitional object derives from the same psychological impetus that lies behind the creation of the symbolical universe. Consequently, the driving need is to internalize the environment, to grip the "external world" and thus to answer the problems of separation and loss with "magic." The "magic" is, of course, psychological mastery, psychological control, which

Roheim termed "dual–unity," or the "magical" condition of having the object at the symbolic level and of relinquishing the object at the level of "reality".[132] Now, when we recall that 1) money is a powerful, complex symbol, 2) that the psychological urge toward the symbolic resides in the separation crises of infancy, and 3) that *that* urge is linked inextricably to the problem of internalization, or the defensive method of retaining the object, and hence, of magically establishing "dual–unity," we recognize that the *exchange* which money is fated to accomplish at the unconscious level will engage the entire separation–individuation problem. Where money is concerned, "exchange" will directly focus on the give–and–take between the physical and psychological boundaries established by individuals and institutions, the whole "business" of "merging" and "withdrawal," the metaphors of the marketplace in all their underlying significance. Indeed, to "exchange" is to touch on the very basis of human existence itself. Eros, for example, draws forth the sexual response between people during nature's essential "transaction," one that leads to the "exchange" between the mother and the infant at her breast. To say that money is a means of "exchange" and "nothing else" is not simply true, it is *profoundly* true; it is true in a way that directs attention to the deep, affective life of mankind. As for the "transitional" implications, they are clear enough: money is a transitional object triggering transitional aims; its complex symbolism reaches down to crucial issues bound up with the crises of the early time, the crises which color all subsequent psychological life.

The customary association of money and food, money and survival, also harbors unconscious significance, also touches upon the problems of union and separation, the oral problems which are forever tied to the maternal object and the breast. It was in the infant's relationship with the mother, one recalls, that Freud postulated the origin of the "oceanic feeling," the feeling in which the boundaries between the "self" and the "other" disappear, the feeling in which one exchanges himself for the other, or is indistinguishable from the other. That money may be exchanged for food, is in a sense indistinguishable from food, not only links economics to psychology, particularly with regard to the mother–

infant interaction, but also links economics and psychology to religion. This is particularly true in reference to religion's mystical aspect where ego boundaries disappear in the divine "exchange" between the individual and the god who is his sustenance, food, wafer. We are not dealing here simply in metaphor but in a metaphoric version of psychological reality. The "oceanic feeling" is grounded in the same bond that religious feeling is, the bond that overcomes separation, and provides the gratifications of symbiosis.

Religion strives to answer the "discontents" of "civilization"—the discontents of separation, anxiety, isolation, loss, mortality, ordinary awareness itself—through its particular method of reconstituting the parental tie, the tie to the good object and to her subsequent transference expression, the good father–god. But the "discontents" of "civilization," of the "dual" aspect of "dual-unity," are also addressed, and paradoxically deepened, by the economical system (religion's ancient adversary!) that works to compensate for the original loss through its own substitute objects—wealth, power, possession.

In the development of Protestantism, for example, the two, economics and religion, formed a joint assault on the basic infantile dilemma, an assault that constituted, at another level, a remarkable attempt to resolve the ancient conflict between god and gold. That conflict was not resolved, of course, because—and this is the point—the enemies, god and gold, are not really enemies at all but "brothers under the skin." As the Upanishads remind us, the face of God is hidden behind a circle of gold,[133] the psychoanalytic significance of which is further expressed in religious ornament. The early Protestants attempted to deny the equivalency by stripping the churches, an attempt that was guiltily rooted in the lust for gold which characterized Protestant life (Max Weber). We begin to spy from this perspective the compulsive or obsessional ground of our economic organization, or the "discontent" of our "civilization" from an economical angle. Offering a version of the maternal object, promising a magical reunion with the breast, the economic order "teases," even "titillates," the unconscious requirements of millions of human beings, for the desired symbiosis is actually over; the longed–for mother is no longer there. In the deepest psychoanalytical sense, then, ordinary religion and ordinary economics are one. Money and the sacred meet in the need to retain the oral tie to the object, in the dynamics of internalization and its subsequent projective creations. Not without transitional significance is the recent discovery that the first banks were temples, temples in which sanctified food was stored.[134]

2.

The oral significance of money, the unconscious connection of money with the objects of the early time, has of late been underscored in a metapsychology that had for decades been mired in an investigation of money based upon the dynamics of the "anal stage." Writes William Desmonde, "the sacrificial bull was often regarded as a fertility spirit or embodiment of the crops emanating from the goddess Earth. The act of eating the bull . . . represented an eating of the goddess, or mother image . . . [It] represented the desire to incorporate the mother, thereby returning to the infantile state of nondifferentiation from the mother."[135] In this way, the "acquisition of money," which admitted the bearer to the sacrificial feasts of the cult,

> represented the finding of a mother substitute which provided an infallible source of emotional security. This is also in accordance with the fact that early coins were also amulets, magical devices for retaining the feeling of omnipotence associated with the oral stage of development . . . Money, which originated in the obtaining and distribution of food, symbolized mother's milk and the various ideas and emotions connected with [the] breast . . . Participation in the communion symbolized by the early monetary forms represented the psychic attaining of an identification with the mother image.[136]

The paternal influence is there, Desmonde notes, as he investigates "food rituals" which "represent . . . the breaking through of irrational hostility toward the father" and which are closely associated with money's primitive uses.[137] This influence, however, is properly understood only when regarded in the light of its maternal antecedents.

Roheim, who strives to demonstrate that individual economic systems reflect the tensions in the familial organizations of particular cultures, puts the matter this way:

> The concept of property, that is, the introjection of part of the external world into the self, comes about through the mediation of a severed part of the body, [and] is tantamount to an erotic tie . . . In those parts of the body that can be severed and are autoerotically cathected, we have the physiological prototype of property.[138]

For Roheim, the basic psychoanalytic meanings of possession and economic organization are to be discovered in the "curious connection between birth and property, between landed property and the mother's body."[139] The "totemistic phase" of primitive society, which stands behind Freud's view of "civilization," has ultimately a projective import. It says, "Mother earth belongs to the ancestors, that is, the mother belongs to the father."[140] The fundamental significance is maternal.

Similar items are underscored in Posinsky's classic study of the Yuroks.

> On a pre–Oedipal level the shell money is certainly equivalent to a positive introject, or 'good body contents'; but it also develops a phallic component which reinforces the previous ones. [Thus,] to be poor means originally to be hungry or empty, but it also comes to mean to be without a penis.[141]

Posinsky goes on,

> There is, again, a danger in emptiness (starvation, lack of love, poverty, castration, death), and a fear of fulness. The danger of fulness grows not only from the projection of oral aggressions onto the mother (and father) and of the consequent fear of retaliation, but also from the ambivalence involved in fulness—which means both

good and bad body contents. Thus, the fear of emptiness makes the
Yurok greedy and retentive, while the fear of fulness makes them
moderate eaters who must keep the alimentary passage open: Death
is ascribed to a visceral constriction, and the material but animate
'pains' are both obstructions and parasites.[142]

The "resulting personality is remarkably akin to the configuration found in a compulsion neurosis."[143] In this way, the
"men" of Yurok society are perpetually involved in "Oedipal
rivalries," or the "never–ending struggle for wealth and prestige."[144]

Such findings are reminiscent of Reich's observation that
money and the size of the penis are often equated in the
unconscious.[145] Large amounts of money equal a large penis. But
this particular equation has ultimately a transitional implication; it
is ultimately a transitional phenomenon. When the objects of one's
inner world breed insecurity, or when one detects the presence of
the bad object within, one seeks support, emotive nourishment or
narcissistic supplies, in the magical, symbolical surrogate that
actually possesses the power to provide "supplies" and "nourishment" in the "real world." Thus, money comes to be unconsciously associated with the internal "system." One is held by money,
reassured, made secure by it, and this security reaches "up" from
the mother to those later "Oedipal rivalries" involving the father
and siblings. As Roheim contends, "castration anxiety" is ultimately related to the "absence of the mother;" the penis is ultimately a "means of reunion."[146] Thus money, like the penis, is a way
back to the object. Even as a source of food it is overdetermined,
for as Roheim points out, "the whole process of food distribution—or of wealth or success—is fraught with anxiety."[147] The
"chief" is sacred because he dispenses food, a function that connects him to God, the provider on the one hand, and to God's
intermediary, the Priest, on the other. At the deepest psychoanalytical level, money as a means of providing food becomes associated with the entire maternal function—sustenance, acceptance,
and protection. As for the power of money, it is measured in inner
as well as in outer terms which correspond precisely to the context.

The powerful, the rich, are secure, secure in the tie to the internalized object and in the "reality" which is an outgrowth, a projective expression, of that tie. Hence, "to distribute things, to feed people," is to be "a good mother."[148] Shell money is discovered in primitive societies "where the excrements of a pig would be expected, and the maternal character of the pig is . . . clear."[149]

Again and again Roheim stresses the crucial connection between money and its tie to the object, particularly with regard to the central problems of power and control. "Money gives one control over others, and that is what really tells the story. A lien upon another person means that you can at your will convert him into a giver. The inability to control the mother was the most signal defeat of childhood."[150] To anticipate a thesis, both the power in money generally, and the power–seeking of the capitalist in particular, are related to this pre–Oedipal conflict. The power desired is power that fulfills magically an infantile or fantastic transitional need for control, control of the maternal figure and of her later substitutes. As for the power of the penis and capital, they are also connected thus; both are ways to the object, used transitionally to compensate for the "signal defeat of childhood." Stinginess and the compulsive desire for money answer "oral frustrations."[151] "Riches and 'mother' are magically identical."[152] "To be rich means to be full of good body contents."[153] In this way, the drive for wealth is closely bound up with the unconscious drive for omnipotence. We "fight" as "adults," writes Bergler, to regain the "sheltered existence of the womb." The "cornerstone of the urge to possess is a compensatory mechanism the purpose of which is to heal a wound to the child's self–love, his narcissism,"[154] and the basic wound, the wound that catalyzes the formation of symbols in an effort to internalize the maternal object and thus discover her presence in other objects, is separation–in–the–widest–sense, both actual separation and the "fantastic" separation which surrounds the existence of the bad (not–to–be–controlled) object, that is, the frustration and imperfection of the early interaction with the parent. Money "denies dependence," Bergler observes, and "stabilizes" feelings of "rejection."[155] It is a "blind for existing and repressed infantile conflicts."[156] But as money is also concerned with religious ceremony, and particularly with the practice of sacrifice, it is important to disclose the motivational dynamics of sacrificial behavior and then look at the role of primitive money therein. This will allow us to make the basic connections among money, religion, establishment of ordinary consciousness, and implications of altered awareness for the psychological forces that link these areas of cultural activity.

3.

Hubert and Mauss point out in their study, first, that

> sacrifice always implies a consecration; in every sacrifice an object passes from the common into the religious domain; it is consecrated. . . . The consecration extends beyond the thing consecrated. Among other objects, it touches the moral person who bears the expenses of the ceremony . . . The devotee who provides the victim which is the object of the consecration is not, at the completion of the operation, the same as he was at the beginning. He has acquired a religious character.[157]

This "acquiring of a religious character," this "transformation" of the "devotee," brings into view the central aim of sacrificial behaviors:

> The thing consecrated serves as an intermediary between the sacrificer, or the object which is to receive the practical benefits of the sacrifice, and the divinity to whom the sacrifice is usually addressed. Man and the god are not in direct contact. In this way sacrifice is distinguished from most of the facts grouped under the heading of blood covenant, in which by the exchange of blood a direct fusion of human and divine life is brought about. (S, 11)[158]

Thus the chief purpose of sacrifice, which is rooted in an act of "exchange"—the very word Gesell uses to express the chief purpose of money—is to establish a tie, connection, or bond, between the individual who feels the need for such a tie and the divinity to whom he directs his need. In psychoanalytic terms, that divinity is a projective version of the internalized object, a creation that emanates from the individual's inner world where an absorption into the bad presence and its derivatives is underway. No longer sure of his inner bearings, experiencing divisiveness, self–alienation, or "guilt," which grows as the "war" between introjections heats up, the "devotee" seeks to find the good object again and thus to strengthen his internal boundaries by altering the areas in which "exchange" is occurring. It is not simply the security of the father's good graces that is sought but a deeper security that resides in the deeper layers of personality formation, a security associated with the object of the early time.[159] Thus, Hubert and Mauss's description would be both anthropologically and psychoanalytically correct were they to write not of the "fusion" of "human and divine life" which sacrifice strives to establish, but of the re–fusion that it seeks.

As for the animal (or "matter") used in the sacrificial action, it is either: (a) a "pure" or "sinless" victim, material offered the divinity in expiation for transgressions committed and designed to facilitate the divine cleansing of the devotee through his oral or manual touching, or (b) a "tainted" animal which through the ministrations of the priest, bears away the sinfulness of the devotee leaving him in a cleansed or pure condition in God's eyes (*S, 28–45*).

This is, of course, a condensation of much material in Hubert and Mauss, a condensation that leaves out many individual variations and numerous customs and rites connected with sacrifice. It requires little psychoanalytical knowledge, however, to recognize that the split nature of the victim taken generally is a reflection of the split nature of the inner world, forged in the dynamics of internalization. The victim, like the god, is either a version of the good object and its derivatives or the bad object and its derivatives. The tension surrounding the victim reflects the tension that accrues in the ambivalent relationship to the object of the early time, the object whose basic threat is loss, abandonment, rejection, and/or

separation. Yet the matter does not end here. So prevalent is this
anxiety in infancy that it often gives rise to the fear of engulfment,
that is, absorption into the bad object. Thus, the sacrificial animal
may actually become, in the logic of the unconscious, a version of
the divinity itself. The internalized object of infancy is explicitly
involved in the projective mechanisms that subsequently "handle"
the conflicts arising from the inner world. In the magic of sacrifice
the devotee is offered a safe or "sublimated" avenue to the fulfilment of his incorporative aims. Victim and god are one (Christ as
lamb).

When Schafer calls the internalizations of infancy "immortal,"[160] he adumbrates the connection between that immortality and
the "immortality of the gods." Both are immortal because in
ordinary consciousness the transitional aim, the transitional mode
of existence, continues throughout life. As Hubert and Mauss
express it, "the notion of sacrifice to the god developed parallel
with that of sacrifice of the god" (S, 90). Gods do not simply "live"
on the substances offered them, they "are born" by them (S, 91).

The sacrificial substance bears a relation to the live–giving
body, the breast, upon which the life of the infant depends entirely.
This parallels the inner, or even actual, life of the sacrificer who
depends on the "refusion" to the "divinity" with whom he addresses himself. When Hubert and Mauss state that sacrifice, at the
deepest psychological level, is a "guarantee against annihilation"
(S, 64), they call to mind the "annihilation" experienced by the
infant during periods of separation from, or loss of, the object, as
well as those periods when he confronts the bad object (often his
own "bad" impulses), and that are also a kind of separation or
rejection. The fear of annihilation appears at the individual's
beginning and is inextricably bound up with separation from
mother at birth as well as with the inevitable ambivalence of early
object relations. Religious, and particularly sacrificial activities,
are employed to cope with that ambivalence, to reestablish equilibrium on the inside and thus, preserve order on the outside. One is
permitted to indulge his ambivalence in his killing and eating of the

victim (scapegoat), yet one is also able to reunite with the good object who, in the magic of the action and through the ministrations of the Priest, will accept one's forbidden desires and judge one "good." Sacrifice enables our repressions, especially repressions of aims associated with the earliest internalizations, to remain flexible and thus, preserves social stability by keeping people in contact with their good objects–by preserving and making psychically comfortable the unity of the "dual–unity situation."

Sacrifice, write Hubert and Mauss, "cuts the individual off from the common life, and introduces him step by step into the sacred world of the gods" (S, 22). This sacred or magical world is a "fantastic" version of the "good" world of one's infancy. Its very existence expresses the human need for that "good" place, the satisfaction and security that comes at the "good" breast, and in the body of the "good" object and her derivatives, the good father, the protector generally. That which the individual experiences in the "sacred world" is closely related to the oceanic experience of union described by Rolland and by Freud, or the "mystical" sense of harmony, merger, well–being that is fundamental to a large area of religious feeling and which was erroneously set aside by Freud as he sought the origin of the religious need.

What all of this makes clear is that religion is a transitional phenomenon, a transitional activity designed to accomplish precisely the end accomplished by the transitional object earlier described, the object which "gives" the child to the universe of culture and symbol at the same time that it "takes" the child away from the universe of the mother, the object which magically allows separation and reunion in the same psychological moment. In this way, the sacrificial animal is not only, or simply, a special object in the sense that it is a version of the internalized object around which swirls the ambivalence of the early time, the anxiety and hostility tied to loss, rejection, separation, incorporation; it is special, too, in the sense that it is a version of the transitional object around which swirl those feelings associated with the child's effort to preserve and retain himself, during the period in which the crises of separation transpire. Hubert and Mauss' observation that the sacrificial animal departs from this world as a spirit designed to "nourish the eternal life of the species" (*S*, 97) will be discussed in the final section of this book.

4.

That money plays a key role in sacrificial activity gets not only at the transitional significance in money's complex symbolism but at the extent to which an economic system devoted to the acquisition of money can exprèss transitional aims, or "echo" the requirements and purposes of the religious system which is ostensibly at odds with the "worldly order." That money is inextricably linked in its origin and function to primitive religion and, in particular, to primitive sacrifice has been indisputably established in the literature and does not require lengthy exposition. Everywhere in primitive culture, writes Einzig, the "sacred" character of money is apparent, as is its role in sacrificial activity.[161] If goods come from god, and if money gets goods, then money is an integral aspect of god's giving or provision. This insight comes to the members of the group as the emotive aims of sacrifice are accomplished, aims concerned with the conflict, tension, and "immortal objects" of the inner world.

Although Weber is correct to suggest that in Protestantism the amassing of wealth and total concentration on riches were used as a means of reaching God and thus, in our terms, a transitional phenomenon with an obsessive or even hysterical cast (the bad object had all but usurped the Puritan), money as a link to god has been there from the beginning. In the characteristic ambivalence of the human animal toward his projected internalizations, money as the bad object, as filth, has also been there from the beginning, perhaps as reaction–formation to the deep–seated need for (and fear of) merger.

What constituted the sacrificial animal in Protestantism, the animal offered the deity as the compulsive concentration upon work and wealth went forward? What but the body of the Protestant himself, his own body, his own senses? As Weber expresses it,

> something more than mere garnishing for purely egocentric motives is involved. In fact, the summum bonum of this ethic, the earning of more and more money, combined with the strict avoidance of all spontaneous enjoyment of life, is above all completely devoid of any eudaemonistic, not to say hedonistic, admixture. It is thought of so purely as an end in itself, that from the point of view of the happiness of, or utility to, the single individual, it appears entirely transcendental and absolutely irrational. Man is dominated by the making of money, by acquisition as the ultimate purpose of his life.[162]

One's own physical organism, one's own sensuous animal, is rendered up in the magical attempt to reach the transitional god.

The psychodynamics of this neurotic behavior emerge more vividly when we recall with Einzig that the word for money in many primitive societies is similar to, or even identical with, the word taboo (*PM*, 72) (something taboo, of course, is forbidden, sacred, power–filled, or awesome, usually in some religious context). What is desired and pursued is also perceived as dangerous, or reflecting a questionable aim. This focuses from still another angle the ambivalence bound up with the pursuit of wealth, with sacrifice, religion, and with the internalized objects that are projectively employed as the foundation of these cultural activities. In some areas of the Pacific, for example, tambu or money can still be offered the gods in expiation for transgression (*PM*, 72). In ancient Athens, money "belonged to," or derived from, the mother of the city herself; Athens and her owl were stamped on the coinage. Rings, too, were frequently used as money in ancient times (*PM*, 191), and rings are obviously concerned with key transitional phenomena, namely bonding, union, marriage, the sealing of contracts, especially with the paternal or maternal substitute. One is "struck," Einzig remarks, "by the frequent association between primitive money and primitive religion . . . In many communities the creation of money is attributed to supernatural powers" (*PM*, 370). Primitive man was guided largely by "religious concerns," and the "evolution of the economic system was itself largely influenced by the religious factor," in particular by the requirements for "sacrifice" (*PM*, 371).

Focusing for us again the transitional significance in Gesell's term "exchange," as well as the transitional significance of sacrificial conduct generally, Einzig writes that "making sacrifice" to the "deity" is "a form of barter between man and his gods" (*PM*, 371). Not only the sacrificial animal but the very objects employed in the sacrificial action—the knife, the axe, the tripod, the cauldron, the spit—were used as money among primitive peoples. Such items created a "unit of account" (*PM*, 73) and could be exchanged for a sacred beast. As for the payment of the priest, it, too, has clear transitional implications in that the priest is instrumental in establishing the tie between the individual and his god. Today, as the "plate is passed" in church, or among the institutions of religion, the transitional use of money is established in modern society. One pays, and then one gets the "good" feeling, the sense of connection with and praise from the "good" object on the inside. As religion evolves, Einzig writes, "donations to the gods" in the form of "precious metals" (*PM*, 373) become an integral aspect of spiritual life, a traditional part of that "sacrifice" of one's property ("let's all make a sacrifice today") which connects one, or re–connects one, with the projective creations of the inner world, with the "divine." Einzig's entire discussion of primitive money is confirmed and deepened by another definitive treatment of the subject, Laum's *Heiliges Geld*.[163]

5.

We are now in a position to bring home the analytic significance of this material, particularly with reference to ordinary consciousness and altered states of mind. We must remember 1) sacrifice is integrally associated with religion's chief aim (re-fusion); 2) religion is integrally associated with the sacred; 3) the sacred is embodied in those symbols (including money) that give a kind of frozen or hieroglyphic expression to mankind's basic conflicts and needs; 4) the symbolic capacity awakens in people not only through the biological response but in the defensive effort (internalization) to answer the problems of the early time, espe-cially separation; and 5) finally, our customary method of retain-ing the tie to the object is to receive and perceive the universe in a symbolic manner, the manner of ordinary awareness, of language in which, as Huxley expresses it, "words are taken for things and symbols are used as the measure of reality."[164] In the symbolified mode of ordinary consciousness the very running on of our thoughts, our symbol–thoughts, becomes our way of ensuring what Roheim designated as the central design of culture—the establishment of "dual–unity." Hence, to alter awareness is to change one's relation not only to the sensorial world, or to the universe "out there," but to the world of ordinary or transitional religion and to the world of ordinary or transitional economics. For if money is a complex symbol with transitional import (sacrifice), if its pursuit and possession signifies at the unconscious level a method of acquiring the power to control the object of the early time, to erase the "signal defeat of childhood," to ensure the connection with the "divinity" within, then the alteration of aware-ness, which is by definition the disruption or truncation of the symbolical world itself, works a kind of psychological alchemy that modifies the "subjective" nature of money by removing it from the symbolical realm.

Concomitantly, the alteration of awareness modifies the tran-sitional nature of the sacred (of which money is an integral part) by substituting for the union with divine symbols that are ultimately derived from the inner world of objects a sacredness which is rooted in the return to the world, in the feeling of direct, immediate contact with the universe "out there" and with one's body as its center of becoming. In this way, the "theology" of money and an economic system based on money goes because the transitional aims that create such theologies no longer press for fulfilment. Thus, the individual is no longer in the "dual-unity situation" which is in the last analysis a kind of madness, a magical, primitive, fantastic solution to the problem of separation; he is, instead, in the unity situation and, therefore, unable to feel the unconscious attraction to wealth as a source of security, as a means of controlling the maternal figure and compensating for castration.

Explained here is the endless, obsessional pursuit of coin. Because the "dual–unity situation" is magical, has no foundation in actuality, and is essentially an all–consuming struggle to retain the object, it needs constant support, buttressing, and psychological "fuel": one is ultimately in the dependent position on the inside because one is still seeking after the object. When the society encourages the strengthening of transitional bonds through the pursuit of wealth by canonizing that pursuit in every imaginable way, the combination of intrapsychic and cultural pressure becomes almost irresistable. Now, when we recall that 1) internalization is the original method of controlling the object; 2) the pursuit of wealth becomes a secondary method of such control by affording the individual the dream of power; 3) the central aim of all systems for modifying consciousness is the acquisition of power on the inside, an acquisition that derives entirely from the disruption of ordinary consciousness on the outside ("stopping one's thoughts"); 4) ordinary consciousness is rooted in the tie to the object; and 5) it is the extension of this tie (Freud's group psychology) which binds the individual to his culture and to his culture's transitional aims, as expressed through economic and religious organizations, we begin to spy the revolutionary implications of altered awareness which is psychologically nothing other than the suspension of the tie to the object within. We begin to spy its potential for bringing about not only the cessation of ordinary consciousness, with its grinding discontentment and boredom, but the cessation of ordinary religion, with its regressive goals and ideological compromise, as well as ordinary economics, with its wastefulness and greed and alienation. To interrupt the power–control–security–transitional connection to wealth is to begin to turn "the system" around. If "the system," as we presently know it, presents a threat to the survival of the species—as it clearly does—then the alteration of awareness emerges as a key, not only to the higher evolution of man, but to the continued evolution of man.

To suggest that through altered awareness one achieves a unity of self, as opposed to a "dual–unity" or transitional unity, is to suggest that in the alteration of consciousness resides the end of what has come to be known as the *causa–sui* project, the unconscious attempt to be the originator of oneself—the mad, endless quest for omnipotence. The *causa–sui* project is ultimately a striving to deny one's dependence on the object, to escape transitional needs and the entire transitional mode of existence, to terminate, in short, the "dual–unity situation."

Ironically, the quest for riches is closely bound up with this project; that is to say, because *money* functions as an agent of control at the deep psychological level, because *money* provides the dependent personality with the dream of unlimited *power*, wealth becomes in the transitional mode a means of accomplishing one's total independence. Were one to *possess* the object entirely, one would not need the object any more. At the same time, because "wealth," as we know it, can only exist in the ordinary realm of awareness, and because ordinary consciousness is itself an expression of the tie to and need for the object, the pursuit of coin can only provide an illusory liberation. On the inside, the "dual–unity situation" has not changed. What promises omnipotence ironically makes bondage. Yet, and paradoxically, the *causa–sui* project is not "an impossibility." That is to say, one achieves it as one reaches the evolutionary or psychological level where it ceases to be a project. By severing the tie to the object within through the alteration of awareness, one terminates the need to deny dependence, to engender one's own existence. The feeling with which the individual is replete in the break—the good, secure feeling of having the self—is the accomplishment, so to speak, of the *causa–sui* project. Out of the transitional mode of existence, one no longer derives from the object within but from the basic connection to the life–giving world of which the parent is only one aspect. The unity that was "dual" and, therefore, unsatisfactory has become the unity that is single and, therefore, sufficient. Money, consequently, is no longer "everything."

Reich often contended that the failure of revolution was not rooted solely in economic factors but in men's characters as well. Ideology was internalized into the personality structure. Until familial organization changed, until sexual repression lifted, until patterns of authoritarianism disappeared, until all individuals underwent psychoanalytic education into the deep–seated origin of their fascistic proclivities, revolution would bring only temporary relief, if that.[165] What this discussion makes clear is the psychological–phenomenological insufficiency of Reich's position, and other similar ones. "Revolution" will not "last" while people remain in the transitional mode of existence, seeking the object and fashioning compensatory substitutes in the form of economic, religious, and political symbols. It is ordinary consciousness itself that predicates the search for the object by trapping the individual in the symbolic approach to "reality" and, thus, reactivating continuously the anxieties and the defensive inclinations of the early time. "Revolutions" will "fail" until individuals achieve in themselves the power to put the universe of symbols "on" and "off " again, the power to truncate the tie to the object within, the power to terminate transitional existence or the "dual–unity situation," the power to receive the world differently and hence to perceive the world differently. In the deepest psychodynamic sense the problem of "revolution" is a problem of perception because perception is an emotive action with social consequences.

Another important point is this: the connection sought for in sacrifice (the connection with the projective version of the internalized object, the transitional aim of religious behavior accommodated by the transitional employment of money) is ultimately a connection between the individual and the alienated parts of his own body. Religious sacrifice is, in large measures, a way to reach a specific kind of mind–body relaxation in which those parts of the organism that "carry" the internalized object are able to discover a stress–free, harmonious interaction with the rest of the body. The alienation of "sin" consists largely in the loss of bodily integration or the loss of a happy feeling in the very chemical, physical composition of the self. The sacrificial action leaves the devotee in a relieved, tensicn–less condition ("now you may relax; everything is going to be all right"), one which may inspire a profound sensation of well–being, mystical delight, joyous bodily, and spiritual existence. The danger one apprehends in the "sinful" state recalls the danger of the internalized bad object to the infantile body–ego. In a very general sense, unconscious awareness of danger (anxiety) takes the form of stress. The oral significance of sacrifice emerges readily in this context. As one achieves relaxation in the body, as one feels the alienated parts of the organism come together, as one reaches the object one transitionally seeks, as one "regresses" behind the splitting of the early time toward a harmonious, undifferentiated state of being, one gets the good feed, too, the feed associated with the mother's breast, maternal security, and comfort.

As was earlier suggested while discussing Max Weber's work, the Protestant sacrifices his body in his all-consuming pursuit of riches. The traditional use of sacrifice, to render up wealth and to achieve, thereby, relaxation in the "new" relationship with the objects of the inner world, is altered in its unconscious emphases. This is a key occurrence in the development of western economics. Since the quest for wealth becomes obsessive, one's body as well as one's money is used in a transitional way. One's life, as well as one's gold, becomes a sacrificial entity, meaning simply: one holds oneself in tension and in stress all the time and gets as a "reward" only the satisfaction that can arise from the superego which may or may not give an affirmative nod to such a scheme. The psychological equilibrium is precariously grounded in an ethical system which vehemently pursues a symbolic version of the mother's body. The particular strain of capitalistic life, a strain that, along with other factors of course, has contributed to two world wars, originates in this departure from the normal or "ordinary" use of religious sacrifice. When one is making a sacrifice of himself in his enormous need for the object, not only is he miserable, he is apt to make others miserable, too.

Chapter 5

KARL MARX AND THE PATHOLOGY
OF CAPITALISM

1.

To discuss Marx in light of what has been said so far is to discover a new mode of understanding his great works, not only in a philosophical, or phenomenological context, which seems appropriate enough in that Marx was influenced so profoundly by Hegel, but in a psychoanalytical context, too, one which gets at fundamental connections between revolutionary economic theory and the revolutionary implications of altered awareness as clarified by the depth psychology of the last eight decades. The degree to which Marx comes astoundingly close to revealing explicitly the transitional dynamics of western economic life and the key role of altered consciousness in a revolutionary program for change is explored below.

Lenin wrote: "Where the bourgeois economists saw a relation between things (the exchange of one commodity for another) Marx revealed a relation between people."[166] In other words, Marx recognized the human, and to this extent the psychological meaning of the economic setup, or the manner in which goods were produced and exchanged. Compare this to Gesell's point that money is "only" a means of exchange. In particular, Marx got at crucial psychological verities through his tendency to regard specific economic practices in systematic terms. At the heart of these were mythic and religious metaphors that touched on the psychoanalytic significance of the entire capitalistic enterprise. Freud always recognized the value of a writer's metaphors in providing clues to the unconscious side of things; indeed, he insisted that to this extent the poets had discovered the unconscious. There is no reason to exclude Marx's analysis of capitalism from this psychoanalytic recognition. One sees in the metaphors of Marx, his deep, intuitive grasp of the underlying nature of the economic order.

2.

Marx viewed the capitalistic system in metaphorical terms which call to mind directly the dynamics of sacrificial conduct, particularly with reference to money's role therein. As Marx expresses it, the capitalist, in his insatiable greed, is willing to "sacrifice human beings," to "sacrifice" the very "flesh and blood," "nerves and brains," of the working man in order to maximize his profit, his "surplus–value" that is derived from human labor and that, to this extent, wears a human aspect.[167] Like the ancient Aztecs, the owners of industries, mines, and factories, are "prodigal with human lives," casual about "wasting" the men and women to whom they believe they have some sort of natural right. "When profits are at stake," writes Marx, "killing is no murder" (*Kap,* III, 106). This is also true in the religious sacrifice of human beings; killing is not murder but a "religious" action, that is, an action whose full meaning is concealed beneath the projective defenses of the unconscious. The Aztecs, just mentioned, are, of course, a prime example.

In capitalist countries, Marx suggests, human beings are not human beings at all but "horses" whose energy and power to make profit become the sole concern of the capitalist. They are even fed certain foods that prepare them for their sacred use as begetters of money (*Kap*, I, 627–628). In terms that recall the animal victim of ancient rites practiced in the Mediterranean area, Marx compares the manner in which the "whole beast" is slain so that his owners might possess a hide to the manner in which the laborer is "converted" or transformed by the capitalist from the human being he is into a kind of "monstrosity" (*Kap*, I, 396). This serves the purpose of providing the capitalist with the gain to whose pursuit he (the capitalist) is totally, indeed obsessionally committed (*Kap*, I, 170).

What is particularly interesting here is that Marx displays in his very earliest writings a deep admiration for sacrificial conduct, sacrificial conduct that derives from an emotive direction completely opposite from the one in *Das Kapital*. In fact, the metaphor of sacrifice informs one of the first expressions of Marx, composed during the formative university years, on the subject of how men should live, on the subject of moral or proper behavior, the ideal ethical life. "The greatest men," he says, "work for the universal," devote themselves to improving mankind's lot, making "the most people happy," ensuring the "welfare of humanity." One's own fulfillment as a person comes solely from this charitable orientation, for other "joys" are but "meager, limited, egoistic by comparison." The best life, says Marx—and here is the term we are looking for—"sacrifices itself to humanity" in an effort to promote the general good.[168] What Marx saw in capitalism, then, was a perversion of the religious ideal connected with the role of sacrifice in human life, a perversion at the center of which stood the transitional object that originated in the act of sacrifice itself—money. Instead of men sacrificing themselves for each other and, thus, reaching a moral satisfaction that itself contains transitional aims bound up with the parents, men in capitalism use each other as sacrificial animals in order to reach their own transitional goals of power and control through wealth. Those who labor for the gain of the bosses are "skinned."

3.

The figures Marx employs to characterize capitalism include, in addition to the metaphors of sacrifice, those which call to mind the broad mythic framework in which sacrificial conduct transpires. Referred to here are the vegetation myths concerning the cycle of the seasons—the "magical" transformations of the year that provide man with his sustenance and directly touch on his preoccupation with fertility and reproduction. These myths are traditionally associated with the mysteries of Eleusis. The spirit of Demeter breathes everywhere in *Das Kapital,* as does the spirit of the transformational gods of antiquity, the fertile line of Israel's children, and even of the life–giving Nile. They are all mentioned explicitly by Marx in a variety of passages and contexts. What is crucial to note is this: just as the actual behavior of men toward one another in capitalism perverts the ideal of sacrifice, the humanistic expenditure of oneself for the species' welfare, so does the actual behavior of men in capitalism pervert the time-honored use of nature. Capitalism undermines the ideal of the production, reproduction, and distribution of nature's goods rooted in the cyclical, vegetational conceptions of mankind—those mythic conceptions ultimately derived from the religious realm and ultimately tied to the dynamics of sacrifice, and money's role therein, as described by Einzig and Laum. Not only does Marx employ mythic metaphors to reveal the unnaturalness of capitalism, but he employs them in such a way as to disclose his own adherence to the ideals of human conduct embedded in the myths, just as he shares the ideal of sacrifice contained in the "proper" use of that institution. In this way, Marx's metaphors of sacrifice form an integral part of his total view of the economic problem in mythic terms, terms which focus through their analytical significance the oral dilemma, the oral problem of feeding and survival that is so "fraught," in Roheim's terms, "with anxiety," and that stands behind the transitional aims of civilization in general and the development of ordinary awareness in particular.

"Just as the working day is the natural unit for the function of labor–power," writes Marx, "so the year is the natural unit for the periods of turn–over of rotating capital. The natural basis of this unit is found in the fact that the most important crops of the temperate zone, which is the mother country of capitalist production, are annual products" (*Kap*, II, 176). Thus, the productions of capitalism are linked to the annual or seasonal productions with which men have always associated their religious conception of world process; more than that, they are linked through the use of a metaphor which calls the mother explicitly to mind, for the heart of the "system" is the crop that arises from the part of the globe that is to be associated with the maternal object herself. But the workings of capitalism, because they move in a never–ending cyclical manner annually are to be linked not only with the metaphors of production, but with the metaphors of reproduction or renewal as well. The author does not refer here simply to Marx's use of the expression "industrial cycle" which appears constantly in his work but to other expressions of a related, yet qualitatively distinct nature, which get at a fundamental figurative aspect of his perception. In words that are reminiscent of the mythic, vegetative conception of nature, Marx writes, "A society can no more cease to produce than it can cease to consume. When viewed, therefore, as a connected whole, as a flowing on with incessant renewal, every social process of production is, at the same time, a process of reproduction" (*Kap*, I, 619–620). Yet a further conceptualization of a metaphoric nature contains his richest insight into the "hidden" quality of the system: his tendency to characterize the cycles of capitalism, the processes of "reproduction," in transformational or metamorphic terms, terms which call to mind the basic religious mystery of magical change. This is the mystery in which the dead god (cut crop) gives rise to life–producing sustenance, food. "Production," "consumption," "renewal," "reproduction," "transformation," "metamorphosis," "natural cycle,"—these are the key terms of the analysis. Not surprisingly, as we shall see, the final metaphor of the capitalistic system as a whole turns out to be the metaphor of cannibalism in which man's vicious orality, out of control, greedily gulps down the body of the earth itself—the body of the mother–provider.

4.

Discussing capital's circulation within the system, Marx chooses the following terms to figuratively describe it: "The Metamorphoses of Capital and Their Cycles" (*Kap*, II, 31). Everywhere is talk of transformation: "Productive capital . . . consumes its own component parts for the purpose of transforming them into a mass of products of a higher value" (*Kap*, II, 45). "Labor–power" is "transformed" into "commodity," into the "money–form" (*Kap*, II, 36–37). The "rotation" as a whole comprises the "metamorphoses" of capital, the "transformation" of its "cycle" for the purpose of "making money" (*Kap*, II, 58–59, 60, 67). Capital can "reproduce itself" simply or on an "enlarged scale." "At the end of the period P . . . P, capital has resumed the form of elements of production, which are the requirement for a renewal of its cycle. The rotation of capital, considered as a periodical process, not as an individual event, constitutes its turn–over" (*Kap*, II, 176). But it is perhaps the following example that discloses most vividly this aspect of Marx's figurative language. When "capital" has "finally passed" through "the cycle of its metamorphoses," it "steps forth out of the internal organism of its life" and, like the butterfly emerging from the chrysalis, or the child from the womb, "enters into the external conditions of its existence" (*Kap*, III, 57).

Clearly, the cycle of capitalism is modeled after the cycle of life itself, the fertility cycle traditionally associated with the cycle of the seasons, the "annual cycle," to use Marx's expression again, which is in turn integrally connected with sustenance and which has always been linked at the mythic level to the image of the mother, who is, through a further transformation, the earth. One thinks, of course, of Demeter (or Ceres) whose precious child,

Kore, a symbolic representation of spring or foison, is dragged to the underworld and raped and imprisoned by the dark god Plutus, the mythic equivalent of the capitalist. That Marx refers to this myth explicitly in the midst of his analysis of capitalism's evil we will shortly see.

In the transformation of labor into commodity and of commodity into money, money ultimately rooted in the value of labor, Marx uncovered what he took to be the principal "mystery" of the entire "religious" system. Indeed, this transformation, this metamorphosis, to use again Marx's mythic metaphor, is the essence— the ugly, immoral, and destructive essence, of the capitalistic order itself. Insisting that money is a "magical" substance surrounded by illusory thinking, by "necromancy" (*Kap*, I, 87), terms which anticipate Roheim, Marx states that money "contains" nothing other than the "labor," the "power" of men, that has gone into producing the "commodity" which is able to fetch the money in the "market" (*Kap*, I, 93–99). Thus, for Marx a "commodity" is, simply, that which holds or "contains" the labor of working people. "Every commodity is a symbol, since, in so far as it is value, it is only the material envelope of the human labor spent upon it" (*Kap*, I, 103). In other words, the commodity, because it contains "labor," is a symbolic representation of the person, and since it leads to money, money itself becomes a symbolic representation of the person, the person who has been sacrificed to bring about the magical working of the cycle, the cycle which provides the capitalist with the powerful substance that promises him the fulfillment of his transitional aims and the cessation of his transitional anxieties. In Marx's own words, money entirely and forever in the capitalistic system is "the direct incarnation of human labor" (*Kap*, I, 105). The capitalist invests in the "very flesh and blood of the laborers" (*Kap*, III, 158). Through the unconscious, defensive disguise of the cyclical order, then, the capitalist devours the bodies of his workers in an unholy version of religious sacrifice. His money is his feed, and as Marx has already expressed it at the level of symbolic representation, the feed is upon an object (money) that contains the body of the worker himself in a hidden or metamorphosed form acceptable to the conscience of the owner. At the level of conscious process, however, the capitalist regards "surplus–value" as the "offspring" of his monetary resources (*Kap*, III, 49), and the "breeding of money" becomes his obsessive concern (*Kap*, III, 462). Indeed, after a certain period of time has elapsed, the investor considers his "money" to be "pregnant" (*Kap*, III, 462). Interest and profit "accumulate," and finally "fulfill" his most "fervent wish" (*Kap*, III, 462). The "social powers of production," accordingly, "sprout from the womb of capital itself " (*Kap*, III, 963) and not from the bodies of men and women. It is an "old story," declares Marx, "capital begets capital" as "Abraham begat Isaac," and "Isaac begat Jacob," and "so on" (*Kap*, I, 637). The sacred nature of capitalist ideology begins to reveal its origin. Just as the symbols of the religious system deal, or cope with, the basic transitional anxieties of men, so do the symbols of the economic system—the "other side" of religion, its "opposite," its unconscious double, deal or cope with those anxieties.

In both realms the symbol leads to the projective version of the internalized parent that is, in the last analysis, the sacred. In religion, money is sacrificed to gain control over, or reunion with, the "lost" object. In economics, which transpire in "society," or the "real" world, man is used sacrificially to obtain the money, to obtain the "gold," which unconsciously represents the security, the power, the potency, required by the individual in the "dual–unity situation," in the transitional mode of existence, in the "reality" of separation from the object. Money means control over the extension of the parent, for that is what "society" is. As we have seen, the tie to the social order, or "civilization," is an outgrowth of the tie to the internalized object—to the parental figure (Freud). The "religious world," said Marx in what is perhaps his most famous utterance, "is but a reflex of the real world." The full, unconscious meaning of this statement derives from Marx's own metaphoric examination of capital, as we shall continue to see.

5.

What must be pointed up here is that the underlying significance of "exchange" as discovered in Gesell's discussion of
money is not only substantiated and supported in Marx but
deepened as well in terms of its human and, particularly, its
transitional meaning. In the context of Marx's metaphorical depiction of capital's "fecund metamorphoses," grounded in the body of
the worker whose energy "breeds" the magical profits of the owner
in a kind of black ritual of fertility, exchange is a psychic phenomenon, one that reaches deep into the character of the capitalist
where preoccupation with compensatory power, power embodied
in the sacred symbol of money, reigns unchallenged. Marx writes,
"the capital which is exchanged for labor–power is itself but a
portion of the product of others' labour appropriated without an
equivalent; . . . this capital must not only be replaced by its
producer but replaced together with an added surplus. The relation
of exchange subsisting between capitalist and labourer becomes *a
mere semblance* appertaining to the process of circulation, *a mere
form*, foreign to the real nature of the transaction, and only *mysti-
fies it*. The ever–repeated purchase and sale of labour–power is
now the mere form; what really takes place is this—the capitalist
again and again appropriates, without equivalent, a portion of the
previously materialised labour of others, and *exchanges* it for a
greater quantity of *living labour*. (*Kap*, I, 639, my emphasis).
Marx goes on,

A particular commodity cannot become the universal equivalent
except by a social act. The social action therefore of all other
commodities sets apart the particular commodity in which they all
represent their values. Thereby the bodily form of this commodity
becomes the form of the socially recognized universal equivalent.
To be the universal equivalent becomes, by this social process, the
specific function of the commodity thus excluded by the rest (*Kap*,
I, 98–99).

And finally, in a particularly incisive utterance, "Since the producers do not come into social contact with each other until they *exchange* their products, the specific social character of each producer's labour does not show itself *except in the act of exchange* (*Kap*, I, 84, my emphasis). It is not simply the overwhelming sense of alienation which emerges from these passages that is striking; it is the manner in which the labor of men is "lost" in the material object that ultimately begets a disguised version of that labor—"money is a crystal formed of necessity in the course of . . . exchange" (*Kap*, I, 97), as well as the manner in which the laborer is excluded from exchanging his own work for its equivalent. The manner in which the exclusion takes place, from a psychological angle, is patently disguised to facilitate the exchange of what would be unthinkable if exchanged directly, that is, human beings—the energy, and life–force, of living human creatures. To this extent, the exchanges of capitalism include the transformational use of people to gain a "crystalized" version of their bodies, namely money whose central role in the process derives from its "magical" ability to confer upon the "exchanger" the *power*, the bodily power, inherent in those who produce the commodities. The "defeats" of infancy and childhood, as well as the anxiety of the "dual–unity situation," are denied again and again by this mastery over other men in the "real" world, a mastery expressed in the owner's control of those other men's bodies, the source of their power. Here is the root of the obsessive, all–consuming aspect of capitalist psychology.

The marketplace is where one deals in power, where exchange provides proof (a term that pertains to the testing of gold as well as to the cogency of evidence) of one's mastery and security in both an actual and symbolic way. Money talks, both consciously and unconsciously; that is, it talks to the whole mind and is thus able to work a magical security in that it attests to control of the external world (the extension of the parent), a control that denies the "defeats" of the early time. "Threats to the narcissistic cathexis of the self . . . exist from the moment of birth," writes Lax, "and stem from the interaction of the child's libidinal and aggressive drives with the demands, frustrations and gratifications of the real world."[169] Such "narcissistic hurts" evoke "feelings of depression and worthlessness, unending ruminations, and a growing sense of perplexity," perplexity that is "answered" by "aggressive, assertive striving," by "achievement" in the "social realm."[170] Unlike the parent's body, which can not be mastered, the body of society—the body of "civilization," the massive collection of living creatures each of whom recalls at the unconscious level the body of the parent—can be. In addition, the sacrifice, abuse, and "exploitation" of the worker provides the owner with unconscious fulfillment of his aggressive, ambivalent feelings toward the internalized parental figure. The worker will be treated as the capitalist was treated during the crises of the early period. The "idealized" object, in the words of Sydney Smith, becomes the "vilified" object as the hostilities of infancy disguisedly emerge.[171] In this way, money not only provides security by denying dependence (*causa–sui* project), by fulfilling transitional needs, it also expresses the capitalist's willingness to destroy the worker in retaliation for previous "defeats." It is this aspect of the "system" which helps us to appreciate more fully the analytic importance of Birnbaum's point that Marx (and Engels) "thought of communism as a religion of humanity. . . . The proletariat, after all, was assigned the role of a surrogate for all of humanity. Humanity could regain itself only when the proletariat, as its most injured part, assumed the task of revolution—a mode of universal historical redemption."[172] Here is a further paradoxical motive for the capitalist's obsession with coin.

That is, as more money and more power are acquired through the employment of labor, more anxiety over aggression accrues through the sacrificial abuse of human beings. Thus, the bad, rejective object is continuously reactivated in the unconscious of the exploiter, an occurrence that prompts, in its own turn, an ever–greater need for power, money, and the good, reassuring feed. Marx's depiction of the capitalist's psychology touches dramatically on this compulsive, and ultimately transitional, pattern. "More and more wealth," he writes, is the "sole motive of [the capitalist's] operations" (*Kap*, I, 170). His "chase" after riches is a "passionate chase"; in fact, the capitalist is a "rational miser," a "rational hoarder." Although his obsession, his "madness," is not conspicuous, or visible in any obvious way as is the hoarder's, it is nevertheless there. "The never–ending augmentation of exchange–value, which the miser strives after, by seeking to save his money from circulation, is attained by the more acute capitalist by constantly throwing it afresh into circulation" (*Kap*, I, 171). Wanting as much power, or its equivalent, money, as he can get for as little "wages" as he can pay, the capitalist's deepest urge is to become a kind of ruler, or king, an omnipotent chief over men, in Marx's own words, a sort of "lord" (*Kap*, I, 623) who is, from an historical angle, related to the "lords" of the medieval world. With special reference to the aggressive component of this urge Marx writes,

> the capitalist gets rich, not like the miser, in proportion to his personal labour and restricted consumption, but at the same rate as he squeezes out the labour–power of others, and enforces on the laborer abstinence from all life's enjoyments. Although, therefore, the prodigality of the capitalist never possesses the bona–fide character of the open–handed feudal lord's prodigality, but, on the contrary, has always lurking behind it the most sordid avarice and the most anxious calculation, yet his expenditure grows with his accumulation, without the one necessarily restricting the other (*Kap*, I, 651).

As for the transitional side of the capitalist, the side that requires the security of profit, the feed of money, the refusion with the parental figure, it emerges most strikingly perhaps through Marx's analysis of interest, an analysis which helps us to understand further the connection between the economic order and the development of ordinary awareness.

6.

The association of interest and time is of course fundamental, and Marx acknowledges it at the inception of his discussion. But the time bound up with interest is for Marx dependent upon the time bound up with the rate of capital turnover as a whole, and in this respect his analysis leaves far behind those who suggest that time begets interest in a simple, straightforward way. He writes,

> With his customary insight into the internal connection of things, the romantic Adam Müller says: 'In determining the prices of things, time is not considered; while in the determination of interest it is principally time which is taken into account.' He does not see that the time of production and the time of circulation enter into the determination of the price of commodities, and that this is precisely what determines the rate of profit for a given time of turn–over of capital, while the determination of profit for a certain time in its turn determines that of interest" (*Kap*, III, 420).

Interest, therefore, is a "part of profit" (*Kap*, III, 421), "surplus–value" (*Kap*, III, 424), and is always to be "measured in money" (*Kap*, III, 421) or in the labor of men of which money is a "crystallized form." Interest goes "down" in prosperous times as "extra profit" and up in times of crisis during the course of which it may reach "a point of extreme usury" (*Kap*, III, 424). These are, in the last analysis, but aspects of the industrial cycle: "condition of rest, increasing activity, prosperity, overproductivity, crises, stagnation, condition of rest, etc." (*Kap*, III, 424). How, then, does this material shed light on the transitional nature of the search for gain?

Interest is not simply an aspect of profit, it is that aspect of profit that is entirely associated with the passage of time in the industrial cycle. As has been shown, time from a phenomenological angle, and particularly the psychoanalytic phenomenology of early development, is inextricably concerned with the infant's relation to the maternal object. Indeed, the coming and the going of the mother is the principal event in the rudimentary growth of the time sense. Security becomes the mother's presence measured in terms of inchoate duration, and "good eternity" is in large measure the blissful sense of timeless well–being experienced in the longed–for union with the breast. It is precisely in the intervals of the mother's absence that imaging achieves a conspicuous intensity as an aspect of the internalizing, symbol–making capacity which is, in turn, the organism's way of holding the mother during those periods when she is not there. Prolonged absence on the mother's part becomes, in Hartocollis' words, an "experience of catastrophic dimensions" for the infant and is closely connected to the individual's apprehension of "bad" time, or "bad eternity," a feature of Hell.[173] It is from this perspective that the transitional meaning of interest as profit begins to emerge. Because interest provides money, because it leads to money after a period of waiting, and because money is a symbol rooted in the drive to control and reunite with the internalized object, interest becomes a kind of psychological scheme to fill time with the magical presence of the maternal figure. One is making money as time passes and to this extent, the emptiness of time is denied, the absence of the object is denied; indeed, the emptiness of time and the object's absence are only illusions. Time is not simply passing, it is breeding money, money that makes one secure in its passing. Thus, the interest in interest attests to the individual's desire to be imaging unconsciously the object of one's security all the time, just as the child has the mother all the time at the level of his primary, internalized holding. The feed of cash proceeds uninterruptedly at the level of transitional need. One "goes through life" with his lips at the breast. These lines of Dylan Thomas get at the phenomenon effectively:

> The lips of time leech to the fountainhead,
> Love drips and gathers, but the fallen blood
> Shall calm her sores.[174]

And when the sum of interest actually appears, when the

"payoff" actually arrives, it constitutes not only the climax to a period of passive ingestion, passive sucking, it constitutes as well the proof that the "stuff" was there. One's good anticipation leads to one's gratification "in reality." Time, intimately associated with the threat of loss, has been mastered. At the level of unconscious processes, the accumulation of interest is a secular version of eternal life.

The psychological passivity of the individual absorbed in the pursuit of interest is sharply adumbrated in Marx's division of capitalists into "money" and "industrial" types. He writes,

> It is indeed only the separation of capitalists into money–capitalists and industrial–capitalists which transforms a portion of the profit into interest, which creates the category of interest at all; and it is only the competition between these two kinds of capitalists which creates the rate of interest (*Kap*, III, 435).

The industrial capitalist, says Marx, is "active," "muscular," ambitious in an obvious, extroverted way; the money–capitalist is more "abstracted," "inactive," "non–participating," (*Kap*, III, 439–440). Again, the industrial–capitalist "reproduces actively" while the money–capitalist—and here Marx employs the oral imagery that has been suggesting itself all along—is content to see the "profits" of enterprise "flow" in his direction. For "active" we might say "phallic" or "striving"; for "abstracted" we might say "passive" or "schizoid." In any case, the psychoanalytic implications are clear. Marx's "industrial–capitalist" expresses the ambivalent attitude toward transitional phenomena and calls to mind the "depressive position" of Fairbairn and Klein in which aggressive behavior is used to cope with anxieties emanating from the internalized presence of "bad" mother. Directly involved in the exploitation of the worker, in the "sacrifice" of "blood and bone" (the cannibalistic feed on profit which, in its form as money, comprises symbolically the body of the laborer), the industrial–capitalist strives not only to deny the "defeats" of the early time but to retaliate on the object as well. The money–capitalist is, by contrast, closely associated with the "schizoid position" of the authors just mentioned, a personality structure characterized chiefly by withdrawal, passivity, and severe dependency needs that disclose themselves in a longing for merger, or symbiotic union with the succoring object and with the breast. Beneath the "style" of each "type"—"industrial" and "money"—lies the disturbance, tension, stress of early object relations, and the transitional aims which arise therefrom.

7.

The psychological feed of interest calls to mind once more the agrarian features of Marx's approach, his association of capitalism with the "cycle of production" in its mythic or archetypal form. Yet for Marx capitalism is not simply a version of the "annual cycle"; it is the vicious or evil version, undermining and destroying the ancient wisdom expressed through the myth in its ideal, pristine expression. The "annual" productions of "nature" that beget the "general stock" of society are unnaturally handled; they are "retained" for the private, egoistical use of the capitalist, and, in this way, the yearly "cycle" becomes a destructive instrument, one that breeds injustice and suffering instead of foison and well–being (*Kap*, I, 533). Marx stated this even more dramatically in the notebooks from which he drew the material for *Das Kapital:* "The circle Money–Commodity–Money, which we drew from the analysis of circulation, would then appear to be merely an arbitrary and senseless abstraction, roughly as if one wanted to describe the life cycle as Death–Life–Death."[175] Referring caustically to the orthodox "political economy" of his day, Marx declares that the "vicious circle" of "capitalist production" may be traced not to a "system" of "primitive accumulation," but to the feudal system in which the control and exploitation of man and nature was more visible, open, and less "mystified" than in the present mode (*Kap*, I, 784–786). As for that system's "lord," he becomes, in the course of industrial development, the "new potentate" of the capitalistic order, as we have seen (*Kap*, I, 786).

The "vicious circle" that Marx describes appears to those who cannot see into the realities of production as a "natural" system using "natural resources." He writes, "Because this power costs capital nothing, and because, on the other hand, the labourer himself does not develop it before his labour belongs to capital, it appears as a power with which capital is endowed by Nature—a productive power that is immanent in capital" (*Kap*, I. 365). But for all its "naturalness" capitalism ultimately "perverts" nature and the order of life, the benign, provisional earthly cycle expressed in the myths that celebrate the world's miraculous, divine ability to provide men seasonally with nourishment, to act as good feeder, good parent, by transforming the seed into the crop or by offering substances that might be transformed into food through specific ministrations, such as heat. Capitalism is, thus, not only a bad feeder, a bad distributor at the individual level, it is a threat to the survival of mankind as a family, as a society; it is a threat to the globe: "Capitalism loses on one side for society what it gains on the other for the individual capitalist" (*Kap*, III, 104). The "transformation" of "surplus–value" into "profit" is a "perversion of subject and object taking place in the process of production" (*Kap*, III, 58).

> The real barrier of capitalist production is capital itself. It is the fact that capital and its self–expansion appear as the starting and closing points, as the motive or aim of production; that production is merely production for capital, and not vice versa, the means of production mere means for an ever expanding system of life process for the benefit of the society of producers" (*Kap*, III, 293).

In times of crisis, and here again the agrarian metaphor is present, "old capital" is compelled to "lie fallow"; production "stagnates"; the capitalists begin to war among themselves: "How much the individual capitalist must bear of the loss . . . is decided by power and craftiness, and competition then transforms itself into a fight of hostile brothers" (*Kap*, III, 296–297). The figure of "hostile brothers" is integrally bound up with Marx's explicit presentation of the capitalist himself as the bad parent, as one who has failed to achieve psychological maturity, who remains at the level of sibling–rivalry as opposed to the level of parental responsibility, who provokes transitional anxiety in the working classes— the members of which not only grip the economic system for reasons similar to those for which they grip ordinary awareness, but also view the owner with a deep–seated ambivalence similar to that with which the owner views them. The medieval "lord" is also the bad object and, as we shall see, a reflection of Plutus, god of the underworld. "Certain individuals," writes Marx, claim to have an "exclusive right" to "certain pieces of the globe" (*Kap*, III, 743), and in the process of turning these "pieces" to their own advantage, they negate an ancient purpose. No one, he declares, "owns" the earth. We all simply "use" it; and our business is to use it justly so that we may distribute its products to all who require them, thus preserving the planet for succeeding generations. To do this is, in Marx's words, to behave ourselves as "the good father of a family behaves himself" (*Kap*, III, 902).

Marx's depiction of the capitalist as bad parent is closely related to his picture of the earth under the spell of the capitalist order. This is a picture where the planet is wasted and destroyed by the irresponsibilities of the obsessive, egocentric owners. It is also a picture where the "annual cycle" of foison and abundance grinds to a terrible halt. The world becomes a permanent wasteland; the ancient wisdom that men have heeded since "time immemorial" is lost (*Kap*, III, 961). The "lord" of the "unnatural" system enters the "bowels of the earth" (*Kap*, III, 898) and takes from them the source of mankind's future wealth; he drains the very "body" (*Kap*, III, 898) of the globe, "consumes" the very "fruits of the earth," and in this way leaves it "barren," a place of "soil" that is finally "exhausted" (*Kap*, III, 946). What is particularly striking about this is Marx's employment of oral metaphors that get further at the transitional significance of the "vicious circle." It is at the oral level that Marx spies the danger, for it is the capitalist's "all–engrossing appetite" (*Kap,* III, 466) that "consumes" the earth's products and similarly empties the mother's "body." Left unchecked, writes Marx, the capitalist would simply "eat up the world" (*Kap,* III, 463), devour and cannibalize it; his conduct marks him as a kind of "wolf" or "shark" (*Kap,* III, 520–521) with an endless hunger for victims. Thus, Marx is ultimately disgusted and outraged by capitalism's greedy mouth, its narcissistic orality which has no respect for the careful approach of the old tradition.

But it is perhaps Marx's explicit reference to a central figure in Greek mythology, and the agrarian myth in particular, that most effectively describes his figurative conception of the capitalistic order. After reminding us that the "ancients" saw in "money" an element subversive to the welfare of society, Marx declares that capitalism has "pulled Plutus by his hair from the bowels of the earth" and set him up as the "incarnation" of its aims, as the "principle of its own life" (*Kap,* I, 148–149). Just as Plutus in mythology raped Kore, the earth's daughter who is symbolic of springtime and renewal, and dragged her to the nether world and kept her among his possessions, so does the capitalist's drive for profit, and money, rape the earth. The myth is given new meaning. Money has returned from the underworld—the bowels of the planet, the maternal object herself—as the voracious consumer of the earth's "fruits," the depleter of the "annual product." But Plutus, in Marx's view, is more than the consuming, devouring parent, the infant–parent gone mad with the power to ingest anything and everything; he is also the "glittering" parent (*Kap,* I, 148–149), the "sparkling" parent, which is to say, the egoistic, narcissistic parent who refuses to give to, share with, care for, his children. Indeed, he is a kind of evil "god" to whom the capitalist sacrifices the workers', or children's, bodies; for as we have seen, it is the body of the worker, his power, of which money is, in Marx, the "incarnation." (It may be noted parenthetically that money is explicitly referred to as a "god" in Marx's early writings.)[176] Surely, it is more than coincidental that Marx describes money as the "incarnation" of the worker's "flesh and blood" in one passage of *Kapital* (*Kap,* I, 105) and Plutus as the "incarnation" of capitalism's deep–seated aims in another (*Kap*, I, 148–149). In this way, capitalism becomes an idolatry, an idolatry in which human beings are offered to an egocentric deity. We are reminded once again of Marx's early preoccupation with sacrificial behavior, as well as of the religious or transitional implications of the problem.

Just as splitting, internalization, ambivalence, and refusion constitute keys to the religious activities of men in which money and sacrifice play a crucial role, so do they constitute keys to the economic activities of men in which money and sacrifice also figure centrally. Moreover, if the bonds of "civilization" and "religion" are rooted in the tie to the parent (as demonstrated in Freud) then the bond between the capitalist and his economic order, or his secular "religion," his "theology" of the marketplace, is also rooted in that tie. The psychological forces that bind workers to the "system" can not be ignored here, for the worker, too, is prone to regard the economic setup as an aspect of the "civilization" to which he is linked at the emotive level. This is the level of transference relations or the level where he is ultimately linked to his ordinary manner of perception itself. All of these "phenomena"—economic, philosophic, and religious—are aspects of a single issue: man's tendency to internalize his environment, cope with his intense transitional anxiety by exploiting his biological proclivity to create symbols, and "get on top" of his world by transforming it into concepts that are charged with defensive energy, and power. The separation crises of infancy and childhood unite with the symbol–making brain to produce the transitional mode of "civilization," the mode that defines the present evolutionary stage of the species.

8.

Marx's revolutionary spirit, as well as his profound recognition of the manner in which capitalism alienates the worker from his life, senses, and body, emerge with striking clarity from the early writings. Focusing on the familiar problem of money in the capitalistic system Marx writes,

> [Its] essence is not primarily that it externalizes property, but that the mediating activity or process . . . becomes alienated and takes on the quality of a material thing, money, external to man . . . the very relationship of things and the human dealings with them become an operation beyond and above man. Through this alien mediation man regards his will, his activity, and his relationship to others as a power independent of himself and of them . . . His slavery thus reaches a climax. It is clear that this mediator becomes an actual god, for the mediator is the actual power over that which he mediates to me. His worship becomes an end in itself.[177]

Marx continues this line of thought in his criticism of Hegel; the passage is lengthy but crucial to the discussion:

> Suppose we had produced things as human beings; in his production each of us would have twice affirmed himself and the other. 1) In my production I would have objectified my individuality and its particularity, and in the course of the activity I would have enjoyed an individual life; in viewing the object I would have experienced the individual joy of knowing my personality as an objective, sensuously perceptible, and indubitable power. 2) In your satisfaction and your use of my product I would have had the direct and conscious satisfaction that my work satisfied a human need, that it objectified human nature, and that it created an object appropriate to the need of another human being. 3) I would have been the mediator between you and the species and you would have experienced me as a reintegration of your own nature and a necessary part of your self; I would have been affirmed in your thought as well as your love. 4) In my individual life I would have directly created your life; in my individual activity I would have immediately confirmed and realized my true human and *social* nature.
>
> Our productions would be so many mirrors reflecting our nature.
>
> What happens so far as I am concerned would also apply to you.
>
> Let us summarize the various factors in the supposition above:
>
> My labor would be a free manifestation of life and an enjoyment of life. Under the presupposition of private property it is an

externalization of life because I work in order to live and provide for
myself the means of living. Working is not living.

Furthermore, in my labor the particularity of my individuality
would be affirmed because my individual life is affirmed. Labor
then would be true, active property. Under the presupposition of
private property my individuality is externalized to the point where I
hate this activity and where it is a torment for me. Rather it is then
only the semblance of an activity, only a forced activity, imposed
upon me only by external and accidental necessity and not by an
internal and determined necessity.[178]

As the sole purpose of this alienated activity is to service the
needs of the capitalist, or engender his profits, man is robbed not
only of his work, but of his "life," his "species–life," his "actual
and objective existence as a species." Alienated labor "changes his
superiority to the animal to inferiority, since he is deprived of
nature, his . . . body."[179] Hence, man "falls under the domination
of his product, of capital." The "sensuous external world" is
denied him.[180] As for orthodox or mainstream "political economy," it conceals the alienation in the nature of labor by ignoring
the direct relation between the worker (labor) and production."[181]
What Marx has perceived and revealed with such clarity in these
utterances is that man has become in capitalism a means to an end,
an object, a thing, used by the owner for egotistical purposes.
Now, when we recall that the system's goal is "surplus–value" or
"money," and when we recall the *transitional aims* bound up with
the acquisition of money, we are in a position to spy the full
grotesqueness, the full psychological disturbance, of the entire
"order." Man in capitalism is not simply an object, he is a transitional object—a transitional object in the literal, psychoanalytic
sense of the term. What was served for man as infant and child by
the "blankie," teddy bear, bottle, kitten, or storybook, is served for
man in his "adult" condition by man himself, by other human
beings. In an economic setup that struggles to cope with the
persistent transitional anxieties of the creature, people disappear
as people. We spy from this perspective, too, the full significance,
the full unconscious meaning, of dehumanization as it emerges

from Marx's work and from the psychodynamics of internalization. What serves the child magically as a "transitional object," as a method of retaining the tie to the parental figure during the time of separation, is a symbol, an external "thing" that, in the "cultural space" of the child's inner world, corresponds to the internalized presence of the parent and becomes the "surrogate." Hence, the transitional need may prompt the child to see other people symbolically, transitionally, as ways to the parent, as parental substitutes, a developmental occurrence which, in its turn, catalyzes the tendency to regard the world in a transitional manner, to look upon "reality," or the "external environment," as a transitional object designed to gratify one's private, transitional needs. Whole groups of people, the "reserve army of workers," for example, become not people but things removed, symbols of economic possibility, "factors" to be "taken into account" in the "passionate chase" after gain. Unable to grow into his full humanity, unable to reach, in Marx's words, the father's level, the capitalist persists in what is essentially an infantile mode of perception, a mode of perception that is connected inextricably to what is taken to be "normal" or "ordinary" consciousness. The termination of a transitional economic system is, then, dependent on the termination of a transitional perceptual system; one is so much a part of the other that it is impossible to try to end one without ending the other. As long as the tie to the object remains firm, and as long as that tie engenders transitional anxiety, and as long as symbolic awareness is linked to the "timeless" goal of refusion, men will be prone to use one another as objects.

9.

As was suggested earlier, the power that binds the individual to the culture, that stands behind all social and religious phenomena, is ultimately drawn from the inner world, from the individual's psycho–physical connection to the internalized objects of infancy and childhood. As was also suggested, methods for altering an individual's consciousness are based largely in the breaking of that tie. To see the world directly, or "face to face," one must regain the *energy* that is habitually invested in the old relationship *within,* the relationship that governs perception by continually awakening transitional anxiety and the symbolical mode of awareness which was itself a defense against the early danger. The "emotional charges" attached to the object, writes Grof, explain "the enormous amount of affective energy" that must be "discharged" before traumatic experiences can be "extinguished."[182] What is particularly striking about Marx's work here, and what links that work with Freud's in a remarkable manner, is the extent to which the analysis of capitalism is ultimately grounded in the analysis of power. "The total labour–power of society, which is embodied in the sum total of the values of all commodities produced by that society, counts here as one homogeneous mass of human labour–power, composed though it be of innumerable individual units" (*Kap,* I, 46). And again, "Productive activity . . . is nothing but the expenditure of human labour–power" (*Kap,* I, 51). That the calculated control of such power constituted in Marx's mind the mastery of "owner" over "labourer" is clear enough: "The process of production has the mastery over man, instead of being controlled by him" (*Kap,* I, 93).

For Marx, then, the "key" to capitalism, to its mysterious, hidden, unrecognized aspect, lies in the *unseen energy,* or power, that stands behind "production," that is controlled or mastered by the owner, and that can be "transformed" into its magical, symbolical "equivalent," namely money which is "really" commodity. The similarities with Freud emerge, for Freud also discovered the "key" to an analysis of "civilization" in the unseen energies, the powers, and drives (triebe) with which "instinct" provides individuals and which "civilization" represses. Such repression gives rise, in turn, to the dynamic unconscious that is set against the aims of "culture" and that often erupts by virtue of the guilt and aggression associated with its frustrated wishes. In both conceptual systems the energies and the powers of men are put to suppressive use, are chained to an order of domination or mastery. In Marx, energy or power is exploited by the "ruling class," and becomes, therefore, an energy that can be used to disrupt the "system," to free itself from "mastery" or "bondage." In Freud, the power and the energy of men is pushed down by morality, by the need for control. The seething unconscious created thereby also harbors a disruptive, "revolutionary" potential. What links Marx and Freud as seers, then, is their recognition and analysis of what is unseen, that energy or power that cannot be perceived in the usual sense and that drives the objects of the physical world, living and non–living, in accordance with principles that ultimately derive from the Newtonian model of attraction and repulsion, the *forces* of classical scientific theory.

Here is where a bridge to the problem of awareness may be made. The energies that are "exploited" in "production" do not present themselves in direct, Newtonian fashion, as "natural resources." Power is available because the worker views the "setup" as a projective expression of his inner world. He is *tied* to "hierarchies" by a psychic extension of the energic bonds that tie him to the objects within. Accordingly, power is not distributed in capitalism; it is redistributed. The initial cathexes transpire on the inside; what is left of the individual's force is then directed toward the external order. It is not simply the withholding of food that makes the system "go"; it is the worker's attachment to infancy as well. Similar motivations stand, of course, behind the owner's "exploitation" of "labor." What is aimed at is what wealth means, namely, the fulfillment of wishes inextricably linked to the "immortal object" of the early time,[183]—the anxieties, defeats, and unconscious aspirations of the transitional years. There are no human energies, there are no instincts, that are not linked to human interactions. Because object relations are internalized into the individual's mind–body, his subsequent expressions of power are fated to reflect his inner life. What was "force" to the classical physicist is "symbol–force" to current psychology, at least with regard to the "motions" of people. To think for a moment on the extent to which the economic organization is, and was in Marx's day, conjoined with the state (that timeless receptacle of men's affects, and "identifications" in the Freudian sense of the term) is to recognize the inclusiveness of the issue. As to how such a system "gets going" in the first place, we must cite once again the work of Max Weber[184] in which specific individuals pursue transitional goals in an active, aggressive manner and in a world that offers both the material *and the psychological* conditions for "success," available natural and human resources in the form of a needy populace energically tied to a hierarchical order reflective of the inner "realm." The point is, ordinary consciousness, rooted as it is in a symbolical perception that preserves the tie to the objects within, constitutes the general human framework in which the projective or transitional attachments "live." Hence, ordinary consciousness constitutes the framework in which power relationships beget their urgency, their magical ability to service the unconscious aims of the individual, to ensure the existence of the "dual–unity situation" originally ensured by religious activities in which sacrifice and money played a central role. What has all this to do with the writings of Karl Marx, specifically his writings? The answer is, a great deal.

Marx stresses again and again the importance of altered awareness and "revolutionary consciousness" in his program for radical change. The chief purpose of his "communistic" activities, he writes in 1843, is to "awaken the world out of its own dream," to "explain to the world its own acts," to induce a "self–understanding . . . of the age concerning its struggles and wishes."[185] Also, the established economic powers have less to fear from the "practical efforts" of revolution than from the "theoretical explication" of "ideas."[186] What holds the exploited classes in bondage are thoughts that come eventually to comprise an "outlook," thoughts which are ultimately "forged" in the "conscience."[187] These, writes Marx, constitute the "chains" from which the oppressed must be released—the chains that must be "torn away" from them.[188] The task of history, thus becomes "to establish the *truth* of this *world*."[189] Marx believes that it is only such an establishment that can free an individual from the mystifying influence of—and called attention to here is the transitional significance of these institutions—"family, religion, state."[190]

To amplify Marx's concept of awareness along lines suggested by the psychology of recent decades, and particularly by Freud's psychology of groups, is to confront directly the far–reaching implications of his position. "Revolutionary consciousness" cannot achieve its purpose of liberating men from their thoughts until it reaches down to the ground of thought itself—the internalization of the world and the formation of symbols. From here derives the emotive power that binds men not only to the economic system, but to the authoritative order of states (present–day dictatorships, both fascist and communist). Thus, as long as "revolutionary consciousness" remains at the surface of the mind, or as long as it lacks a radical psychological emphasis, it cannot diminish social and economic bondage in a permanent manner.[191] While power is still available in a transitional way, while transitional needs still press for fulfillment, there can be no escaping the transitional mode of social organization. As soon as those who seek control discover a method of manipulating those who "follow," the transitional intent will rule the new "order." "Revolutionary consciousness" must break the source of the power "chain" from within the individual to the projective, symbolic level outside the individual. As the internalization of the parental figure and the establishment of ordinary or symbolic awareness are, themselves, the sources of that power, the development of "revolutionary consciousness," in the deepest Marxian sense, derives precisely from the individual's truncation of the tie to the object within.

Detached from internalized forces that impel him to perceive the external world in a symbolic, "ordinary" manner, the individual is no longer available to the transitional setup "out there." Free on the inside, he can begin to work toward lasting freedom on the outside. What must be stressed above all at this juncture is that the "truncation of the tie to the internalized object" will not be brought about by "psychoanalysis," the "talking cure," or the individual's conscious realization of his bondage, but by methods traditionally associated with religious or mystical "schools."

These methods focus on the individual's body into which the parental object has been internalized. It is not enough that there be "ego" where "id" was, as Freud recommended; the ego in its development is as unconscious as the id. Equally insufficient, for similar reasons, is Reich's "Freudo-Marxism"; no matter how much "character–armor" an individual has shed, if he/she remains in ordinary awareness, without the ability to put his world of symbols on and off again, nothing of final significance will have been accomplished. For as we have seen, "the truncation of the tie to the object within" consists by definition in the cessation of ordinary consciousness and the symbolical sight which is its inevitable counterpart. To perceive the world differently is to receive it differently. This suggests reference to Marx's famous assertion that religion is "the opium of the people."[192]

We have explored in previous sections the transitional significance of religion and drugs. Marx, treating metaphorically the workings of the capitalistic order, particularly with reference to the "passionate" pursuit of "surplus–value," has disclosed at the dynamic level of the analysis what might be termed the transitional aspect of the economic setup. It is not only religion that constitutes "opium," it is money as well. What emerges with striking clarity at this point in the discussion is that ordinary awareness is itself a kind of "opium," a kind of drug that stands between the individual and his apprehension of the world. The "reality" of man's "normal waking consciousness," to employ William James' famous expression,[193] is as much a "fetish" at the level of unconscious processes, as much a "deity" transitionally clung to, as "commodity" or the transference figures of the church. That he is treated as an object economically is a source of man's "alienation." But that source is rooted, in turn, in an alienated method of perceiving the external and internal environments. The return to the self, so precious to Marx,[194] cannot be realized as long as the individual remains in a perceptual, ontological stance that, by its very nature, affirms the governing influence of the internalized object and divorces him from direct, sensuous contact with the universe, including his own body. The "dual–unity" of the species is ultimately a dualism, a "symbolism" in which an alienated manner of "seeing" not only presents itself as "given" but actually breeds the transitional aims which place men in the marketplace among the other objects of legitimate pursuit. The slave of wages is ultimately a slave of the transitional world–mind which enslaves us all. Opium, religion, commodity, wealth, symbolic or "ordinary" perception, these constitute a kind of psychological family away from which the species has yet to grow.

Chapter 6

OUR NEW INDUSTRIAL STATE
Dr. Galbraith and Psychoanalysis

1.

To what extent does this analysis of Marx apply to the modern economic "setup?" In one respect, of course, this question is rhetorical. Obviously, the author considers Marx's writings to be profoundly relevant to the present. In another respect, however, this question is "real," for the pertinency of a position taken many decades ago cannot be fully recognized until it has been applied to a specific, detailed account of current practices. To this end, Galbraith's *The New Industrial State* will be examined. It is not colored, openly or covertly, by an identification with the "establishment," or the "status quo"; it is not burdened with tendentious, ideological interpretations calculated to nudge individuals toward the acceptance of a particular "view." Needless to say, it is a controversial book; but then, books in this area tend to generate controversy. Around the economical sphere of human activity swirl powerful emotions that reach back to the very origins of our affective life, emotions that are integrally tied with the parental figures. That *The New Industrial State* has been so widely read, so "influential" as is said, adds a certain spice to the task.

What emerges overwhelmingly from this volume is the degree to which current economic procedures are designed to control or master aspects of economic anxiety in the capitalist camp, and the degree to which "the public" is controlled and manipulated in the effort to accomplish the aims of those who attend the corporate power structure, the structure that counts in our world. "The forces inducing human effort have changed," writes Galbraith,[195] and while this change may "assault the most majestic of all economic assumptions, namely that man in his economic activity is subject to the authority of the market" (*NIS*, 25–26), it must, nevertheless, be faced. "We have an economic system which, whatever its formal ideological billing, is in substantial part a planned economy" (*NIS*, 26).

He continues, "Nearly all communications, nearly all production and distribution of electric power, much transportation, most manufacturing and mining, a substantial share of retail trade and a considerable amount of entertainment are conducted or provided by large firms" (*NIS*, 28), firms that comprise in Galbraith's expression, the Industrial System (he estimates that there are approximately 600 such organizations at the center of the picture). The planning of these "giants" ensures that their expansion, their "success," will transpire without hindrance. Accordingly, the large corporation strives to control the supply of raw materials by expanding its activities into areas out of which it formerly kept. Instead of haggling with the supplier, it becomes the supplier; instead of waiting for workers of other firms to iron out their problems with their bosses, it buys the firms; instead of struggling to obtain capital, it creates its own capital and, therefore, "concedes no authority to outsiders" (*NIS*, 55); instead of waiting to see whether the public will buy its products, it manipulates the public on a massive scale so that they will buy them; instead of praying that the government will not interfere with its activities, it aligns itself with government by including "joint" investment in its own projects (subsidy and/or partnership) and, thus, makes the welfare of the state dependent on its own welfare. In addition to all this, it influences legislation in such a way as to make the burden of the tax structure fall on those from whom it actually begets its profits through the control of pricing. Everything, in a word, is arranged; nothing is left to chance as far as this is humanly possible:

> From the time and capital that must be committed, the inflexibility of this committment, the needs of the large organization and the problems of market performance under conditions of advanced technology, comes the necessity for planning. Tasks must be performed so that they are right not for the present but for that time in the future when, companion and related work having also been done, the whole job is completed. And the amount of capital that, meanwhile, will have been committed adds urgency to this need to be right. So conditions at the time of completion of the whole task must be foreseen as must developments along the way. And steps must be taken to prevent, offset or otherwise neutralize the affect of adverse developments, and to insure that what is ultimately foreseen eventuates in fact (*NIS*, 34–35).

Nearly every facet of our current economic organization can be traced to this method of "doing business."

It hardly needs to be pointed out that the end of this control, planning, or "sophisticated" economic activity, is exactly what it was in earlier decades—the acquisition of money. As for the meaning of money today, it represents precisely what it represented in Marx's own day, and in days long before that—power over men and events, power that ultimately derives from the labor of human beings, the people who make the setup "go." In this way, Galbraith's analysis suggests that the "modern" capitalist has had time to learn what is likely to impede the satisfaction of his transitional needs, and has striven to remove such impediments, much as the child learns to master the "reality" that interferes with the satisfaction of his own aims. Grown up at the "top," the capitalist has remained precisely the same at the "bottom." He is devoted to the endless acquisition of wealth and to the control and power that such wealth brings. Taught unforgettably by the Great

Depression, or as it is called, the Great Panic, that his "system" could break down, that the transitional feed of riches and power could be interrupted, he strove to devise methods for completing his mastery and assuring his longed–for "security" (*NIS*, 246).

The capitalist's "opium," the capitalist's "hit," is the same today as it was before; today, however, he makes sure of his "supply." Indeed, as Galbraith points out, profits themselves are limited by the Industrial System so as to provide a steady flow and expansion, and protect the owners "against" the "loss" that might occur in a "free" and "open" market (*NIS*, 250). The capitalist, then, does not have to suffer the interruption of his "habit." Without anxiety, he can wrest from the "order" the substance that serves as surrogate for the "lost," primary object. Thus, in a very real way, the profit–making of the present arrangement recalls the interest–making of Marx's era: to master time, control the future, ensure the steady, uninterrupted flow of gain, and fill the emptiness with the mother's presence, these appear to be the major goals of the "system."

That the methods of the capitalist have actually diminished his anxiety is highly improbable; in all likelihood, they have only increased it. For the need to control breeds uncertainty, breeds doubt; it also breeds an ever–greater desire for more control. No matter how much one tries, one cannot be sure. And bigger investments mean potentially bigger catastrophes. Not only is "planning essential," writes Galbraith, it is "difficult" as well (*NIS*, 37). Enormous amounts of money are "at risk," and "many things" can "go wrong." The underlying possibility of "disaster" is always there (*NIS*, 38). Psychoanalysis has stressed that one can "get hooked" on being anxious, and on being in the "state" one has grown up with and become accustomed to. Paradoxically, the capitalist's "security" is assured by his "planning" and removed by his "planning." As Michael Harrington expresses it, "capitalist life" is "particularly schizophrenic" in that the "system" is "increasingly scientific as to details" but "irrational as a totality."[196] The attempt to do the impossible—to control the entire market— speaks not only for the disturbance in the behavior but for the transitional purpose in the behavior as well. One will be secure in an uncertain world. One will have the riches that mean control and refusion. Time will succumb to the manipulations of "reason." The psychological importance of Galbraith's analysis vividly emerges from his presentation of the motivational factors that compel the members of the so–called "technostructure," from the "workers" at the "bottom," to the "executives" at the "top." Of particular significance is his use of "identification." He writes,

> The mature corporation is a large and complex organization, and individuals align themselves with its goals in response to diverse motives . . . The worker, unlike the stockholder, lives in immediate daily association with the organization. This is itself an inducement to identification; an individual comes to think of himself as an IBM man, a Corning Glass man or a Sears man (*NIS*, 154–156).

Moreover, as the corporation has come to recognize that the identification of the worker increases through decent treatment, through a "living wage" and security benefits, and that such identification is good for profits, it has acted accordingly, which has had the effect of deepening the worker's identification with the company. The worker is tied to his job emotively, and we have in this tie a version of the group tie earlier depicted in the writings of Freud.

"Next," Galbraith continues,

> as one moves inward, are foremen and supervisory personnel and the clerical, sales and other routine white–collar personnel. These merge at their inner perimeter with technicians, engineers, sales executives, scientists, designers and other specialists who comprise the technostructure. Beyond these at the center are the executives or management" (*NIS*, 157).

Galbraith then notes, "as one moves through these inner circles identification and adaptation become increasingly important" (*NIS*, 157). In fact, "barriers to identification" tend to "disappear." There is "no sense of compulsion and thus no bar to voluntary adoption of the goals of the employing organization" (*NIS*, 157). What is the question "automatically" asked when two individuals meet on a plane? " 'Who are you with?' Until this is known," writes Galbraith, "the individual is a cipher. He cannot be placed in the scheme of things" (*NIS*, 158). Thus, "he surrenders to organization because organization can do more for him than he can do for himself . . . 'How can you overwork,' executives ask, 'if *your work is your life?*' " (*NIS*, 158–159, my emphasis). Thus, the technostructure "meets a large share of the needs of the individual" (*NIS*, 159). The transitional implications of this material are obvious. The corporation that seeks the money, profit, and substitute object, is psychologically adhered to by those who form a part of it. Identification permits the magical belief that they, too, are reaching the transitional goals after which the corporation chases; they, too, are part of the large, powerful "structure" that gets the huge wealth and that, in association with other large "structures" (surrogates), controls "reality" or "the world." Money received in wages derives from this source and, thus, provides, in the "fantastic" arrangement characteristic of this era, not only an avenue back to the maternal figure but a "part" of that figure herself. Indeed, workers are nudged in this psychological direction by management's offering token shares in the company, actual "pieces" of the corporate "body." Hence, each worker is transformed into a little capitalist, and the "system" as a whole is characterized less by "war" between rival segments of society than by identification within one large "capitalist" class.

For all this, of course, the "order" is essentially the same as the "order" of earlier decades; it has merely softened relations to get cooperation. The worker is still exploited, as he was in the nineteenth century; his exploitation is simply concealed by propaganda, shibboleths, a car in the garage, a chicken in the pot, a union contract, and, perhaps, a few shares of stock (this in "good" countries and "good" times; in "bad" countries and/or "bad" times things are very different). His capacity to identify with the symbol of power is exploited along with his labor. Before he was simply "skinned." Now he is psychologically seduced and skinned. The main point, however, is this: there can be no genuine progress, or evolutionary development for the species, within such a "system." For all the softening of industrial relations, for all the "benefits" accorded "working people," the rape of the earth, the pollution and debasement of the planet, the egocentric pursuit of wealth, and the irresponsible distribution of resources—the perversion of the ancient wisdom embodied in the agrarian myths—are every bit as visible in our own time as they were in the time of *Kapital*. They are perhaps even more visible if one has the ability to see through the fulsome, propagandistic screens of the large corporations ("finding new energy for *you!*"). As in the past, human beings are infantilized on an enormous scale, urged to exist in a transitional attitude toward creation—still seeking the parental figure, clinging to ordinary reality, tied to the forces of the inner world, wasting their power, their capacity for maturation, on the surrogate objects of the marketplace. Identification with the corporate structure, or with the state of which it forms an integral part, does not change the result; identification is by definition a transitional phenomenon. Man cannot have himself when he belongs to another power, either through coercion, as in Marx's day, or through "identification," in our own.

In modern capitalism, Galbraith writes (with a strikingly inverted syntax), "to the desire of the individual to mold the world to his goals, a thoughtful providence has added the illusion of a great ability to do so" (*NIS,* 161). Compare this to the words of Omar Khayyám, the medieval Persian poet:

> Ah, love! could you and I with him conspire
> To grasp this sorry Scheme of things entire,
> Would we not shatter it to bits—and then
> Remold it nearer to the Heart's Desire?

In this economical instance, the "heart's desire" metaphorically expresses the regressive dream of union with the object of the early time, or the power to control her. By aligning himself with the large corporation, the modern seeker believes he will discover the narcissistic supplies he requires. His capacity to create symbols, his biological ability to make a concept–reality out of an affect, allows him to continue, magically pursuing this "illusion" to the end of his days, and to the detriment of his surroundings, including the people therein. When an individual maintains that his "work" is his "life," as our executive maintained a few paragraphs earlier (*NIS*, 159), one can safely replace "life" with another word, for there is only one "object" in one's "life" that is that important, and the needs associated with her are frequently transferred to one's precious "employment." Moreover, the word "life" as it is used in the foregoing passage focuses from yet another perspective the element of sacrifice, with its multiple religious and transitional meanings, in the current economic order. Absorbed in his responsibilities, the corporate employee is eager to devote his energy, power, body, and his very "life," to the powerful "structure" of which he forms a "part." Can the significance of altered awareness as a revolutionary instrument be missed at this juncture, altered awareness that consists in the severing of the tie to the object within, the tie that comprises the psychological ground in which "identification" is rooted?

2.

One significant element lacking in Galbraith's analysis is an awareness of the ambivalence with which transitional aims are pursued by the corporate employee, and even by the "higher–ups" themselves. The procedures and techniques associated with mass production, writes Pederson–Krag in a definitive treatment of the issue, foster in the worker a kind of existential "fatigue" by according him a "status" that corresponds in the unconscious to the "conditions of infancy."[197] Although the individual is "integrated" into the organizational "structure," he is also obliged to undergo the reactivation of unpleasurable affect, a considerable amount of it in fact.

The relationship between individuals . . . is based on fear of
aggression from strangers (competing companies) which makes
each person submit to the authority of his superior. Superintendents
exhort subordinates to work more efficiently to outstrip the production of other firms. This is the equivalent of stimulating the workers'
rivalry with unknown competitors to overcome their resentment of
authority and aversion to effort.[198]

Pederson–Krag continues,

superintendents report to the manager of a department which produces either one complicated product or several of the same nature.
The manager is subordinate to a vice–president who surveys not
only manufacturing but allied problems such as cost, design, and
demand. The president gives an account of the whole procedure to
the chairman of his board of directors. The organization resembles
the feudal system, with the squire commanding the peasants, the
baron the squires until the final authority, the king, is reached.[199]

And then, in a key observation, "the corporation is like a vast
pregenital mother who gives her brood security and nourishment,
but who loves the eldest and strongest (the top executives) best,
since she gives them the most. The weaker and inexperienced
newcomers get promotion and wage increases, favors from the
mother, only if they are deserving and their superiors approve."[200]
As for the junior executives, although they express their "rivalry"
toward "colleagues," they "prefer" a "protecting, maternal organization to independence. When the pregenital mother plays favor-
ites, and becomes too closely identified with the strong men at the
head, a new mother, the union, takes her place and forces her to
feed the hungry young."[201] Clearly then, although the corporation
is gripped in a transitional way, there is ambivalence and fear in the
gripping. Adhered to and "loved" for its "bodily contents," it is
vilified and "hated" for its debasing, authoritarian method of
organizing human relations.

The corporation does more than reactivate old wounds; it
breeds a sense of failure, or regressive attachment, in the now of
life. At the deepest emotive level, the individual betrays himself in

his identification with the surrogate object, in his desire for protective, essentially infantile merger. What was bodily alienation and, to a lesser degree, psychological alienation in Marx is psychological alienation and to a lesser degree bodily alienation in our own time. The "tiredness" of the corporate employee, a tiredness which is, as Pederson–Krag expresses it, out of proportion to his "expenditure of energy,"[202] measures his enormous investment of power in the internalized objects of his inner world, the objects "exploited" by the corporate structure in its vast effort to control its "staff." To be a Corning Glass man may not be quite as "smooth," or quite as tolerable, as Galbraith appears to imply.

3.

Discussion of *The New Industrial State* would be conspicuously incomplete were it not to include Galbraith's analysis of "consumerism," that aspect of the present "order" directly engaging the "citizency" as a whole. What emerges here is clear: everything in the "system"—and that includes the state—is geared toward manipulating the "consumer" into an uninterrupted, endless urge to buy products, purchase "items," possess things. Indeed, it is precisely this manipulation that stands at the center of the entire scheme. To accomplish such an end, to "bring it off," the controllers of the marketplace must operate behind the illusion that nothing is going on "out there" except the exercise of choice, that the individuals in the society, the "targets," are perfectly free to make their own decisions. "It is possible," writes Galbraith, "that people need to believe that they are unmanaged if they are to be managed effectively" (*NIS*, 217).

And then, going to the heart of the matter,

> along with bringing demand under substantial control [management] . . . performs yet another service; . . . it provides, in the aggregate, a relentless propaganda on behalf of goods in general. From early morning until late at night, people are informed of the

services rendered by goods—of their profound indispensability. Every feature and facet of every product having been studied for selling points, these are then described with talent, gravity, and an aspect of profound concern as the source of health, happiness, social achievement, or improved community standing. Even minor qualities of unimportant commodities are enlarged upon with a solemnity which would not be unbecoming in an announcement of the combined return of Christ and all the apostles. More important services, such as the advantages of whiter laundry, are treated with proportionately greater gravity. The consequence is that while goods become ever more abundant they do not seem to be any less important. On the contrary, it requires an act of will to imagine that anything else is so important (*NIS*, 208–209).

The point is, of course, that

goods are what the industrial system supplies. Advertising by making goods important makes the industrial system important. And therewith it helps to sustain the social importance and prestige that attach to the technostructure. As the landowner and the capitalist lost prestige when land and capital ceased to be socially decisive, so the technostructure would soon sink into the background were the supply of industrial products to become routine . . . This would have happened long since had not advertising . . . kept people persuaded to the contrary (*NIS*, 208–209).

In this way, the well–being or the "health" of the "industrial system" is totally dependent on the public's continuous expenditure of money. Not only is it vital to get "them" to spend, it is a genuine "danger" to allow "them" to save. "The individual serves the industrial system . . . by consuming its products" (*NIS*, 53). The very system of taxation itself, and even the rate of inflation (*NIS*, 57–60), are, accordingly, managed to insure the steady flow of profit to the companies: "The state uses its power over taxation and expenditure to provide the balance between savings and their use that the industrial system cannot provide for itself. It supplies the missing element in the planning of savings" (*NIS*, 58).

Lest one believe there are genuine material needs attached to

this "business," that individuals actually require what they purchase, Galbraith has the following:

> Most goods serve needs that are discovered to the individual not by
> the palpable discomfort accompanying deprivation, but by some
> psychic response to their possession. They give him a sense of
> personal achievement, accord him a feeling of equality with his
> neighbours, divert his mind from thought, serve sexual aspiration,
> promise social acceptability, enhance his subjective feeling of
> health, well–being or orderly peristalis, contribute by conventional
> canons to personal beauty, or are otherwise psychologically reward-
> ing . . . The industrial system serves wants which are psychological
> in origin and hence admirably subject to management by appeal to
> the psyche (*NIS,* 201).

And again,

> though a hungry man cannot be persuaded as between bread and a
> circus, a well-nourished man can. And he can be persuaded as
> between different circuses and different foods. The further a man is
> removed from physical need the more open he is to persuasion—or
> management—as to what he buys. This is, perhaps, the most
> important consequence for economics of increasing affluence (*NIS,*
> 202).

There is no need to continue. We live in this "system," and we
know the extent to which it devotes itself to getting people to
consume things. What must be stressed above all is the profound
social consequence of the psychological connection between this
activity and the exploitation of the worker's capacity to identify
with corporate power.

Just as the employee's adherence to the company provides
him with transitional reward, so does the consumer's obsessive
purchasing of goods. The very vocabulary Galbraith employs
adumbrates the transitional end. Buying and possessing mean
acceptance (rejection's opposite), achievement, sexual fulfillment, well–being, escape from thought (a "bad object"), and a

host of other psychologically gratifying items. Power and security, the goals of Marx's "capitalist," immediately come to mind, particularly in reference to their "psychic" connection with money as a primary version of "good body contents." Thus, capitalism in its current, "Galbraithean" form is able to exploit the psychological equivalence of money and goods in such a way as to lay the accent on goods, goods that represent money, and are money at the level of unconscious mentation. As Roheim observed (pages 109–112), it is not merely "coin" as such that comes to signify the body of the object, either as a direct substitute (in primitive culture), or as a symbol of control (in the capitalistic order). Wealth in any form can serve a "magical" purpose (dual–unity) by becoming a surrogate for the mothering figure. It is precisely in this sense that the Marxian transformation of "commodity" into "riches" not only remains with us but expands to include the manner in which the "citizenry" as a whole is "skinned." The transitional circle of the "industrial state" closes through the identification of the worker and consumer with symbols whose maternal or "religious" significance is obvious (the company and the product). An entire population, directly under the influence of state and "private" management, struggles to fulfill its transitional needs, and to allay its transitional anxieties, through, on the one hand, identification with the corporate "body," and, on the other, the expenditure of a substance that begets in the end but a version of itself. Needless to say, through the firm, punctilious control of price and of wage, the steady flow of profit is guaranteed further.

Remarkably, then, it is not only the worker who is transformed into a little capitalist; everyone in this "one–dimensional" system undergoes the transformation. The emotional malaise that Marx discovered in the character of the "primitive" capitalist spreads through the whole population. Exploited for profit and, at the same time, given access to "goods," each member of the "order" is strenuously encouraged to pursue the transitional dream. Not only can everyone have a chicken in the pot, everyone can possess the traditional symbols of the owner (symbols that signify power and security) in their fake, middle–class form: a big, cheap version of a luxury carriage (the "motor car"), an imitation–crystal chandelier, a credit–card that speaks for hidden resources, or "backing," a neighborhood home with a "plantation" facade, many pair of shoes, jewelry. The "passionate chase after riches" that formerly characterized the "capitalist" becomes the passionate chase after goods that at present characterizes the "consumer." Existence is sacrificed to the begetting of possessions which, in contrast to "religion," become the new "opium" of the "industrial" community.

It all seems perfectly natural, of course; not simply because the transitional longings are real (and endless), but because both sides of the power structure receive a transitional reward, a transitional "hit." The owner gets his profit, the consumer gets his stuff. But the system is "natural" only in the way in which labor power appeared "natural" in Marx's own day. To grasp the "system" in its underlying meaning is to grasp its infantilism, wastefulness, danger to the growth and evolution of the species, and its irrational, "religious" character. When Galbraith tells us that laundry soap is advertised with a seriousness that would be appropriate to the return of Christ and the apostles (*NIS*, 209), there is more than a rhetorical truth in the comparison. "If we continue to believe," he writes, "that the goals of the industrial system—the expansion of output, the companion increase in consumption, technological advance, the public images that sustain it—are coordinate with life, then all of our lives will be in the service of these goals (*NIS*, 382).

One could not ask for a passage that more vividly points up the compensatory, sacrificial, and sacred nature of the order. Everywhere beneath the surface of the entire "organization" the quest for transitional reward is visible. Genuine evolutionary significance is not lacking in Galbraith's final statement that steps to combat the current form of madness may, if we are lucky, work our general "salvation" (*NIS*, 383).

When he alludes to the "public images" that support the "industrial state" Galbraith calls to mind Freud's revolutionary insight into the nature of group solidarity. Goods are not simply offered to the members of the public as personalized indications of power and security, as psychological avenues to transitional fulfillment at the level of individual need; goods are offered in such a way as to become loved and worshipped as symbols of the national purpose. In the prevailing ideology of "the new industrial state," what the corporation produces, what the consumer purchases, and what "the nation" is "accomplishing" are linked inextricably at the emotive level (*NIS*, 381–383). The significance of altered awareness as a revolutionary tool emerges once again. For as Galbraith explicitly declares, the entire transitional setup with which the populace identifies is directly dependent on the established powers maintaining an "access to the minds" of individuals (*NIS*, 210). Like Marx, Galbraith recognizes the key role of consciousness in the present, indeed in any economic organization. To effectively diminish the "values" of the "culture" one must first of all achieve the ability to sever the energic tie to the object within, the tie that triggers the desire to grip whichever transitional symbols are currently being offered, and that, thereby, enables the prevailing forces to manage human beings as responsive objects. When he is able to put his symbolic mentation on and off again, when he has achieved that control, detachment, and mastery, the individual will have become conscious of the extent to which his history, and particularly the history of his economic life, has been written in the language of his transitional needs—the language of his "immortal," internalized objects, the language, in short, of his ordinary "reality."

Part IV

THE GOAL OF LIBERATION

Chapter 7

ANXIETY, LIBIDO, AND REPRESSION

Further Comments on Freud and Brown

1.

Promised in an earlier chapter was a discussion of Freud's treatment of the death drive, ambivalence, guilt, and anxiety in *Civilization and Its Discontents,* a discussion in what might be called analytic–phenomenological terms, terms that demonstrate the integral connection between the problem of ordinary awareness and specific psycho–dynamic issues.

The "discontents" of "civilization," said Freud, are related inextricably to the "neurosis" of the individual, and particularly to the manner in which his "narcissistic libido" gets entangled with his "compulsion to repeat." The "life instincts," accordingly, may extend themselves outward toward the world in a productive, "happy" fashion or backward toward the "subject" in what Freud regarded as a kind of psycho–biological "conservatism." His postulation of a "destrudo," or "death instinct," derives from this analytical perspective.

I drew the conclusion that, besides the instinct to preserve living substance and to join it into ever larger units, there must exist another, contrary instinct seeking to dissolve those units and to bring them back to their primaeval, inorganic state. That is to say, as well as Eros there was an instinct of death.[203]

This controversial concept will be evaluated during the remainder of the discussion, chiefly in regard to the way in which other writers have chosen to approach it. What must be stressed at once is that Freud's effort to "hook" the individual neurosis to the malaise of the "culture" is considerably eased when the unconscious assumptions of ordinary awareness are kept firmly in mind. The individual's struggle to establish and maintain "dual–unity" binds him to the objects of his inner world and, hence, to an overestimation of external objects that "automatically" become projective exemplifications of either acceptance or rejection, in other words, psychological symbols. Always seeking to compensate for the wounds and defeats of infancy and childhood, always seeking a security that will remove forever the angst of early separation and loss, the ambivalent, divided human is drawn toward the domination and exploitation of others, and identification with surrogate parental "structures"—the church, state, corporation, the group generally. He is also drawn to sexual acting–out, withdrawal into fantasy, narcosis, private "tripping," and a host of other emotive occupations that characterize the conduct of mankind.

The point is, ordinary consciousness as a tie to the object, or a transitional employment of the biological capacity to make symbols, constitutes a neurosis in itself. To give up the world of ordinary awareness is to give up the internalized presence, the primal foundation of an emotive security the precariousness of which is conspicuously, indeed, overwhelmingly apparent. It is here that a fresh perspective of Freud's "instinct" of "death" may be gained. Human beings adhere to their "discontented" world, their destructive, mad projection of internalized affect, not because they have a "drive" to resume an "inorganic mode of existence" but because they fear detachment from the powers within.

They are "conservative" regarding "dual–unity" no matter how much "discontentment" the need to maintain it involves. In the deep, unconscious sense of the term, a sense integrally concerned with the development of object relations, they are superstitious. Because Freud did not fully fathom the connection of internalization to the crises of the early period, the connection of the early period to the attainment of symbolic awareness, and the connection of symbolic awareness to the advent of ordinary mentation or the sense of "reality," he attributed to instinct what arose in the course of human interaction—the capacity to suffer and make others suffer, too. The "destrudo" of the species is the individual's unwillingness to drop his emotive, energic attachment to the objects of his inner world and the projective aims that arise therefrom.

Even the operation of human sexuality, which is more obviously linked to the instincts, or "drives," than is "death" (*CD*, 54), cannot be divorced from transitional issues, or the overriding influence of internalization in the development of human behavior. As Lichtenstein has demonstrated,[204] each person begets from those around him during the course of his early experience what might be termed an "identity theme," an affective, qualitative conception of himself which he eventually brings to his adolescent and adult relations and which governs the manner in which he employs his sexuality in "culture." The "instinct" is put to a human purpose and defines the individual's "style" of interacting with others. If the internalized "identity theme" suggests that one is unlovable and fated to isolation, there could be a certain desperation in the use of one's sexuality to gain contact and positive response. If one has internalized "privilege" and "special consideration," sexuality could be used in a manipulative manner for purposes of power and control. Remarkably, Lichtenstein's major illustration of the connection between sexuality and "identity" focuses on a prostitute and, through her personage, on the psychological interrelation of libidinal and economic matters, an interrelation long stressed in the analytic literature.[205] The point is, just as money is tied inextricably to the problems of internalization, symbol formation, dual–unity, and ordinary consciousness, so is sexuality tied to these issues. Ordinary sexuality is transitional sexuality, sexuality in which the partner is not only a reflection of the object within but an avenue back to that object, in short, another symbol in the symbolical universe. To sever the tie to the internalized presence, achieve the ability to put the world of symbols on and off again, or alter one's awareness in the classical sense, is to liberate sexuality along with perception generally. Sexuality is, in the final analysis, an aspect of one's total perception; it is fundamentally rooted in the apprehending organism—the body in which all stimulations are received. One's response to stimuli and one's reception of stimuli are "twins."[206] When one has terminated the "object relation" on the inside, one's partner, finally, *is there*.

2.

Freud's analyses of guilt, ambivalence, and anxiety in *Civilization and Its Discontents* are integrally connected to his understanding of internalization, an understanding which is, in spite of its originality and brilliance, unable to lead us to the pith of the matter. Striving to explain how it is that a person "comes to have a sense of guilt," the feeling that he has done something wrong or "bad," Freud closely focuses on the infantile situation. A person's own feelings would not bring him to this pass, he notes; consequently, there must be an "extraneous influence" at work (*CD*, 61). The essence of the issue resides, for Freud, in the dependency and helplessness of the infant and child, a dependency and helplessness that cause his paramount "fear" to be precisely that "loss of love" (*CD*, 61).

If he loses the love of another person upon whom he is dependent," writes Freud,

> he also ceases to be protected from a variety of dangers. Above all,
> he is exposed to the danger that this stronger person will show his

superiority in the form of punishment. At the beginning, therefore, what is bad is whatever causes one to be threatened with loss of love. For fear of that loss, one must avoid it. This, too, is the reason why it makes little difference whether one has already done the bad thing or only intends to do it. In either case, the danger only sets in, if and when, the authority discovers it, or when the authority would behave in the same way. This state of mind is called a 'bad conscience'; but actually it does not deserve this name for at this stage the sense of guilt is clearly only a fear of loss of love, 'social' anxiety (*CD*, 61–62).

When the "authority" is internalized, Freud maintains, a "great change" takes place; through internalization, the "super–ego" is established and conscience reaches a "higher stage" of development (*CD*, 62). The individual is now "in charge of himself."

It is here that Freud offers a crucial set of remarks. In spite of his postulation that the individual achieves a "higher stage" of development through "internalization," Freud declares that "things" remain "fundamentally" the same in the sphere of conscience (*CD*, 62). How can this be? Here is the explanation:

> It is true that the seriousness of the situation from a real point of view has passed away, for the new authority, the super–ego, has no motive that we know of for ill–treating the ego, with which it is intimately bound up; but genetic influence, which leads to the survival of what is passed and has been surmounted makes itself felt in the fact that . . . things remain as they were at the beginning. The super–ego torments the sinful ego with the same feeling of anxiety and is on the watch for opportunities of getting it punished by the external world (*CD*, 62).

What Freud's explanation makes clear is this: as things remain "fundamentally the same" because of the "genetic influence," the problem of "guilt" remains a problem of separation, loss, and anxiety. The "loss of love," in which "guilt" originates, persists into the "higher stage" and prevents that "stage" from "really" being "higher" at all. The sole difference between the early and late "fear of loss" is, according to Freud, the extent to which the late fear is internalized. As we have seen, however, internalizing mechanisms are at work within the individual long before the stage of the "super–ego" is reached. Early "fears" are taken into the "psychic structure" quite as readily as late ones, if not more readily. Hence, the way is open, through a modification of Freud's emphasis, to demonstrate the transitional aim which stands behind "civilization" as a whole. This is the aim Roheim recognized and wedded to his concept of "dual–unity." The "institutions" of "culture"—its religious and economic organizations—are forged by a creature who seeks to master anxiety, who seeks security on the inside where his "immortal objects" reside. It is when "guilt" is understood for what it actually signifies in Freud's book that the importance of his assertion, "the sense of guilt [is] the most important problem in the development of civilization" (*CD*, 71) is properly comprehended.

The progression of Freud's logic virtually begs him to explore the role of separation in the genesis of culture. As is invariably the case when he confronts pre–oedipal material, however, he shifts the matter to a "higher level" and discusses the "father" and the "primal crime." Accordingly, as his analyses continue, so do his misemphases. For if things remain "fundamentally the same in the sphere of conscience," as he says they do, then, surely, the origin of guilt must have everything to do with that all-determining influence that keeps them "the same"; the origin must be consistent with its product, with those affects derived from the "fear of loss," anxiety, the dread of separation, the powerful bond to the maternal figure who stands at the center of the infant's existence. Yet, such affects are not found in Freud's presentation. Although "innate constitutional factors" unite with "influences from the real environment" (*CD*, 67) to produce conscience in man, the influence from the real environment "goes back to the killing of the primal father" (*CD*, 69), back to "an inclination to aggressiveness against the father" (*CD*, 69) which is repeated in each generation and automatically, as it were, produces the sense of guilt in human beings. In this way, when men group themselves together they do so out of "Eros," or the desire to unite; yet as soon as they do unite, their "aggressiveness," or "primordial ambivalence of feeling toward the father," emerges to disrupt their unity (*CD,* 69). It is precisely this aggressiveness, and ambivalence, that catalyzes the feeling of "guilt" in them, a feeling that provokes their "discontent" and which leads, in turn, to the sad history of human relations (*CD,* 69). Freud, here, lays the emphasis on guilt as a fear of punishment, punishment in the sense of retaliation and restriction (*CD,* 69) rather than guilt as a fear of "loss of love." Remember, this in spite of the fact that things "remain the same."

What such a scheme ignores is that which people are doing in their religious and economic activity, their daily, "ordinary" existence; both continually disclose the anxiety that persists in the mind until the stage of the "father" is reached. Freud declares that individuals are always feeling some measure of guilt because of their ambivalence toward the male parent, and that the presence of this guilt provides them with woe. What he does not seem to realize, and, therefore, fails to make plain, is that because this guilt is actually anxiety, or a fear of "loss of love," individuals are constantly experiencing anxiety and striving to overcome it through compensatory conduct. This conduct bespeaks a need to reach the object, to control it, and rediscover the way to power and security (economics, religion, the state, sexuality). In short, Freud's analysis makes no sense as it proceeds from loss of love, to "primordial ambivalence" in the group, to remorse, and to fear of punishment, rather than from loss of love to the attempt to overcome that loss.

By attributing the urge to "unite" to an erotic "impulsion" (*CD,* 70) that is present at birth and remains relatively constant in the exingencies of the "environment," Freud, in effect, leaves out this vital step in human development. He does not see people "in their everyday lives" coping with transitional problems. He sees them in their unhappiness, leaves them alone in their usual activities, and then sees them again in their wars and destruction, as if what happens in the middle (society itself) does not count. What our "civilization" reveals, is that what happens "in the middle"

.is what actually counts "the most." Our lives are spent consuming, making money, getting married, going to church, having children, striving for success, beauty, and friendship, identifying with heroes or with powerful groups, and when we cannot "make it" or feel threatened in our transitional pursuits we *aggress*, withdraw, seek comfort, or deny. In other words, aggression is one way of coping with "guilt" (fear of loss of love) after the primary, transitional way has been tried. This makes sense: one fears separation and tries to overcome it. It is when one fails to overcome it that he may "get nasty." Like sexuality, aggression is used to answer transitional needs. There is no such thing as "thanatos" in the sense of an urge for death. Eros and the loss of Eros is the first concern of human beings, and when they feel they have lost it, they try to get it back. The concept of "dual–unity," then, merges with Freud's "sense of guilt" in both its originative and resultant aspects. Carried to its logical conclusion, Freud's theory of conscience is consistent with a transitional view of culture as a whole.

The same applies, of course, to his emphasis on "ambivalence" as another cardinal feature of mankind's "civilized" condition. Experiencing "primordial ambivalence" toward the "father" (*CD,* 69), human beings are replete with guilt, guilt that creates intolerable psychological pressure (*CD,* 70) and, in combination with the "destrudo" or the aggressive drive, leads to further "uncivilized" wishes and deeds (*CD,* 73–74). In keeping with the logical extension of Freud's description of guilt as "fear of loss," however, we are obliged to suggest the following: if the "guilt" of the individual precedes the development of his "ambivalence," and if that guilt is in reality a "fear of loss" that "persists" into the "higher stage," then such a "fear" must not only precede "ambivalence," it must have something to do with it, too, of a structural nature. For as Freud declares, the "sense of guilt" exists before the "primal crime" is accomplished and, hence, before the advent of "remorse" in human affairs (*CD,* 69). Now, when we recall that internalizing tendencies are in operation prior to the accomplishment of Freud's "higher stage," we are in a position to achieve a genuine understanding of the matter. The divisiveness of the individual's feeling toward the parent is inextricably tied to his internalized object, the "good" and "bad" figures of the early time who promise bliss and fulfillment on the one hand, and rejection and loss on the other. It is precisely what the individual "takes in" during the first years of his life that provokes his habitual "fear" and, hence, those transitional behaviors that reveal an aggressive intent. Ambivalence is not "primordial"; like everything else, it has a history. The "primal father" was "hated" and "loved" (*CD*, 69) out of the inner world of his "sons." As we recognized during the course of the analysis of Marx earlier, the capitalist "exploits" his workers at the same time that he "passionately" pursues his riches. Here is ambivalent conduct that engenders social unrest. The employee who "hates" the corporation at one level, identifies with it at another; he feels resentful and "fatigued" at the same time he feels "secure." The religious enthusiast discriminates against others for their gods while at the same time he orally clings to his own god through a "mass" or similar rite. Ambivalence, as Freud suggests, certainly has everything to do with the "discontents" of "civilization"; but it is ambivalence rooted in the world of internalized objects rather than "primordial drives." An animal that is hopelessly split on the inside can hardly be expected to fulfill his social potential on the outside. It is from the transitional dilemma as a whole that the malaise of the culture derives. Until the individual's "fear of loss" is considerably lessened through a disruption of the emotional tie that breeds it, a disruption that is solely and precisely the aim of altered awareness, a "group" of "ambivalent" creatures will forge its divided world.

3.

Freud returned to the relationship of guilt and anxiety in two subsequent sections of *Civilization and Its Discontents*. This may have been because he was uncomfortable with his analyses. Indeed, in one striking passage he lays the matter bare by candidly confessing his confusion.

> Our patients do not believe us, when we attribute an 'unconscious sense of guilt' to them. In order to make ourselves at all intelligible to them, we tell them of an unconscious need for punishment, in which the sense of guilt finds expression. But its connection with a particular form of neurosis must not be over–estimated. Even in obsessional neurosis there are types of patients who are not aware of their sense of guilt, or who feel it as a tormenting uneasiness, a kind of anxiety, if they are prevented from carrying out certain actions (*CD*, 72).

And then, puzzled himself, Freud declares, "It ought to be possible eventually to understand these things; but as yet we cannot" (*CD*, 72). He then relies on anxiety once again and reiterates a conclusion which he presented earlier: "Here perhaps we may be glad to have it pointed out that the sense of guilt is at bottom nothing else but a topographical variety of anxiety; in its later phases it coincides completely with fear of the super–ego. And the relations of anxiety to consciousness exhibit the same extraordinary variations" (*CD*, 72).

As he strives to clarify these "variations," Freud comes as close as he ever did to a sense of the transitional problem and to a breakthrough that might, conceivably, have enabled him to grasp the origin and nature of "civilization's discontents." Ultimately, however, he falls short of the mark. Here are his words:

> Anxiety is always present somewhere or other behind every symptom; but at one time it takes noisy possession of the whole of consciousness, while at another it conceals itself so completely that we are obliged to speak of unconscious anxiety or, if we want to have a clearer psychological conscience, since anxiety is in the first instance simply a feeling, of possibilities of anxiety. Consequently it is very conceivable that the sense of guilt produced by civilization is not perceived as such either, and remains to a large extent unconscious, or appears as a sort of *malaise*, a dissatisfaction for which people seek other motivations" (*CD*, 72–73).

Now, it is precisely this "dissatisfaction," "malaise," or kind of general uneasiness that derives from the initial "fear of loss of love," from the separation crises of the early time, from the presence of the bad, rejecting object within, and from the doubtful, imperfect, precarious institution of "dual–unity" as the solution to the original dilemma. Of course people will seek "other motivations" for "guilt" when symbolic awareness itself, ordinary consciousness itself, "reality" no less, comprises the nub of the issue. Individuals are ambivalent in "civilization" not only because they are trapped within a mode of perception that presents them with the same "reality" over and over again and, thus, cuts them off from direct, immediate contact with an inexhaustible universe, but also because that mode of perception (which is supposed to provide an opportunity to separate from the parents) affirms and strengthens in its very operation (symbolical sight) the tie to the internalized parents, or "objects," from which the individual's "malaise" actually springs. The "discontent" of "civilization" is the double–bind of humanity striving to escape the fears and defeats of early life through the pursuit of substitute objects which can come into existence in the first place only through a mode of perception that keeps those very fears and defeats alive.

As for the "solutions" mentioned by Freud (the "answers" through which people strive to cope with their "discontentment" in "culture"), they emerge from the spheres of religious, economic, and interpersonal activity. Indeed, such activity is, in large measure, precisely what "civilization" is. The "discontent" and its institutional reply are not really as separate as Freud's analysis would indicate. What one does seeking transitional gratification through economic, religious, and sexual behavior, is what one actually is as a social creature. "Dissatisfaction" breathes from the individual to these "institutions" and from them back again to the individual in a kind of discontented symbiosis that reflects, at the level of unconscious process, the wounds, terrors, and longings for union characteristic of the early period.

Freud comes very close to confirming this by the manner in which he touches upon religion in his book. He writes,

> Religions . . . have never overlooked the part played in civilization by a sense of guilt. Furthermore—a point which I failed to appreciate elsewhere [The Future of an Illusion]—they claim to redeem mankind from this sense of guilt, which they call sin. From the manner in which, in Christianity, this redemption is achieved—by the sacrificial death of a single person, who in this manner takes upon himself a guilt that is common to everyone—we have been able to infer what the first occasion may have been on which this primal guilt, which was also the beginning of civilization, was acquired (*CD*, 73).

Once again, the emphasis of the argument shifts away from guilt as anxiety, or as fear of loss of love, and back to guilt as awareness of wrongdoing, or as "sin." This shift characterizes the final pages of *Civilization and Its Discontents*. If guilt is "actually" anxiety over loss, as Freud insists, then why does he not say Christ takes upon himself through his sacrifice not our sinfulness but our fear of separation? Why does he not say He works not our redemption but our security? And if our redemption is our security, then why is that not underscored in keeping with Freud's inclination to underscore the fact that anxiety is "really" guilt? Could it be that this matter, like the other one, is destined to be understood "eventually"; that "as yet we cannot" (*CD*, 72)? That Freud *is* thinking here in terms of guilt as fear of punishment and sin as unacceptable aggression is confirmed, of course, by his reference to the father's murder, to the "primal guilt" over the "primal crime" from which the individual's unease derives and in which our "civilization" supposedly begins. The point is, Freud is unable to grasp the unconscious significance of religious phenomena because he is unable to grasp the manner in which guilt, which is actually anxiety, operates unconsciously within the individual. He cannot see the enormous longing for connection. Hence, for all his amazing and historic penetration of the meaning of words, he fails to comprehend the words religion uses in their deep, unconscious significance. Ironically, he is prone to take religion at its word in *Civilization and Its Discontents,* to believe what it says at the surface or "doctrinal" level. Had he been able to "follow" the workings of anxiety through those puzzling "variations", had he spied the manner in which "guilt" or "sin" invariably reactivates the original dread of loss, and, most of all, had he connected that event to the religious inpulsion about which he writes from the father's perspective, he would not have become the "believer" he turns out, unwittingly, to be.

The consequence for the "beginning of civilizaton" (*CD*, 73) emerges with striking clarity here. If "guilt" is at bottom "anxiety," then it was not the "primal crime" in which "civilization" originated but the "fear of loss of love," that "fear" that is integrally tied to the maternal figure and to the "oceanic" need in which the religious impulsion resides, the need to belong to the other, to belong to a higher power that ultimately contains and controls one's existence. As La Barre expresses it, God is the "Caretaker," not the "fallible conscience."[207] There is no reason to exclude the entire maternal influence from Freud's view of civilization's "beginning" when the genuine significance of "guilt" in his study is examined. What an anthropologist such as Bachofen discovered before Freud had written his book, namely the existence of a matriarchal strata beneath the ancient patriarchal setup, is precisely what Freud stands upon the verge of perceiving in his seminal work. This author believes he came as close to the matter as his resistances would allow him.

4.

The limitations of *Civilization and Its Discontents* can now be examined thoroughly. Internalization for Freud, as we have seen, commences after the crises of the early period have passed, during the course of a "higher stage" in which the "super–ego" is finally "set up." Yet, because of a "genetic influence," nothing in the sphere of the "super–ego" has really changed; the early fears over "loss of love" persist, and "guilt" becomes, in Freud's cumbersome scheme, a "variation" of anxiety whose unconscious operations are not genuinely, or "as yet," understood. Can anyone doubt that the reason Freud was forced to call one thing another ("guilt"

= "anxiety") and at the same time to insist that it was something other than what it was ("guilt") lay in his failure to recognize that, as we have also seen, 1) internalizing mechanisms are at work within the individual long before the advent of the "super–ego"; 2) the person is developing as a person (as an internalizing human animal) long before the "passing" of the "Oedipus complex" and; 3) the so–called genetic influence is, in reality, the influence of the persistent, "immortal" internalized objects of infancy and early childhood? As the "level" of the "super–ego" is attained, the parental figure is internalized into a self that has already been taking the world in on an enormous scale; the "super–ego," accordingly, merges with earlier "objects"—the good and bad presences of the inner world that became part of the individual's character during precisely the interval when the problems of merger and loss surrounded the maternal figure. This was also the interval when "matriarchal" organization predominated "on the inside." The history of the psyche, as Freud suspected, certainly does impinge on the history of "civilization," particularly in the sphere of "moral awareness," which is tied inextricably to the repressed, "discontented" aspects of "culture." But it is a history in which the maternal presence underlies and influences the later, paternal one.

The "higher" issues of "sin" and "guilt" are always comprehended in the whole mind, at all the levels of "psycho–sexual development." This inevitably "reduces" those issues to their "lowest common denominator"—the "fear of loss of love." This discussion begins at that point. The sacrificial conduct of the Christ to which Freud refers as an "echo" of the "primal" crime has, at its deepest foundation, a transitional purpose—to permit the sacrificed god to rediscover his source and to permit the "religious" individual (through that sacrificed god or in that sacrificed god) to rediscover his security, his "salvation," his "heaven," and his "home." The aggression in the rite, the "murder" on the cross, manifests the frustration, the "ambivalence" of the "people" in their lost or "fallen" condition, after their expulsion from the "garden" and before the way to refusion was opened to them (we must view the myth *in toto*). As Jim Swan puts it,

The later, oedipal conflict appears to be the development of a conflict already shaped in an earlier mother–infant (or nurse–infant) relationship. In a relatively oversimplified manner of speaking, we may say that the early split between good, pure, nurturing mother and ugly, sexual humiliating mother gets redistributed in the later relationship between good mother and humiliating father.[208]

The sacrifice of the "god" carries all this unconscious material in all its manifold "variations."

Today, we recognize that a passage such as the following from the researches of Dr. Spitz has everything to do with the development of conscience and guilt, those topographical varieties of "anxiety" with which Freud struggled in his effort to explain the "discontents" of "civilized" man:

> Obviously, nursing is not the only ministration of the mother during which the baby can stare at her face. We are rarely aware of the fact that, whatever we may do with the infant, whether we lift him up, wash him, diaper him, etc., we always offer our face straight on for the baby's inspection, fixating him with our eyes, moving our head, and mostly saying something. It follows that the face as such is the visual stimulus offered most frequently to the infant during the first months of life. In the course of the first six weeks of life a mnemonic trace of the human face is laid down in the infantile memory as the first signal of the presence of the need–gratifier.[209]

And it is precisely the absence of the "need–gratifier," or the "good object" (an absence measured by a "bad," rejective staring) that constitutes a sizeable portion of the affect that has come to be known as "guilt" in psychological circles today. We will now turn to Freud's methodological schemes for removing the discontents of civilization.

5.

What we have here is meager indeed. As a matter of fact, what we have here in the main, and in terms of explicit pronouncements, is bare hope, hope that Eros, or "love," will "emerge triumphant" from the battle with death. By implication, of course, we also have the entire psychoanalytic tradition which devotes itself, ideally, to awakening men from their "conscious dreaming," from their destructive "acting–out," and restoring them to what Freud would characterize as "reason." In *Civilization and Its Discontents*, however, the promise of the discipline is hardly conspicuous. It is toward the conclusion of the volume that Freud discusses the issue and once again the initial emphasis, which serves as the way into the argument, is guilt, not guilt as anxiety over loss but guilt as it derives from one's aggressive and, in particular, one's self–aggressive inclinations. In every case where the analyst deals with a sense of guilt, writes Freud, he deals "with an aggressiveness which had been displaced inwards" (*CD*, 75), in short, with an expression of what was earlier termed the "death drive" (*CD*, 56). Guilt as an expression of Eros, as a seeking of the lost object, as an anxiety over separation (*CD*, 72), is no where to be found. Freud is careful to point out—and for us the observation is crucial—that this conflict in the individual, the conflict between Eros and Thanatos, is not directly reflected in the individual's struggle with "society," for "society," says Freud, provokes a struggle over the distribution of one's "libido" (*CD*, 78). This struggle is concerned with the extent to which one must repress his erotic urges. Thus, "culture," at the theoretical level, is able to "accommodate" people, to offer them a life that is less at odds with their instinctual nature than the one being offered them currently. Amelioration in the libidinal sphere would lessen people's antagonism toward the social order and, to this extent, create a kind of "mastery" over the "instinct to aggression," the "instinct" that provokes such disturbance in both individual and communal existence (*CD*, 82). "One day," writes Freud, "someone" will "embark" on the "pathology of cultural communities" and thus commence the process of amelioration so long, and so painfully overdue (*CD*, 82). His final, rather gloomy words are these: "But who can foresee with what success and with what result?"

Freud's ultimate, ameliorative "vision," then, is of an innately aggressive, guilt–ridden creature pacified or "tamed" by an enlightened society sympathetic to the expression of erotic needs and therefore "wise" regarding the degree of "instinctual renunciation" that can safely be imposed on the human being. The trouble with this final analysis derives from the same psychological direction from which the troubles of Freud's book have arisen all along. The culture that breeds repression is a culture to which individuals are bound through the process of identification, through the energic, libidinal *tie* which Freud himself outlines in his earlier work, *Group Psychology and the Analysis of the Ego*, that "potentially liberating tract," as Ernest Becker recently described it,[210] which purports to uncover the essence of collective relations. Yet here, with the accent on aggression and guilt, guilt not as "fear of loss of love" in keeping with the original definition, but as remorse and fear of reprisal, the "hope" of "civilization" becomes the lessening of repression rather than the lessening of identification. It is as if the conclusions of the earlier work, which profoundly bear on the problem of anxiety and, hence, on the problem of guilt, or what becomes of that enigmatic "fear of loss of love" (it is transferred to parental substitutes), are swept entirely aside, particularly with reference to their ameliorative implications. Moreover, as guilt and repression can develop within the individual only when he is identified with the cultural realm through the internalizations of the early period that link him to the parental objects, the effect of the dilemma—a nasty, destructive breed of animal—is mistaken for the principle cause. No wonder the future seems gloomy.

With the accent on guilt as anxiety, however, one sees the "other half" of the "story," the half that Freud leaves out by failing to trace anxiety through those trying, and maternal, "variations." Because the tie to the culture is forged in the tie to the object (the primal defense against annihilation), and because the "sickness" of "cultural communities" stems directly from the nature of that tie (religion, economy, state as synonymous with culture), the core of the ameliorative issue is radically altered. Freud's cautious hopes give way to a genuine method for change. Instead of "embarking" on a "pathology," or waiting for "Eros" to conquer "death" while a "civilized" world teeters at the edge, one can lessen the tie to the objects within, the tie in which institutional configurations are grounded. Not only would such a procedure disrupt those passionate, transitional "chases" which unconsciously reactivate the inadequacy, dependency, and insecurity of the individual and trigger, accordingly, the exploitation and manipulation of others, it would also disrupt the ordinary or symbolical mode of mentation, the alienating, habitual method of "sight" underlying the "cultural malaise" itself, the very "reality" Freud set about examining. In other words, had he applied the conclusions of his psychology of the group to the final pages of his psychology of "civilization," Freud may well have spied the possibility of progress through a diminution of that regressive, "desexualized libido" which holds the present "reality" together by indulging the persistent anxiety of the individual, by creating institutional avenues to "dual–unity," by assuaging the fear of being left alone in the dark instead of *working* through that fear. For after all, he *said* guilt was anxiety; had he followed it through, he would have recognized that anxiety was culture's chief problem, not guilt and repression. Too, because anxiety is not an instinct, there would not have been the pessimism, or the emphasis on "fate," the "death drive." The "dual–unity situation" does not constitute "civilization" or "culture"; it constitutes our civilization, our culture, at this point in our evolutionary development as a species of life on earth. There is, then, a method for change implied in the work of Freud, a method that would emphasize the detachment of the creature from the "immortal objects" of his inner existence. How can the world inherit itself while the individual has still to inherit himself? As long as the world continues to inherit the individual's version of his parent, it will stand on the verge of inheriting the wind.

In a brief, but fascinating, reference to economic factors that focus on the problem of "civilization and its discontents," Freud writes near the conclusion of his book,

> I . . . think it quite certain that a real change in the relation of human beings to possessions would be of more help in this direction [of ethical progress] than any ethical commands; but the recognition of

this fact among socialists has been obscured and made useless for
practical purposes by a fresh idealistic misconception of human
nature (*CD*, 80).

The point here, of course, is that "possessiveness" cannot be
"changed" until the tie to the object is changed, for economic
activity is, itself, an expression of that tie. What is more, the
economical system taken as a whole is inextricably bound up at the
emotive level with the state and religion, that is, with the other
key, cultural "institutions" which reflect the regressive orientation
of "group" members and which will not alter positively on the
"outside" until individuals alter positively on the "inside."

What is encouraging is that psychoanalysis in its investigations of internalization and the early period, in its completion of
the ideas adumbrated by Freud in his psychology of the group, can
now offer the "socialist" a conception of "human nature" that is not
pessimistic or defeatist, born of "instinct" and the "death drive," or
"idealistic" and impractical, unable to further the advent of positive change. Indeed, the "socialist" currently has the advantage of
seeing the extent to which the economic setup bespeaks transitional aims as they press toward fulfillment in the owner, worker, and
in the consuming, unthinking public who comprise the "one–
dimensional" heart of the "new industrial state." He can allow the
revolutionary implications of this knowledge to find a way into his
programs, into the manner in which he endeavors to wean the
corporate infants from their colossal profits, the legislative powers
from their collusive rationalizations, the laboring people from
their regressive identification with the "company" and its "goods."
Able to grasp the hardest fact of all, that the current disturbance of
"mankind," in both the "east" and the "west," is rooted in its very
mode of awareness, in its tendency to "immortalize" regressive
goals by apprehending the world through the "eyes" of the object,
the "socialist" will strive, as he has striven for decades, to raise the
consciousness of those around him and to create the prospect of a
genuinely human future. His task, needless to say, is enormous,

but at least he has more to go on here than Freud's bare hope. This brings us, once again, to Norman O. Brown's *Life Against Death*.

6.

Stressed earlier was Brown's sensitivity to the overwhelming importance of pre–oedipal factors in human development and, hence, in the history of civilized life. Also stressed was Brown's failure to explore these pre–oedipal factors in his own analyses. Grounding his investigations in Freud, in what might be termed the classical libido theory, rather than in those followers of Freud who were at the time of Brown's book shedding considerable light on the dynamics of the early period, Brown offers an examination of culture the crucial limitations of which he is himself fully aware. As one might suspect, the ultimate difficulty with *Life Against Death* in reference specifically to its ameliorative potential, to its proposed methods for the improvement of "man's lot," is firmly related to this crucial limitation.

To begin, Brown's adherence to Freudian theoretics gives rise to an erroneous conceptualization of what might be termed "the pleasures of childhood." He writes, "How can a fundamentally narcissistic orientation lead to union with objects in the world? The abstract antinomy of Self and Other in love can be overcome if we return to the concrete reality of pleasure and to the fundamental definition of sexuality as the pleasurable activity of the body."[211] And then,

The answer is contained in Freud's doctrine of the peculiar ego–structure, the sense of one's relation to the outside world, which is developed in infancy and which, like the rest of infantile sexuality, is repressed but never abandoned in the adult. In the unreal, protected situation of human infancy, the infant develops an unreal sense of reality. Reality is his mother, that is to say, love and pleasure; infantile sexuality affirms the union of the self with a

whole world of love and pleasure. . . . The infant develops a pure
pleasure–ego instead of a reality–ego (*LAD*, 45).

Hence, "the human libido is essentially narcissistic, but it
seeks a world to love as it loves itself. . . . 'The development of the
ego consists in a departure from primal narcissism and results in a
vigorous attempt to recover it' " (*LAD*, 46). These concepts are
not only acceptable to Brown, but they color the entire shape of his
subsequent analysis, including, of course, his methodological
recommendations for change.

What they lack, however, is an appreciation of the anxiety the
infant experiences along with his "pleasure" during the early
period. "Reality" may well be the infant's "mother," but "mother"
includes the bad, frustrating and omnipotent objects. "Reality"
also includes, accordingly, the infant's fear of separation, his
longing for merger, his anger and his terror as triggered by the
imperfections of maternal care, feeding, handling, and the like,
not to mention the painful reintrojection of affect originally and
defensively projected.[212] What is hidden from Brown, as it was
hidden from Freud, is the entire ambivalent shape of the infantile
years—their threat of engulfment, annihilation, loss alternating
with their promise of bliss and well–being. The upshot, of course,
is clear. As the nature of infantile aims is missed, so the nature of
subsequent aims is missed, too. Individuals in their "adult" condition may possibly be seeking "bliss," but they are seeking it
anxiously, transitionally, even ambivalently, out of the internalizations of the early time, out of the tie to the object within, out of
the wounds and rages and fears, as well as the "pleasures" and
"joys," which characterize their initial interaction with the world.
People strive to get bliss at the same time that they strive to get rid
of, master, compensate for, or overcome, the "bad stuff" derived
from the "bad" side of infancy. Indeed, it might be suggested, as a
balance to Brown's basic misemphasis grounded in Freud, that the
"seeking of pleasure" is by definition a seeking to shed the infelici-
ties of "childhood" in order that one might find "pleasure" in his

"body." This would suggest, in turn, that the social institutions which comprise and express the "seeking" of human beings are created precisely to cope with, nay more, to undo, the early, internalized damage. The economy, the state, religion, wealth, the pursuit of power, patriotism, sacrifice, redemption—these are, in large measure, "cultural inventions" designed to ease the distress of infantile existence. They seek to establish and ensure what Roheim termed "dual–unity," the compensatory connection with the "good" parental surrogate.

More specifically with reference to Brown's "subsequent analysis" mentioned earlier, the gist of the matter is this: in *Life Against Death*, Brown depicts people as alienated and "dying" in a culture that is unconsciously tied to repression and death. Men and women "lose" their bodies, and, hence, their deep, animal grati-fications, through a variety of restrictive measures born of the oedipal syndrome; as a result, they end up "worshipping the devil" in the form of money, or "filthy lucre"; in other words, they "sublimate" their loss of "life" through an identification with, and an obsessive pursuit of, gain. Such a view constitutes a direct outgrowth of Brown's proclivity to regard the early time as pleasurable. It is that, precisely, which prompts him to regard the loss of pleasure as the chief "existential" feature of the later years. In this way—and the parallels with Freud and Reich suggest themselves immediately—the lifting of repression, as opposed to the mitigation of aims derived from the internalized object, comes to comprise the core of his ameliorative suggestions, the essence of his reparative scheme. Brown cannot see mankind tied to culture in an unconsciously purposive transitional way because he cannot perceive the actual shape of the infant's interaction with the parent. Moreover, he cannot see culture as a method of handling anxiety as opposed to sublimating repression. Indeed, the entire concept of "sublimation" in Brown (and in Freud) is misleading as a result of the theoretical link that is made with repression. The individual does not seek to "sublimate" his "repressed libido" through a variety of "fantastic" obsessional pursuits as described in *Life*

Against Death; rather, he seeks to magically deny the wounds of the early period by engaging in cultural activities which unconsciously restore the good object to him, or unconsciously offset the rejection and loss associated with the "bad" maternal presence. It is not arrested bodily pleasure that is "sublimated" but persistent feelings of anxiousness that express their urgency in the individual's very mode of perception—in his implacable need to view the world in symbolical terms and, hence, keep open a psychological avenue back to the mothering figure. This psychological avenue is "born" in the same psychological "practice" that initially ensures the connection with the need–gratifier, internalization.

Recent investigation on the part of Roy Schafer and others has established beyond doubt that our tendency to identify with symbols, symbols such as those with which individuals identify in the pages of Brown's book, such as possessions and money, is an outgrowth of our tendency to incorporate and introject the environment.[213] Indeed, identification, on which Brown constructs one side of his theoretical edifice, must be regarded as an aspect of the internalizing tendency as it establishes its influence during the first years of life. To place our emphasis here allows us to construct a straight theoretical line between internalization and "sublimation." What the individual "sublimates" in his "mature" behaviors, in his "identification" with key, cultural symbols, are aims that reach back to the "object relations" of infancy and very early childhood. These are "compromised," fated to receive a disguised expression in the sphere of "cultural" conduct. The notion of repression leading to "sublimation" simply jettisons the overwhelming role of internalization in the course of early development by suggesting that the urge to take the world in psychically commences at a relatively advanced stage, as the "Oedipus complex" gets under way. Through such an approach, the transitional nature of "civilized" activity is lost, not to mention the deep, unconscious significance of the human being as a symbol–making animal, an animal that uses its cerebral powers to hold, and possess, the world.

7.

Brown is not oblivious to what can be termed the "transference elements" in man's "civilized" existence. On the contrary, his entire book is based on this concept. "Culture does for all mankind," he writes, "what the transference phenomena were supposed to do for the individual" (*LAD*, 155). But he bases this "service" not in the early time, or in the seeking for the maternal object, the transitional as opposed to the transference "phenomena"; rather, he bases it in the later, oedipal configuration. It is the "Oedipus complex" that continues to "exist" in the form of its "cultural derivatives"; and it is the "Oedipus complex" that "perpetuates" the "infantile flight from death" (castration) that presses itself into adulthood as the chief item in the system of human "repression" (*LAD*, 155). Our "reality," hence, is "based on repression," repression that we "sublimate" into private "versions" of the Oedipal syndrome (*LAD*, 56). Thus, although Brown's emphasis is on the "transference," it is not on "identification" as a key to the transference; "sublimation" answers repression, and repression, therefore, becomes the chief instigator or catalyst of the transference behaviors that are "culture." Brown writes,

> If repression were overcome and man could enjoy the life proper to his species, the regressive fixation to the past would dissolve; the restless quest for novelty would be reabsorbed into the desire for pleasurable repetition . . . Man, the discontented animal, unconsciously seeking the life proper to his species, is man in history: repression and the repetition–compulsion generate historical time. Repression transforms the timeless instinctual compulsion to repeat into the forward–moving dialectic of neurosis which is history (*LAD*, 93).

And again, "The abolition of repression would abolish the unnatural concentrations of libido in certain particular bodily organs—concentrations engineered by the negativity of the morbid death instinct, and constituting the bodily base of the neurotic character disorders in the human ego" (*LAD*, 308). But repression itself is rooted in the early time, in the taking in, and internalization of the object. One represses when he "listens" to the "voices" of the inner world—the world that began when internalization began. One represses when he seeks to avoid confrontation with the "bad," inimical, or the seducing, alluring aspects, of those whom we "took into ourselves" during the primal years. In short, there can be no "repression" unless there is, first, unconscious identification, either positive or negative, with the parental figures, who were the initial and fundamental controllers of our being.

Moreover, because the infant has no choice in his helplessness and dependency (not to mention his biological urges), but to identify, and "listen," because taking the world in constitutes his "way," he is fated to "get hooked" on those with whom he identifies. Because of those to whom he "listens," he undergoes a splitting, or an alienation from himself, that passes for "repression" in the eyes of those who fail to trace the dynamics of "character" development back to their beginnings. During life's elemental stages, it is affect that is internalized into the body of the infant, into what Kernberg calls, after MacLean, the "visceral brain."[214] Later, it is the image of the parent to which the child becomes tied, along with the "transitional objects" of his fantasy and play. Eventually, in the "grownup," the universe of culture as a whole, including, of course, the universe of words, the "ordinary reality" in which we have our "existence," succeeds to the transitional role. Here is where "biology" and "culture" join, as Freud said they did, to create the "discontents of civilization." It is not only the newcomer's defensive proclivity to internalize the universe around him, but his biological and evolutionary proclivity as well—the legacy of his neotenous brain. To find the origins of repression here is not simply to grasp the nature of "man's" persistent, "neurotic" seeking, or the nature of his so–called sublimations; it is also to grasp the essence of what is perhaps the most dramatic turn in the psychoanalytic thinking of recent decades: the "Oedipus complex," in which "repression" ostensibly finds its roots, is also the outgrowth of early "object relations," the cul-

mination of an intensive, human interaction that has been transpir-
ing between parent and internalizing infant for many months.[215]
What Oedipus did to Laius on the highway, and to his mother in
Thebes, is what those of us who have been sorely mistreated as
infants—rejected, mutilated, abandoned—are likely to "dream"
about doing.[216] As for us "ordinary" mortals whose infancies are
considerably less traumatic than Oedipus', we also experience, to
one degree or another, the imperfections and anxieties that are
characteristic of the early period. We ceaselessly "seek the past"
not, as Brown suggests, for reasons that are best described as
"Oedipal," but for reasons inextricably linked to the unconscious
affect that precedes and gives rise to the famous "Complex" itself.
The conclusion, it appears, is inescapable. The "Oedipus complex" is not "the past" in the sense Brown says it is. Like Freud's
"primordial ambivalence," it, too, has a "history." If we are going
to offer the human species a genuine "way out," we cannot place
our emphasis here. Which puts us in a good position to examine
Brown's remarks on the method for achieving positive change.

8.

Since "fallen," discontented lives are "based on repression,"
and since the key to "getting better" is the "lifting" of repression,
"culture" becomes, in *Life Against Death,* a sort of villain, or "the
one who is to blame," for it is "culture" that provides the sorry
human animal with "derivatives" of the "Oedipus complex." It
also encourages his neurotic obsessive seeking, his "compulsion to
repeat." Hence, to liberate man we must liberate "culture." We
must concentrate our efforts on changing culture's goals and
"values," its tendency to "worship" the symbols of "repression,"
to elicit the "sublimation" of psychosexual "fixations." When the
body is permitted to "exist" again, when "culture" offers a "less
repressed" life to men and women, and when "Dionysius" returns
to earth to join with "Apollo" in a grand synthesis of body and
mind, the "sickness" of "civilized man" will begin to diminish at

last. Unrepressed, he will delight in the forces of "life" and, in doing so, will drop his fascination with the forces of death and destruction of which "filthy lucre" is, of course, an unconscious manifestation. As for psychoanalysis, it, too, must undergo a radical transformation so as to be able to play a major role in the amelioration of mankind. In other words, current psychoanalysis, in its conservativism, identification with the status quo, and blind, "automatic" hostility toward transcendent or "religious" inclinations in individuals, is, itself, a "part of the culture" and as such a part of the problem.

Brown writes in a crucial passage:

> The relation between psychoanalysis and religion is not the simple polarity of science and wishful thinking, as suggested by Freud's title, *The Future of an Illusion*. Lutheranism can be explicated not only as theology but also as psychoanalysis. Luther, like a psychoanalyst, penetrates beneath the surface of life and finds a hidden reality; religion, like psychoanalysis, must say that things are not what they seem to be. And psychoanalysis must admit that the hidden reality revealed in religion is the same as the hidden reality revealed by psychoanalysis, namely the unconscious: both psychoanalysis and religion represent phases in the return of the repressed to human consciousness. . . . If we take seriously the position that human history is the history of a neurosis, then psychoanalysis . . . is inside the neurosis, and the neurosis itself must always have contained those 'attempts at explanation and cure' which Freud at the end of his life came to regard as the only basis for therapeutic hope (*LAD*, 231–232).

And then, in what can be taken as the culmination of the entire discussion, "There is a particular need for psychoanalysis, as part of the psychoanalysis of psychoanalysis, to become conscious of the dialectical, poetical, mystical stream that runs in its blood" (*LAD*, 320). Now, the emphasis on religion, mysticism, and healing reminds us that the essence of these practices or "institutions" lies, and has always lain, squarely in the area of detachment as opposed to the "lifting of repression." We spy here a "lead" to the underlying significance not only of Brown's work but of

Freud's work, too. Moreover, we spy here a link between "repression" and "religion" that both men could not perceive because of their avoidance of the early period and the problems of internalization. What we must remember is this: the very heart of that transcendent, "mystical" being which returns man to himself lies not simply in detachment, but in detachment from the objects of the inner world. These are the objects out of which the attachment to "the world," and the "derivatives" of infantile existence, takes its egotic origin. As Brown remarks in another place,[217] the "ego" is "our mother in us," and the seeking of the ego (the seeking which comprises the essence of man's "transference," the essence of his "fallen" activity) is a seeking for a "sublimated" version of that "mother," or for a way to reply to the "discontentments" of her care.

The point is, both "repression" and the "mystical stream" in the "blood of psychoanalysis" are best gotten at not through an emphasis on the dynamics of the "Oedipus complex," as Brown says, but through an emphasis on internalization and identification. For there can be no "revolutionary" psychoanalysis, "liberating" psychoanalysis, or "religious" psychoanalysis until psychoanalysis makes up its collective mind to free man from the tie to the object within and from the "egoistic" seeking that is the expression of that tie. Moreover, it must decide to make its actual aims and methods correspond to the aims and methods of those "therapeutic religions" to which it aspires. "Detachment from the ego psychology" not "ego psychology" must reside at the center of its theoretical future. Concomitantly, there can be no "lifting of repression" and resultant "return to the body" until the source of repression, that is, identification with, or adherence to, the "voices" of the inner domain, is terminated in a radical manner. The overwhelmingness of this last point emerges when we recall that 1) the object of the early time is internalized into the body; 2) the conversion process is a bodily process; and 3) the loss of sensuous delight in the universe, of the "mystical" capacity, originates and transpires in the infantile organism's vulnerable and traumatized "visceral brain." Those "concentrations of libido" in the "organs of the body," which Brown connects with "repression" (*LAD*, 308), are concentrations of affect, both negative and positive, which bind the human being to his split, divisive world, and to the "good and bad objects" of his early experience. In this way, the loss of one's body is firmly grounded in the defensive methods of life's first years. The return to the body is entirely dependent on the relaxation of those original defenses. "Liberal" cultures composed of tense, anxious creatures still attached on the inside to their versions of the parent can offer the human species only further varieties of "death."

9.

To express the matter from another angle, there is no "religion," "mysticism," or transcendental doctrine or discipline that grounds itself in the "lifting of repression." That includes psychoanalysis, which only thinks it does. What psychoanalysis is striving to do at a level that it can not (or will not) perceive is to free individuals from the emotive forces that tie them to the presences within. Yet every religious, "mystical" school is grounded in the achievement of detachment, detachment from the "ego," or the objects that comprise it, because every religion recognizes—referred to here are not the transitional or ordinary religions but the higher religions of altered awareness—that repression can not "go" until the tie to the object ("reality") goes. Consequently, an individual can not be free, whole, sensuously and spontaneously in the universe, until he belongs to himself as opposed to the internalized other, until he is able to decathect the world as projective symbol (parent) and see it afresh in its naked, eternal "suchness." That psychoanalysis did not know what higher religion always knew at the level of intuition, revelation, and practice is, of course, psychoanalysis' problem; that psychoanalysis is currently beginning to know may well constitute its "salvation," and mankind's.

Merleau–Ponty, in his phenomenological studies, declares that the "oneness of man and the world is not . . . abolished but repressed by everyday perception."[218] Although he does not put the word "repressed" to its full, psychodynamic use, Merleau–Ponty, nevertheless, reminds the reader that "repression" in its defensive, bodily signification is ultimately a mode of awareness. It is a mode of perception learned in the vicissitudes of early object relations and fated to direct the person's interaction with the world after the initial establishment of "character." The connection of this concept with what might be termed the orthodox precepts of psychoanalytical thinking is considerably tighter than one might imagine at first glance. When Freud declared that repression constituted the cornerstone of psychoanalysis, he was saying that it concerned itself with the relationship between man's conscious and unconscious apprehension of the world, and with the manner in which the person perceptually handled what he encountered in his experience as a living, cognizing organism. As has been maintained and demonstrated from the outset, ordinary awareness, or everyday, symbolical awareness, constitutes a perceptual tie to the object, an avenue back to the internalized parent; to this extent, it binds or confines one ("repression") to the projective "spaces" that are energically inhabitable within the inner universe. As has been seen through the development of Roheim's anthropological investigations, as well as Freud's revolutionary analysis of the group, the tie to the culture ("identification," grounded in earlier, or more "primitive," internalizing techniques) is also a method of preserving the tie to the object, of establishing and maintaining what Roheim termed "dual–unity," the emotive basis, and purpose of "civilized" existence. In keeping with this, culture itself can be regarded as an expression of the level of awareness that we, as a species, have reached at this particular stage of our earthly development. To suggest that our culture is repressed is, then, to suggest that our awareness, our mental and bodily capacity to fully exist in the universe, is severely limited, or, conversely, that our defensive inclination to perceive the environment symbolically, as a projective version of the parental figure, alienates us not only from ourselves and from each other, but from the entire creation or the "world out there," as well.

To stress the perceptual connection between individual and social cathexes—the tie to the object within as the ground of the person's awareness of both himself and his human environment—is to underscore a central idea that was developed in Parts One and Two and that requires a reemphasis here, namely that the question of the individual's involvement in culture is ultimately a question of power. People are tied to the "institutions" of their "society" out of the tie that binds them to the parental figures within. The projection of internalized affect into the symbols of security and control, or more properly, the epiphenomenal eliciting of internalized affect by the existing symbols of cultural life, is an energic event that cannot be altered until the forces at work are significantly redistributed. The disappointment of *Life Against Death,* with reference to its methodological suggestions for change, comes from this direction. Because he bases his operations on a Freudian foundation that stresses the dynamics of the "Oedipus complex," because he can not appreciate the extent to which the problem of "repression" is a problem of awareness, and because he chooses to ignore, through his theoretical orientation, the energic nature of human bonding in infancy and, hence, in subsequent "civilized" experience, Brown can not get down, in the end, to the elemental issue of power. For this reason, he has nothing to offer in the way of concrete, methodological techniques for improvement. How, we must ask, is "civilization" supposed to "lift" its "repression?" Surely not by thinking, even along the lines Brown so forcefully presents, for thought in this regard is but a straw in the wind. Nor can "psychoanalysis" help, mystical or otherwise, for psychoanalysis is essentially a talking cure and no matter what kind of talking goes on between the doctor and his patient there is nothing, whatsoever, in talk that will enable the individual to alter his actual perception of the world, to achieve the genuine, bodily ability to put his universe of symbolic apperceptions on and off again at will. We are not dealing here with "understanding," regardless of how profound it is. We are dealing with the actual redirection of power. Thus, in the last analysis, *Life Against Death* is a kind of desperate vision within the wilderness of early analytical concepts.

All that Brown can really do in his book is prophetically urge the body on us. He spends hundreds of pages depicting the "disease" then calls out at the end for the return of Dionysius, as if the call, thrilling though it might be, will actually bring the god back. What is remarkable, yet hardly fortuitous when we think upon Brown's failure to explore those pre–oedipal questions the significance of which he deeply realizes, is that the methodological solution to the dilemma of "civilization" (or at least a methodological solution consistent with the tracing of repression to its roots)—detachment from the objects within leading to the alteration of conscious-ness—may be discovered in the very religious, mystical tradition he believes is the key to the future "psychoanalysis" of mankind. We realize that the alienation of man, both in himself and in his culture, does not constitute a "dream of repression" as Brown, following Freud, would suggest. It constitutes, rather, a dream of transitional awareness where the object of infancy is projectively sought in a dependent, ambivalent cathexis of the world. As we may now recognize, there is a way to terminate this dream.[219]

Chapter 8

NIRVANA AND PLAY

A Critique of Marcuse's Radical Critique

1.

The return to Marcuse will keep sharply in focus problems discovered in Freud and Brown; at the same time, Marcuse's political, Marxist approach, not to mention his profound originality, urges an analysis that takes up his work as distinctive in its own right, as transcending, finally, its initial terms of reference. What must be stressed immediately is the religious, even mystical connection between Brown and Marcuse that is created by the former's enunciation of the "mystical stream" that runs in the "blood of psychoanalysis" and by the latter's employment of the concept of "Nirvana" as a modification of Freud's emphasis on the "death drive" and as a key to the understanding of mankind's predicament in culture. Marcuse writes,

> Freud is driven to emphasize time and again the common nature of the instincts prior to their differentiation. The outstanding and frightening event is the discovery of the fundamental regressive or

'conservative' tendency in all instinctual life. Freud cannot escape
the suspicion that he has come upon a hitherto unnoticed 'universal
attribute of the instincts and perhaps of organic life in general,'
namely, 'a compulsion inherent in organic life to restore an earlier
state of things which the living entity has been obliged to abandon
under the pressure of external disturbing forces'—a kind of 'organic
elasticity' or 'inertia inherent in organic life.'[220]

But "more and more," Marcuse continues, the "inner logic of
the conception asserts itself. Constant freedom from excitation has
been finally abandoned at the birth of life; the instinctual tendency
toward equilibrium thus is ultimately regression behind life itself.
. . The pleasure principle appears in the light of the Nirvana
principle—as an 'expression' of the Nirvana principle" (*EC*, 23–
24). Yet for Marcuse, the contradiction remains: "The primacy of
the Nirvana principle, the terrifying convergence of pleasure and
death, is dissolved as soon as it is established. No matter how
universal the regressive inertia of organic life, the instincts strive
to attain their objective in fundamentally different modes" (*EC*,
24).

He asks, "Does Eros, in spite of the evidence, in the last
analysis work in the service of the death instinct, and is life really
only one long detour to death? But the evidence is strong enough,
and the detour is long enough to warrant the opposite assumption.
Eros is defined as the great unifying force that preserves all life"
(*EC*, 25). What, then, is Marcuse's conclusion? "The ultimate
relation between Eros and Thanatos remains obscure" (*EC*, 25).

In an effort to remove the obscurity Marcuse postulates the
following:

> The quest for the common origin of the two basic instincts can no
> longer be silenced. Fenichel pointed out that Freud himself made a
> decisive step in this direction by assuming a 'displaceable energy,
> which is in itself neutral, but is able to join forces either with an
> erotic or with a destructive impulse'—with the life or the death
> instinct. Never before has death been so consistently taken into the
> essence of life; but never before also has death come so close to Eros
> (*EC*, 27).

Hence, "if the 'regression compulsion' in all organic life is striving for integral quiescence, if the Nirvana principle is the basis of the pleasure principle, then the necessity of death appears in an entirely new light. The death instinct is destructiveness not for its own sake, but for the relief of tension. The descent toward death is an unconscious flight from pain and want. It is an expression of the eternal struggle against suffering and repression. And the death instinct, itself, seems to be affected by the historical changes that affect this struggle" (*EC*, 27). Undoubtedly, Marcuse's modification of the "Nirvana principle," a modification that suggests the expression properly indicates not an instinct for death, as in Freud, but an urge toward the "relief of tension," cessation of misery, want, pain, or the evasion of distressing "historical conditions," moves him closer to the religious signification of the term and further away from Freud's instinctual, biological meaning. "Nirvana," in Marcuse, denotes a sorrowful, defensive, life–denying escape from the inequities of "civilization"—the denial of a "reality" that reflects "domination" and control (*EC*, 33). It also denotes the "neurotic" use of the "religious" tendency to regressively search for the "good object" and, in the finding of that object, to remove oneself from the harshness of the world. To the extent that one has evaded "reality" one has gravitated, or inclined, toward "death." Thus, in Marcuse, "Nirvana" suggests psychological as opposed to biological escape, if one is willing to accept the distinction. And indeed, Marcuse confirms the connection between "Nirvana" and the search for the gratifying object when he writes in a subsequent section, "Perhaps the taboo on incest was the first great protection against the death instinct: the taboo on Nirvana, on the regressive impulse for peace which stood in the way of progress, of Life itself. Mother and wife were separated, and the fatal identity of Eros and Thanatos was thus dissolved" (*EC*, 69). Clearly then, "Nirvana" and the mother are integrally related in *Eros and Civilization*. As the search for the mother is, in turn, integrally related to the religious inclinations of the human species, the underlying connection between religion and "Nirvana," and, hence, between the work of Marcuse and Brown, is established.

As it emerges from the pages of Marcuse's book, however, the emotive significance of the term "Nirvana" is ultimately transitional in nature; it ignores the "higher" denotation of the term, the denotation that indicates affective detachment not simply from the sorrows and illusions of the world, but from an ego which is rooted in the object, in the mother, and which is, ultimately, a source of the "miserable" environment.[221] Marcuse's mother–seeking, religious "Nirvana" is the "Freudian" equivalent of Marx's religious "opium"; it is an answer to "reality" that finds "relief of tension" in a regressive position whose very existence is grounded in an assertion of the first parental bond. Moreover, by virtue of its regressiveness, and life–denying nature, it precludes the achievement of the individual's sensuous, bodily potential—the expression of his animal capacities in their widest, life–affirming sense.

Once again with Marx in mind, Marcuse's "Nirvana" is largely derived from the "classical" concept of "alienation," particularly as it emerges from Marx's writings of 1844. By contrast, the "Nirvana" achieved through the alteration of awareness, through the truncation of the tie to the internalized object and to a world which "arises" from the projection of that tie, restores the individual to his body, his senses, and to a non–egotic view of the universe around him. It offers a perception that diminishes "tension" by diminishing anxiety, by removing the old, endemic threat of separation, as well as the precarious "dual–unity situation," the species' magical reply to the fear of "being left alone in the dark." To press the matter further, there can be no genuine, lasting "relief of tension" until the origin of tension (the internalized object) is removed from the body through actual methods associated with the attainment of transcendental consciousness— the very "Nirvana" of which Marcuse writes, but in its healthy, non–regressive character. Such detachment, however, not only provides the individual with a fresh perceptual universe, a release from the stale, rigid "reality" predicated by ordinary, everyday awareness, and a return to the body, but also mitigates the urge to identify with the powerful "establishments" of the social order—with, on the one hand, those forces of domination that encourage the expression of one's ambivalence toward the objects within and, on the other, with regressive institutions that encourage the withdrawal of those who are exploited, controlled, and made to suffer. In this way, detachment from the objects of the inner world, which looks like death to the "ordinary" person and seems to entail annihilation as it shuns the symbolic channel that leads back to the life–giving, parental figure, actually constitutes the rebirth of the individual, the readoption of his original, bodily self, the shedding of his regressive, vicarious existence in the other (identification). The irony, or perhaps the mystery in the deep religious sense, is certainly compelling, but if one looks at it analytically, he will recognize that the relationship of Eros to "Nirvana," or Eros to Death, is disclosed right here—in the application of object relations theory to the traditional disciplines of altered awareness. Consequently, the "common origin" of the two great "instincts" (*EC*, 26) may be spied in the dynamics of internalization. We must look closely now at the psychodynamics of infancy as they bear on the concept of "Nirvana."

As the infant takes in the human objects around him, as he strives to "contain" the "badness" of an environment on which he depends for his survival, as he comes to experience both sides of the mother, as well as both sides of his own passionate nature, he undergoes an experience of primordial ambivalence, a splitting of character reflecting "the inside" of the loved and hated nature of the objects "out there." The anxiety bred of this early "syndrome" (which immediately succeeds the trauma of birth) catalyzes the energic, emotive quest for what Roheim called the "dual–unity situation"—the magical, "impossible" struggle of the human animal to have the other, remain in contact with the other, and to please and to gratify the other, at the same time that he strives to have himself, remain in contact with himself, and to please and to gratify himself. The psychodynamics of the early period, particularly with reference to internalizing mechanisms, place the human creature in a hopeless "double-bind"—seeking on the one hand the full development of his person (Eros) and on the other a defensive symbiosis with the object ("Nirvana" in Marcuse's signification of the term).

The upshot is clear. The initial and primal "domination" of human experience is the "domination" of the individual by the objects within—the "immortal objects" whose persistent, implacable influence stands squarely behind those forms of "domination" that eventually characterize the social world where the individual has his "mature" existence. In a very real sense, it is ordinary consciousness that constitutes "Nirvana" in Marcuse's limited use of the expression, for it is ordinary consciousness that, as we have seen, provides the individual with a universe of symbols which keeps open the avenue to the maternal figure, and that affirms a peculiar, perceptual behavior which echoes the chief defensive practice of infancy, internalization. The desperate, pathological search for the object (psychosis) and the mentally "diseased" indulgence in "Nirvana," is only a deepening of the regressive urge embodied in the adherence to "reality" itself, and to the social institutions of the ordinary world—the "symbolical" versions of the parental figure created out of the transitional mode of perception. It is precisely when the protective casing, the "armor" of "dual–unity" erodes, and when the "universal neurosis of mankind" which is the "dual–unity situation" gives way to a severe disturbance forged in the anxiety over loss and isolation, that the search for "Nirvana," in the regressive sense of the term, comes to usurp the behavior of the person. The wish for total merger, the loss of what is called "ego boundaries," the absorption of the individual into the presences within (engulfment), even the suicidal flight from "reality," the lethal, ambivalent attempt to discover (and/or punish) the longed-for caretaker by "taking care of oneself,"—these are the exaggerated versions of the transitional dilemma as they emerge into the "light" of actual symptomatology. As Freud contended—although from a radically different perspective—the disturbed individual simply has more of what we all have to a considerable degree. Thus, the "common origin" of the two great "instincts," Eros and Nirvana, is disclosed in the power of detachment (detachment from the object, from the source of "domination") to heal the split of the early period, transcend the limitation, the double–bind of "dual–unity," and to end the ambivalence and the hostility toward creation that predicates the exploitative organizations of society, and to open that "physical universe" where the organism finds its perceptual existence. The "instinct" toward "death" becomes the "instinct" to remain in the tie to the object within, to live out the internalized will of the other, either "ordinarily" in what is described as "dual–unity" (neurosis) or psychotically in the total absorption of the self in the other's projective existence ("Nirvana" in the extreme, regressive sense). The "instinct" toward "life" (Eros) is the urge to break that tie, end the internal psychological domination that breeds the miseries of the egotic world, and allow the self to freely resume its development as a live, autonomous entity. To the extent that internalization is born of instinct, of the brain's proclivity to retain the world and, thereby, achieve a natural advantage over other, competing forms of life, "death" is "instinctual." To the extent that detachment is also a natural urge, a sophisticated, defensive, homeostatic capacity rooted in the physiological development of the brain, Eros is instinctual, too. Both tendencies are probably best regarded as drives, and the ability of the human being to choose between them, to exercise control over the quality of his experience— dualistic death–in–life ("dual–unity") as opposed to direct, non–transitional involvement—will become increasingly apparent as the evolution of the species continues. The entire problem, life against death, Eros against "Nirvana," bespeaks the attempt of mankind to pass beyond symbolic, transitional awareness to new modes of apprehension and, of course, communication.

The revolutionary, "Marxian" potential of *Eros and Civilization* is, then, enormously enhanced by the concept of "Nirvana" in its liberating, non–regressive character, as detachment from the objects of the inner world. Far from weakening the forces of change, as Marcuse suggests in one place (*EC,* 98), "Nirvana" in its full, transcendent development undoes the emotive, energic ties that bind the individual to the existing order. From this perspective it is possible to see why "the establishment" of a culture such as ours invariably encourages "transitional" religion and invariably discourages transcendental disciplines—disciplines based on the disruption of those urges that guide the individual toward "the group," and "identification" with institutions that unconsciously replace the relinquished parent. These institutions keep the transitional mode alive. Indeed, it is precisely this identification, this "Nirvana" in the infantile sense, that makes the individual's power available to the exploitative "establishments" that use it. Although one significant danger to the "setup" is the exaggerated expression of regressive needs, or what is usually—and sympathetically—described as "maladjustment," the greatest danger or threat is the mitigation of those needs in higher development, the transcending of the "system" in altered awareness. When that happens the individual has a choice, a genuine choice, and he may choose to go, and take his body, his power, with him. He may even choose to stay and to work toward the accomplishment of another kind of "order." Thus, the "system of repression" that Marcuse explores is ultimately rooted in the transitional dilemma, or the "passionate" effort to regain the object through a mixture of passive and aggressive behaviors in the religious, political, and economic spheres. The ambivalence of the species is everywhere because projective expressions of the "immortal" objects are everywhere. "Never before has death been so consistently taken into the essence of life; but never before also has death come so close to Eros" (*EC*, 27). It is "Nirvana" in its highest, transcendent signification, the "Nirvana" that means the death of the ordinary, or "historical," world, that gives Marcuse's words their most revealing import.

2.

Time and power, concepts that stand at the very center of Marcuse's discussion, are considerably clarified by concentration on the transcendent significance of "Nirvana." As *Eros and Civi-*

lization makes plain, there can be no development of genuine human freedom until the tyranny of time over life is "broken." For "the fact that time does not 'recur' [Marcuse is following Neitzsche here] sustains the wound of bad conscience: it breeds vengeance and the need for punishment, which in turn perpetuate the past and the sickness to death" (*EC,* 109). Disclosed here, above all, is Marcuse's inclination as social philosopher to view temporality along what might be called a patriarchal or paternal continuum, in terms of punishment, guilt, the superego, the "return of the repressed." What blights the existence of the individual destroys the possibility of progress for the species. Civilization "returns" from revolution to "repression" because guilt is inherent in the use of force, and those "lower down" in the hierarchical order are invariably "ambivalent" toward those who have assumed positions of "authority." Man will "come to himself," Marcuse maintains, only when "eternity" is present "here and now" (*EC,* 110). Recent analytic investigation, however, has revealed the crucial, psychological link between the development of the time sense and the early interaction with the maternal figure.[222] "Time" is forged in close association with "the object," and it is precisely the absence of the object that catalyzes the inchoate recognition of duration. In a very real way, to hold onto the absent parent, initially through the internalization of affect and later, through a combination of affect and imagery, is the perception of time in its basic, bodily character. In keeping with the discussion of *Civilization and Its Discontents*, time as a formidable "power over life" (*EC,* 109) has far more to do with the problem of anxiety than it has to do with the problem of guilt. Our temporal gripping of the world is a major facet of what we know as "dual–unity." The point is, the cessation of time is accomplished as the tie to the object within, the tie out of which the time sense originates, is "broken." It is precisely the breaking of that tie, as we have seen, that constitutes the achievement of transcendent "Nirvana." Although it may be exhilarating, even revolutionary, to talk about "eternal recurrence" and the triumph of "the present," it must be remembered that symbolic awareness, which comprises the core of ordinary, temporal awareness, predicates the existence of time by keeping open the emotive, perceptual channel that binds the individual to the objects of the inner world. The persistence of the symbol and the persistence of time are mutually interdependent, largely because, as Freud recognized with such candidly confessed puzzlement, anxiety persists so implacably beyond the initial stages of human development. It is duration that permits the "thing" to be transformed mentally into "the symbol," into that which is able to harbor psychologically the affective dilemmas of the "subjective" position, into that which, in short, will serve as a receptacle for the projection of psychological "contents." We may invoke "eternal recurrence" forever; until we achieve in actuality, however, a method of putting the world of symbols on and off, there will be no "breaking" of the "power of time" over "life" (*EC,* 109).

More specifically with reference to the Marxian concerns of *Eros and Civilization*—concerns that bear directly on Marcuse's philosophical position—it is the symbolical significance of money as a "disguised" representation of the maternal object (object in both an epistemological and psychological sense), as a version of the "good body contents," that breeds the power motive in "civilized" society and, hence, the "repressive" economic order in which the majority of the world's inhabitants exist. It takes bodily, emotive, psychological power to transform the "object" or the "thing" into the symbol at the perceptual level (internalization giving rise to the ordinary world); it takes the physical, muscular, labor power of men to create the symbols of wealth at the socio–economic levels, to transform "things" or "materials" into commodities, commodities that are, as Marx showed, only "mystified" versions of money. Here is the connection Marcuse seeks between time and the repressions of the economic order, a connection that emerges in earnest when the transcendent signification of "Nirvana" is stressed, and when time's role in the process of symbol making (internalization) is underscored, in a word, when time as the basis of transformation is disclosed in a specifically economic, analytical context. As suggested earlier, the urge to "dominate" others expresses the power of the internalized object over the

212 CULTURE AND CONSCIOUSNESS

individual as he acts in the world. To transform men into things by using their power to make wealth (in time) is to reply in a magical, ambivalent manner not only to the wounds of the early period but to the current narcissistic defeat that resides in the person's subordination of himself to the will of the "immortal" other inside. Although it is true in capitalism that time is money, it is equally true that money is time, or that which keeps open the emotive channel that binds the person to the presence within. The recent tendency to think of money in terms of absence, in terms of debits incurred along an infinite continuum of corporate time,[223] does not offset the analytic importance of the issue. On the contrary, the pressing need to maximize "intake" in order to offset an enormous "outlay," together with the uncanny, intangible quality of what modern corporations consider to be wealth, only fuels the urge for control and power, the inclination to regard people as "factors" in the quest for monetary advantage, the drive to diminish uncertainty (angst) and, hence, to master time. This clearly suggests that class conflict, itself, springs from an anxiety that is both the cause and the result of Marcuse's "domination." Those who have power, and who actively seek the transitional reward, exploit those who don't have it. This, in turn, causes the "exploitees" to either rise against the exploiter as "bad object" or to search for transitional comfort in the regressive "Nirvanas" of consumption and religion. These are the "escapes" Marcuse refers to when he uses "Nirvana" in its limited sense. The upshot is clear. Unless we broaden the definition to include the transcendent element, the "instinct" for death will only apply to a portion of mankind, and specifically to the portion which is not, from an historical angle, precipitating most of the trouble and destruction in the world. Is the urge to "dominate" others an instinct for "life?" What unites the species in its appetite for "death," in its regressive longing for mastery and merger, and at the same time permits us to fathom its divisiveness, and antagonistic separation into classes—controllers and controlled, exploiters and exploited—is the persistence of anxiety into everyone's "maturity" and the different kinds of transitional behaviors that are used to cope with that disturbing affect. The "dialectic of civilization," repressive order to liberation to repressive order (*EC*, 79), will "persist" as long as that anxiety "persists."

3.

Patriarchal "values" are, for Marcuse, a source of "discontent" in "civilized" society. To serve Eros, mankind must adopt a "principle" of "reality" that reflects the maternal realm, a "principle" where a premium is placed on "pleasure" as opposed to the fatherly concepts of "duty" and "performance." Accordingly, the phallic component of the "Oedipal wish" is less important here than it is in the work of Freud and Brown. It is possible that the call for a mother–centered world serves in *Eros and Civilization* what the call for Dionysius serves in *Life Against Death*. At any rate, Marcuse writes, "If human happiness depends on the fulfillment of childhood wishes, civilization, according to Freud, depends on the suppression of the strongest of all childhood wishes: the Oedipus wish. Does the realization of happiness in a free civilization still necessitate this suppression?" (*EC*, 186). Marcuse thinks not. Indeed, the "social instincts" as described by Freud in *Group Psychology and the Analysis of the Ego* suggest

> an idea of civilization very different from that derived from repressive sublimation, namely, civilization evolving from and sustained by free libidinal relations. Geza Roheim used Ferenczi's notion of a 'genitofugal libido' to support his theory of the libidinous origin of culture. With the relief of extreme tension, libido flows back from the object to the body and this 'recathecting of the whole organism with libido results in a feeling of happiness in which the organs find their reward for work and stimulation to further activity.' The concept assumes a genitofugal 'libido trend to the development of culture'—in other words, an inherent trend in the libido itself toward 'cultural' expression, *without* external repressive modification. And this 'cultural' trend in the libido seems to be genitofugal, that is to say, away from genital supremacy toward the erotization of the entire organism (*EC*, 189–190).

Such a development, Marcuse maintains, would be furthered by encouraging a "maternal" as opposed to a paternal "attitude" toward nature. The emphasis would be placed not on the "domination" of the environment but rather, integration with it. "For example, if work were accompanied by a reactivation of pregenital polymorphous eroticism, it would tend to become gratifying in itself without losing its work content" (*EC*, 196). Society now has the material means, he declares, to permit this psycho–cultural change to occur (*EC*, 197). And with the recovery of pleasure, the "return of the repressed" and, hence, the urge to "dominate" others (including nature) would gradually lose their hold upon the shape of "civilization."

The difficulty with Marcuse's ameliorative scheme derives from his peculiar conception of the early stages of human development. This is true of Brown's work, also. There is simply no way to "reactivate pregenital eroticism" without reactivating the anxieties and discomforts taken into the body of the organism during the infantile years as well. Return to the "source" does not mean only recovery of the good maternal object, it means recovery of the bad object, too. To "allow the libido to flow back from the object to the body" is also to allow the negative affect to "flow back," for it is not merely "libido" that is invested in the "object," it is, in addition, the entire range of unpleasant emotions which arise within the person as he experiences both sides of his primal environment, oceanic security, polymorphous eroticism, and the all–important "fear of loss of love." Indeed, the very "tension" Marcuse would "relieve" resides in the "object" he offers as a source of relief. It does not make theoretical sense, then, to go "behind" the "Oedipal wish" to the "maternal figure" in seeking out solutions to the malaise of "civilization." The "badness" of the mother is there, and must be faced. Ironically, in fact, the "reactivation" of the early period in which Marcuse places such emphasis occurs constantly and is the actual, emotive origin of the societal "order" that he deplores and wants to change. It is precisely the anxiety that "persistently" emanates (reactivation) from the negative side of the internalized object that the "repressive" and "regressive" institutions of society reflect; they are the early period in its "mystified," "sublimated" form. The only real way to resolve the problem is to return to the time with which Marcuse is concerned, not to derive from it the "libido" of the object, for that would only breed increased ambivalence and tension, but to break with it completely, to sever the connection out of which develops the passionate urge to dominate and regress. Rather than "re-cathect" the "entire organism" with lost, repressed affect, one must decathect the internalized object with genuine methods of detachment. The "social instincts" would then gain their most considerable advantage. What Freud offers in his *Group Psychology,* and what Marcuse relies on in his definition of "social," is not, we must be careful to note, truly social at all. It is, as a matter of fact, a species of identification, a transitional "technique" defensively developed in response to early crises of dependency and loss. It is a symptom of anxiety with an expressly egotic aim. Moreover, it thrives on power, the power of the leader (party, establishment, state and their derivatives) over the individual, or the power of the individual's emotive alliance with the leader who is ultimately and unconsciously a version of the parent. To place any hope whatsoever in that putative social instinct is to remain in the old trap of "culture," to extend, or prolong an already endless procession of transitional phenomena. In short, it is to perpetuate the ancient "dialectic of history," the legacy of the split, "immortal" objects themselves. The truly social instinct "arises" when attachment to the object goes, when what is popularly regarded as "the ego" goes, and when the individual actualizes his innate, physiological ability to put his world of symbols on and off again (to date his most remarkable and forward–looking evolutionary accomplishment). In detachment, or transcendent "Nirvana," he is able to see his fellow creature not as a potential fulfiller of some inner, transitional need but directly as a wondrous organism, valuable in itself, and engaged in the very real business of achieving its highest potential as an advanced form of life. Thus, Marcuse is correct in going "behind" Freud to the maternal, pre–oedipal area. He simply fails to perceive that area in its negative as well as positive character and, hence, fails to go all the way to emotive detachment from it. Until the self in which the individual has his existence no longer derives from the object within, until the hold of the internalized presence is finally "broken," the "reality" he fashions in the universe around him will express his egotic and regressive, as opposed to his social, "instincts."[224]

4.

Similar theoretical difficulties inform Marcuse's emphasis on "play" as a key to the amelioration of culture. "The senses," he writes, "are not exclusively, and not even primarily, organs of cognition. Their cognitive function is confused with their appetitive function (sensuality); they are erotogenic" (*EC*, 167). Accordingly, "civilization has subjugated sensuousness to reason in such a manner that the former, if it reasserts itself, does so in destructive and 'savage' forms, while the tyranny of reason impoverishes and barbarizes sensuousness" (*EC*, 170). The "reality principle" is not reflective of "reality" but of a specific cultural reality where the accent is on "performance" rather than "pleasure" (*EC*, 178) and where the individual's capacity to play, to indulge his sensuousness in the deepest, most integrated manner (Marcuse denies the distinction between body and mind), is repressed. In this way, "freedom" is not simply inner or intellectual freedom but freedom in the reality that comprises the individual's bodily life. "The reality that 'loses its seriousness' is the inhumane reality of want and need, and it loses its seriousness when wants and needs can be satisfied without alienated labor. Then, man is free to 'play' with his faculties and potentialities and with those of nature, and only by 'playing' with them is he free" (*EC*, 171–172). "His world is then 'display' (Schein), and its order is that of beauty" (*EC*, 172). "The truth of art is the liberation of sensuousness" (*EC*, 168). But the psychological developments of recent years have taught us to consider play in a manner that links it to the cultural project, inextricably. One learns to play with substitute objects in the transitional space that succeeds the symbiosis with the parent. Winnicott writes, "Play is . . . neither a matter of inner psychic reality nor a matter of external reality . . . if play is neither inside nor outside, where is it?"[225] Reminding us that the transitional object "is a symbol of the union of the baby and the mother . . . at the point of the initiation of their state of separateness" and that this "separation is not a separation but a form of union," Winnicott declares,

> the place where cultural experience is located is in the potential space between the individual and the environment (originally the object). For every individual the use of this space is determined by life experiences that take place at the early stages of the individual's existence. From the beginning the baby has maximally intense experiences in the potential space between the subjective object and the object objectively perceived . . . In order to study the play and then the cultural life of the individual one must study the fate of the potential space between any one baby and the human (and therefore fallible) mother–figure who is essentially adaptive because of love.[226]

Winnicott concludes, "Given the chance, the baby begins to live creatively, and uses actual objects to be creative into. If the baby is not given this chance then there is no area in which the baby may have play, or may have cultural experience."[227] It is no coincidence that Marcuse's analysis of play occurs in his chapter on "The Aesthetic Dimension" and that Winnicott's examination of the transitional nature of play should emphasize the baby's growing creativity. However pleasing the bodily, aesthetic rewards of "higher sensuousness," however creative the individual in the "space" of his "cultural experience," play, as Marcuse and Winnicott see it, fosters and strengthens the transitional mode of existence by enhancing symbolical awareness and hence the tie to the object.

The individual cannot discover himself in play because play is, finally, a transitional activity. It begins in the separation crises of infancy and leads, inevitably, to culture in the old, regressive sense. It only returns us, in fact, to Roheim. As Winnicott declares, the "culture" in the form of the "symbol" succeeds to the mother's role, resolves the problem of separation magically by proferring the substitute object ("dual–unity"), and thus perpetuates the problem of separation at the same time that it solves it by "hooking" the individual upon his projective symbols. This discourages his subsequent return to himself as opposed to his adherence to the object within. What allows the individual to "grow up" also prevents him from "growing up." Thus, Marcuse's concentration on play and on the pre–oedipal object do not go far enough. Play in its highest evolutionary sense is ultimately related to the concept of "Nirvana" in *its* highest evolutionary sense. People play 1) when they are "free" of the objects within, 2) when the ordinary world no longer governs their perception, 3) when their senses discover new modes of apprehension (the expansion of mind), and 4) when their physical organisms are "liberated" from the effects of internalization. This does not occur as the tie to the object is deepened in the "aesthetic dimension." On the contrary, it occurs as one gains the capacity to put all symbols, including art, aside, to see them "face to face" as "things" that have been given emotive significance by the identifier, to play with the very business of play. To express the matter from another angle, a certain degree of seriousness invariably (and ironically) creeps into the kind of play Marcuse recommends because one is playing seriously with the "objects" of his choice. Separation, after all, is serious. As symbolic awareness commences defensively in reply to the traumas of separation, the seriousness of separation perforce comes to underlie not only the religious, economic, and political pursuits of people, but their artistic or "aesthetic" pursuits as well. Notwithstanding the enjoyment or "sensuous" pleasure it brings, "the truth of art" (*EC,* 168) is ultimately a serious truth to mankind—a serious aspect of its "cultural heritage." Although the "aesthetic" may "challenge" the "prevailing order of reason" (*EC,* 168) it cannot finally defeat the prevailing order of seriousness; in the sense that Marcuse uses the word "play," play and seriousness go together ultimately. In the *objet d'art,* despite the fact that it "shines," the reflection of the parental object lurks.

We should ponder with care, then, Marcuse's observation that mankind must be "free" not only on the "inside" but also in the "reality" in which it discovers itself. As we have seen, that "reality" is largely the projective reflection of *internalized* "good and bad contents." Accordingly, "civilization" as we know it and experience it at present (including the "aesthetic dimension") is based on the splitting of the formative years, the defensive proclivities of the anxious human, the schizoid and aggressive promptings of the conflicted inner world. To the extent that the "reality" on the "outside" encourages transitional aims, the goals of mastery and refusion through the celebration of symbolical objects, and the "acculturated" game of identification, it will not be in a condition to support genuine, substantial change. Although the "aesthetic dimension" can, in unusual moments, offer the individual a sensation of "freedom," or even awaken within him an impulse toward the self, it can never *be* "freedom" simply because it preserves the tie to the object, its actual, emotional source.

Indeed, the object of art may easily impede the individual's achievement of selfhood by draining his power to alter awareness through intensive involvement with aesthetic creations. Art must finally drop, as W. H. Hudson once suggested, like an excrescence from "the human plant," to be taken up again, or not, at will.[228] This can only happen when "the human plant" has attained the psychological capacity to be separate, employ its symbolic potentialities freely and autonomously rather than defensively and automatically, and detach its roots from the culture's familiar, familial soil. "Art, I suppose, is only for beginners, or else for those resolute dead–enders, who have made up their minds to be content with the ersatz of Suchness, with symbols rather than with what they signify, . . . [it is] a home–made substitute for Suchness."[229] The "aesthetic dimension," in the last analysis, is another version of the transitional mode.

Much the same reasoning bears on Marcuse's declaration that

the "senses" are not "primarily" organs of "cognition" but of "appetite" and that "civilization" has "subjugated" their "sensuousness" to "reason" (*EC,* 167). The fresh, remarkable, "liberated" use of the "senses" is, and always has been, directly linked to the alteration of ordinary consciousness. It is when the world no longer reconfirms "automatically" the existence of perceptual "categories" developed defensively during the crises of the early period, or when the world no longer constitutes the "ordinary," symbolical "place" that binds the individual to the source of his "security" (the phenomenological equivalent of Roheim's cultural "dual–unity"), that the sensual channels rediscover their "primitive" powers. The dull, "cognitive" employment of the "senses" derives "primarily" from the inclination to recognize (re–cognize) the world and hence to feel protected and safe within it. The "aesthetic dimension," and this is the point, is based in the very symbolic, linguistic proclivities which comprise the foundation of the "cognitive" function, the enemy of "sensuousness" in Marcuse's own "system." As the symbolic, transitional mode is put off, as the tie to the internalized other is severed through actual, specific, bodily procedures, the "object" returns to itself. What the eye beholds, to use a visual example, is only what is there and not what it "re–cognizes." In this, it achieves its highest "sensuous" bent. It sees. It is no longer hazed with recognizing what it is prone to suspect (angst) will be there. Because the world is new each time it is apprehended, and because the cessation of symbolical sight permits the "senses" to play forever with a nascent universe, one's bodily existence itself becomes creation—a transcendent "Nirvana" of perpetual invention, a "destiny" of "freedom." Thus, there *is* in the "aesthetic" a capacity to draw the individual away from "performance." That capacity, however, emerges as the "aesthetic dimension" of Marcuse is "dropped," after the tie to the object, symbol, "art" and culture, is "broken," to be reconstituted again, or not, at will. In this way, the perceptual significance of ordinary consciousness ultimately underlies the issues of the "aesthetic dimension" and "play," issues that are, in turn, intimately concerned with the question of "civilization and its discontents." Until "everyday" consciousness ends, the solutions to the problems will keep them around because they perpetuate the transitional mode of awareness. Although there is considerably more methodological sophistication in Marcuse's promulgation of aesthetics than there is in Brown's invocation of "Dionysius" (particularly with regard to the contexts out of which their suggestions arise), the concept of "art" as an ameliorative device is finally unacceptable on methodological grounds. It is not simply the difficulty of getting the individual passionately in pursuit of transitional rewards to focus his keen, existential attention on the formal "displays" of the aesthetic realm; it is that such focusing, were it achieved on even a large scale, would leave the individual's tense, converted body in an unchanged condition at the deep, unconscious level where the "bad object" roots itself. By contrast, to get the individual to alter his awareness is not only feasible on a substantial scale, as the current move toward meditation clearly demonstrates, the bodily alteration that such a procedure entails is able to "touch" the actual organs, the actual musculature, and the actual chemistry that grievously, or perhaps "nervously" attests to the pathogenic ordeals of the early period. Everywhere in *Eros and Civilization* Marcuse points toward the life of the body, resumption of sensuous, fully human existence, and rejection of an alienated, exploitative mode of "culture" that suppresses the physical gratification in the world. But the return to the body, senses, and world, cannot be achieved while the body belongs to the other who has been internalized into the individual's life. One cannot be "free" on the outside until one is free of the object's "domination" on the inside.

5.

Marcuse's concentration on the "aesthetic dimension" and "play" culminates in his call for what he terms a "new ego"—an ego that is rooted in a fresh revolutionary consciousness, that has been educated into knowledge of "erotic" as opposed to repressive social orders, and that is willing to express, and "exploit," its "primary," healthy, narcissistic urges. The "new ego" Marcuse recommends is overwhelmingly derived from his "new" evaluation of the timeless human urge to readopt the "narcissistic–maternal attitude" toward experience. He declares, with Loewald,

> the development of the ego is development 'away from primary narcissism;' at this early stage, reality 'is not outside but is contained in the pre–ego of primary narcissism.' It is not hostile and alien to the ego, but 'intimately connected with, originally not even distinguished from it.' This reality is first (and last?) experienced in the child's libidinal relation to the mother" (*EC*, 210).

And then, proceeding to the heart of the critique,

> in the light of the paternal reality principle, the 'maternal concept' of reality here emerging is immediately turned into something negative, dreadful. The impulse to reestablish the lost Narcissistic–maternal unity is interpreted as a 'threat,' namely the threat of 'maternal engulfment' by the overpowering womb. The hostile father is exonerated and reappears as savior who, in punishing the incest wish, protects the ego from its annihilation in the mother. The question does not arise whether the Narcissistic–maternal attitude toward reality cannot 'return' in less primordial, less devouring forms under the power of the mature ego and in a mature civilization. Instead, the necessity of suppressing this attitude once and for all is taken for granted. The patriarchal reality principle holds sway over the psychoanalytic interpretation. It is only beyond this reality principle that the 'maternal' images of the super ego convey promises rather than memory traces—images of a free future rather than of a dark past (*EC*, 210–211).

Consequently, the reader is back to the very same problem that occurred in Marcuse's earlier call for a mother–centered social organization (*EC*, 181). Because 1) the child's relation to the maternal object is not entirely "libidinal"; 2) the original "reality" is in some measure "hostile and alien to the ego"; and 3) the early period is profoundly dissimilar in its affective significance to the model on which Marcuse's critique is based, the "re–establishment of the lost Narcissistic–maternal attitude" is no more accept-able as an ameliorative device when applied to the individual human being than it is when applied to the problems of society. This does not mean, of course, that one must adhere to the "paternal reality" to which Marcuse refers; on the contrary, it means something entirely different. As long as the tie to the object is preserved, as long as it is strengthened by "egoistical" sugges-tions, the transitional aims of the individual will persist to engen-der the power motive, the need for compensatory striving, the magical, schizoid longing to rediscover an idealized version of the "good" maternal split. Just as society will not change until the transitional mode is dropped, so the "ego" will not change in any genuine, fundamental way until the tie to the internalized object ("domination") is "broken." Just as a "new" culture cannot "come to pass" without "new" human beings to comprise it, so a "new" ego cannot come to pass until the ego achieves the "mystical" capacity to detach itself from itself. The way to get out of egoism is to get out of the ego. Moreover, as was demonstrated earlier, much of what Marcuse attributes to the "paternal reality principle" is derived from affect originally developed in the child's relation to the "bad" maternal figure, or to the "bad" or unacceptable im-pulses in himself (endogenously and/or exogenously provoked) that discover their projective expression in the world "out there." What appears to be overwhelmingly "paternal" is frequently but a "higher" or "sublimated" expression of the primary, ambivalent mother–infant interaction. Of course the "paternal realm" exists;[230] it is not implied here that it does not. What is implied, however, is that it cannot be reached until one gets down to the root. Once again, from Swan:

> The later, oedipal conflict appears to be the development of a conflict already shaped in an earlier mother–infant (or nurse–infant) relationship. In a relatively oversimplified manner of speaking, we may say that the early split between good, pure, nurturing mother and ugly, sexual humiliating mother gets redistributed in the later relationship between pure mother and humiliating father.[231]

From this angle, perhaps, one appreciates more fully the causal, psychological factors which stand behind a blunt truth of the historical record, namely the existence of a good many grisly matriarchal as well as patriarchal societies.[232] What is "social" in human experience, or what is receptive, sensuous, "soft," intuitive, nurturing, is simply derived from the "good" side of a maternal split that is not overwhelmingly pathogenic in its character, a maternal split that is relatively less lethal than the kind we have described in Chapter Two. To place hope in a simple return to matriarchy is to leave the anxiety of the "dual–unity situation," the anxiety from which the malaise of "civilization" springs, fundamentally intact.

We may also appreciate more fully from this angle a certain limitation in Marcuse's powerful critique of "genital supremacy." He writes,

> The organization of sexuality reflects the basic features of the performance principle and its organization of society. Freud emphasizes the aspect of centralization. It is especially operative in the 'unification' of the various objects of the partial instincts into one libidinal object of the opposite sex, and in the establishment of genital supremacy. In both cases, the unifying process is repressive—that is to say the partial instincts do not develop freely into a 'higher' stage of gratification which preserves their objectives, but are cut off and reduced to subservient functions. This process achieves the socially necessary desexualization of the body: the libido becomes concentrated in one part of the body, leaving most of the rest free for use as the instrument of labor. This temporal reduction of the libido is thus supplemented by its spatial reduction. Originally the sex instinct has no extraneous temporal and spatial limitations on its subject and object; sexuality is by nature 'polymorphous–perverse.' The societal organization of the sex instinct taboos as perversions practically all its manifestations which do not serve or prepare for the procreative function (*EC,* 44).

According to Fenichel, Marcuse points out, "genital primacy" is a "prerequisite" to "culture" (*EC,* 44). But this is to deemphasize a rather crucial point, a point that can guide us to a view of the issue considerably more liberated than the one Marcuse develops here. The societal "order," including psychoanalysis, does not reject "polymorphous perversity" and elevate "genital supremacy" simply because it is performance oriented, repressive, "protestant," or "conservative." Rather, it sees the regressive, infantile aim in the orality and anality and rightly decries the pathological symptom, whatever the underlying economical motivation might be. In other words, there is a measure of truth in the "old" analytic position. Does this mean that Marcuse's assertions should be set aside? Certainly not. It means only that his assertions must be complemented by an accurate assessment of the nature and influence of infancy, the manner in which the negative aspects of the early period persist in the unconscious and, hence, in the unfolding of one's "sexual" urges.

This is not merely to italicize the work of Lichtenstein where sexual behavior is unquestionably linked to the manifestation of an "identity theme" established during the course of the mother–infant interaction.[233] It is to suggest a good deal more: as long as the individual exists in the transitional mode of awareness, in the anxiety of the "dual–unity situation," the "polymorphous perversity" that Marcuse supports, the free, open, unrepressed indulgence in all the sensual potentialities of the organism, all the "zones" of the human body, will not discover genuine expression. As long as the individual lacks the capacity, as well as the emotive, perceptual, and bodily power to sever the tie to the object within, "polymorphous" sexuality will reflect a regressive, infantile goal, will comprise an emotive effort to rediscover the "good" object, or to fulfil the "forbidden" aims of the "bad," alluring object. What this implies, of course, is that psychoanalysis, although it recognized the regressive nature of the so–called pre–genital desires, had neither the theoretical strength nor the independence of will to discover a satisfactory solution to the issue. The very orthodox sought to "work through" the disturbing, "polymorphous" inclinations of the person, to adjust him to the culture; that meant, of course, to the "higher" transitional ends of the "paternal" or "genital" order. The more radical psychoanalysis, associated with

Ferenczi and Roheim and aware of the unconscious pre–genital
urges inherent in the genital organization itself, also sought to
decathect infantile obsessions, not to the end of encouraging the
individual to firmly plant himself in the world of men, or, in the
case of females, to accept one's traditional "place," but to the end
of allowing the disturbed human being to exist more consciously
and comfortably in the "primary narcissism" of his "infantile"
character, in the "maternal attitude" of which Marcuse writes. The
point is, both orientations seek to strengthen "dual–unity," the
transitional mode of existence, the tie to the version of the object
that is acceptable to the analyst's own defences and to the cultural
world in which he discovers himself. In this way, both orientations
unwittingly encourage the "persistence" of that anxiety that is
crucially connected to the "discontent" of civilization and the
repression of "Eros." In both the "higher," genital organization of
the analytic establishment, as well as in the "lower," narcissistic–
maternal attitude of the breakaway theoreticians from whom Marcuse takes his lead, the bad object of the early time is allowed to
live on and corrupt the happy expression of the human being's
"polymorphous" inclinations. It is not merely the "narcissism" of
the "maternal attitude" that is "primary." The primal ambivalence
of the early period is "primary," too. The "good and bad objects"
of infancy and childhood are quite as much there as the "narcissistic" bent. Is not the upshot clear? To free sexuality, and liberate
Eros, is to "decathect" not only the paternal, but the maternal
influence as well. In a very real sense, there is no "regression in the
service of the ego." There is only regression in the service of the
ego and the object that has been internalized into the ego.

Recent analytic investigation is inclined to regard "perversion" not as the pathologic expression of pre–genital sexual aims
but as a "clinically definable entity, representing a special type of
transference."[234] The emphasis is squarely on the object relation.
But what psychoanalysis has still to digest is the extent to which
ordinary consciousness, ordinary symbolical awareness, itself,
evinces "transference" features, and constitutes a way back to the
parent. Ordinary or "repressed" sexuality (what Marcuse desig-

nates as "genital primacy") transpires within the context of the individual's total sensual participation in the world. The achievement of "polymorphous perversity" is but an aspect of that total return to the senses—perception and awareness—that characterizes the "break" with symbolic or "parental" mentation. When the whole perceptual world is restored in the truncation of the tie to the object, one's sexual behavior becomes an integral aspect of one's perceptually free engagement with the universe. The "mature civilization" (*EC*, 211) that will ostensibly permit the "return" of the "Narcissistic–maternal attitude" (*EC*, 211) is the kind of "civilization" that will "arise" when detachment from that "attitude" is gained. As we have seen, psychoanalysis' abhorrence of pregenital sexuality (*EC*, 45) is surpassed only by its abhorrence of detachment, of the "occult," of the "spiritual" development that is traditionally associated with the "mystical" practices of the east and the west.[235] Because the liberation of Eros is integrally tied to precisely this sort of detachment we cannot ignore the psychoanalytic attitude toward the "occult" when discussing the psychoanalytical attitude toward Eros. This is what the author is suggesting: at a deep, almost imperceptible level Freud and his followers did not want to discover a way to liberate Eros because to liberate Eros is to detach the individual from those psychological forces upon which, as they viewed the matter, the existence of civilization is based. The members of the psychoanalytic community did not want the individual to be genuinely free in expressing himself or the aims of his sensual nature, because the accomplishment of such freedom, as they viewed the issue within the limited framework of their libidinal theories (as well as within the context of their own defences), entailed the permanent loss of those bonds that connected the individual to the parental figure, the "basis" of macrocosmic and microcosmic "organization." The "analyst" was not willing to give the "patient" the final control over his own body, the freedom to put his world of symbols on and off again at will, the detachment actually to see—which means to feel—the mutable foundations of his own affective life. Accordingly, "regression in the service of the ego" became a means to "successful" treatment. That the "ego" was largely the object *in* the ego was ignored, or perhaps denied. Also ignored or denied, of course, was the fact that the advancement of civilization, the positive evolution of "culture," actually depended on the individual's achievement of just that inner freedom—that inner mastery which is an integral aspect of altered awareness, "transcendental Nirvana," detachment. *Eros and Civilization* takes its place in this history of psychoanalytic ideas. Finally, with reference to Marcuse's economic concerns, the "Narcissistic–maternal attitude" is not without its own peculiar dangers. As leisure time increases, as the "work week" of neo–capitalism undergoes a progressive shortening, the "powers that be" may very well recognize the advantage of encouraging the individual's "regressive" sexuality. To have the "worker" occupied "polymorphously" while removed from the place of his employment is to get him back nice and breasty on "Monday morning" when the four–day weekend, or the "holiday," is over. The tie to the object within is never a solid foundation for the achievement of genuine change.

6.

Marcuse's program for social advancement is, like Marx's, closely concerned with the development of revolutionary awareness in the individual. The "chains" that "bind" the human creature to the "establishment" are ultimately forged in the mind; until consciousness changes there can be little hope for creating a just society. Everywhere in *Eros and Civilization,* and particularly in Chapters Seven through Nine, this thesis is forcefully underscored. But it is in a later work, *One–Dimensional Man,* that Marcuse discloses what can safely be described as the crisis of modern political and economic consciousness. Here is a book that is about awareness, and as such, harbors an enormous potential to clarify further this discussion. Marcuse writes, in Marxian terminology, that the "dialectical process involves consciousness, recognition and seizure of the liberating potentialities. Thus it involves freedom. To the degree to which consciousness is determined by the exigencies and interests of the established society, it is 'unfree'; to the degree to which the established society is irrational, the consciousness becomes free for the higher historical rationality only in the struggle against the established society."[236] And again, "all liberation depends upon the consciousness of servitude" (*ODM*, 7). But for modern man the dilemma resides in the fact that the universe of ideas, the universe of awareness, is closing and closing fast:

> Social controls have been introjected to the point where even individual protest is affected at its roots. The intellectual and emotional refusal 'to go along' appears neurotic and impotent. This is the socio–psychological aspect of the political event that marks the contemporary period: the passing of the historical forces which, at the preceding stage of industrial society, seemed to represent the possibility of new forms of existence (*ODM*, 9–10, my emphasis).

Hence, and this is a key statement, that private, inner "space" from which oppositional or "negative" consciousness ordinarily springs, is being "invaded and whittled down by technological reality. Mass production and mass distribution claim the entire individual, and industrial psychology has long since ceased to be confined to the factory. The manifold processes of introjection seem to be ossified in almost mechanical reactions. The result is not adjustment but mimesis—an immediate identification of the individual with his society and, through it, with the society as a whole" (*ODM*, 10). The "loss" of this "space," the loss of this dimension in which the "power of negative thinking" is "at home," is the "ideological counterpart to the very material process in which advanced industrial society silences and reconciles the opposition" (*ODM*, 11). Thus, "one–dimensional man" is man "assimilated" into the "rational, materialistic" orientation of his "affluent" culture; it is man unable to cognize outside the established order of the prevailing "reality," so thorough is the manipulation of his awareness, so total his identification with the "social" realm. In Marcuse's own definitive statement,

> Today's novel feature is the flattening out of the antagonism be-
> tween culture and social reality through the obliteration of the
> oppositional, alien, and transcendant elements in the higher culture
> by virtue of which it constituted another dimension of reality. This
> liquidation of two–dimensional culture takes place not through the
> denial and rejection of the 'cultural values,' but through their
> wholesale incorporation into the established order, through their
> reproduction and display on a massive scale. . . . The greatness of a
> free literature and art, the ideals of humanism, the sorrows and joys
> of the individual, the fulfillment of personality are important items
> in the competitive struggle between the east and the west. They
> speak heavily against the present forms of communism, and they are
> daily administered and sold. The fact that they contradict the society
> that sells them does not count. Just as people know or feel that
> advertisements and political platforms must not necessarily be true
> or right, and yet hear and read them and even let themselves be
> guided by them, so they accept the traditional values and make them
> part of their mental equipment (*ODM*, 57).

What all of this signifies in phenomenological terms (phenomenological terms which harbor psychoanalytical implications)
is that ordinary reality itself has come to be inextricably associated
with political and particularly ideological events.

The ordinary consciousness of the individual is no longer
relatively neutral with reference to its symbolical apprehension of
the world. Indeed, the neutral area is fast diminishing to the point
where ordinary awareness, or ordinary symbolical perception, is
becoming ideological awareness, direct and all–pervasive political
perception. The "domination" of ordinary reality that commences
"on the inside" through the tie to the object, through the anxiety of
separation, through the elevation of symbolical sight to the status
of "rational" or "normal" mentation, in a word, through the union
of biological capacity and defensive purpose, is complemented
"on the outside" by the "dominant" interests of neo–capitalism and
communist dictatorship, the interests of those who control the
"mass media" and hence, the "propaganda machines," including,
of course, advertising. In the past, one's symbolical perception or
"ordinary consciousness" frequently "touched" the ideological

area; now, it is becoming the ideological area. Thus, the alteration of awareness, the cessation of symbolical or "ordinary" sight, the achievement of what has been termed "transcendent Nirvana," is *also* becoming directly linked to political and ideological matters. To truncate the tie to the object within can no longer be regarded as a purely therapeutic procedure (or bourgeois indulgence). It has entered the political arena as an oppositional tool—a method of negating ideological influence that seeks to "dominate" perception itself. Technique for the attainment of the individual "utopia" becomes technique for the denial of socio–economic control and, in this way, for the recovery of human freedom. The days of "purely perceptual problems" are over. Perceptual problems are political problems, and from all indications they will continue to be. As for Marcuse's apparently contradictory statements that "social controls" are being "introjected" as never before and that "introjection" appears to be "ossifying" into a kind of "mechanical reaction" (*ODM*, 9–10), they are probably attributable to a shifting signification attached to the term "introjection." The extent to which the expressions "introjection, internalization, incorpora-tion, and identification" are used interchangeably (and confusing-ly) in psychoanalytical exposition has recently been examined at length.[237] In any case, Marcuse is not suggesting that the anxieties and ordeals of the early period have suddenly ceased to make their influence known. Because ordinary awareness has always been linked to the object within, because ordinary awareness has always constituted an avenue back to the parental figure, because the symbolical world of language and image has always derived from those very processes of internalization which were originally em-ployed in a defensive cause ("dual–unity"), the way has always been open to control the individual at the perceptual level, and exploit his proclivity to think along symbolical lines. It is not what one perceives that becomes the issue of the day, it is how one perceives, for what one perceive depends for its efficaciousness precisely on the mode of our perception. The "flattening out of the antagonism between culture and social reality" (*ODM*, 57) to which Marcuse refers, is properly understood as the spreading out of the object's influence across the cultural realm as a whole. It is the inner life of the individual that is being "exploited" along with his "external existence." Here is the origin of "one–dimensionality."

The extent to which the explicitly political symbol "touches" the symbolical version of the object, the extent to which, in other words, ideological reality is becoming ordinary reality, is captured indirectly (and unforgettably) in Edelman's book, *The Symbolic Uses of Politics*. Striving to depict the essential nature of the current political symbol so that one can grasp the manner in which politics work in the world, Edelman writes,

> [The symbol] could not serve as conveyor of [our] fears and aspirations if it were simply a tool or mechanism which we all had the power and knowledge to manipulate for our own advantage. It is central to its potency as a symbol that it is remote, set apart, omnipresent as the ultimate threat or means of succor, yet not susceptible to effective influence through any act we as individuals can perform.[238]

Edelman's words describe exactly the original "symbol," the internalized object of infancy whose "persistent," all–pervasive influence governs the individual's substitutive participation in group or cultural symbols and, hence, offers him to the "society" that uses him. The object of the early time is also "set apart"; it is "omnipotent" as a "means of threat or succor," and "not susceptible" to our "acts" as "individuals." This is not to imply, of course, that the "symbols" of the past worked differently; it is to suggest that the connection between ideology and internalized object, political symbol and internalized symbol, ordinary perception as governed by the presence within and ordinary political perception as governed by the symbolified version of the presence within, is "rising" to the conscious level. This is the level at which one can recognize not only the link between "introjection," to use Marcuse's term, and the "political symbol," to use Edelman's, but the significance of altered awareness as a method designed in its essence to truncate the "power" relation (Edelman's term again) that allows the manipulative "establishment" to bind the individual's very mode of perception to its obsessive, pathological pursuit of transitional goals, such as money. The detachment of altered awareness becomes detachment from that "inner space" (*ODM*, 10) which Marcuse sees being "assimilated" (*ODM*, 27) into the "social reality" (*ODM*, 27) of the political–industrial order.

One–Dimensional Man is not without passages that indicate Marcuse's sensitivity to the problem of perceptual modes as a key to the future. He writes in one place, for example, "The given reality has its own logic and its own truth; the effort to comprehend them presupposes a different logic, a contradictory truth. They belong to modes of thought which are non–operational in their very structure; they are alien to scientific as well as common–sense operationalism" (*ODM*, 142). And again, "what is at stake is not the definition or the dignity of philosophy. It is rather the chance of preserving and protecting the right, the need to think and speak in terms other than those of common usage—terms which are meaningful, rational, and valid precisely because they are other terms. What is involved is the spread of a new ideology" (*ODM*, 178).

Now, the kind of awareness that could fundamentally "transcend" the existing "operational" awareness of the "establishment," the kind of awareness which is by definition "non–operational" and "non–common–sensical," is the kind of awareness that has been traditionally associated with transcendence, with the negation of opposites (the "yin and yang" of ordinary logic), with the establishment of mind–body integration as an end in itself, and with a view of the cosmos in which dynamic activity is an expression of pure being rather than egoistical power.[239] That this kind of altered awareness should be linked directly to the psychodynamics of "introjection" (*ODM*, 9) (which are, in turn, linked inextricably to an ordinary, operational awareness which reflects ideological concerns at the level of symbolical expression) makes it clear that to take Marcuse's revolutionary consciousness, or "new ideology" (*ODM*, 178), "all the way," is to take it to altered consciousness where the symbolical, operational, ideological mode is put off through truncation of the tie to the object. Had psychoanalysis' abhorrence of detachment, of the "occult," of the "mystical," not prevented it from discovering the emotive connection between "dual–unity" and ordinary consciousness, between "dual–unity" and "common sense" (*ODM,* 142), it would have offered Marcuse not only the "radical" conclusion to his emphasis on "modes of thought" (*ODM,* 142) but the actual, bodily method for the accomplishment of freed perception (Chapter 2).

7.

Marcuse's discussion of Brecht is closely related to the issue of cognitive modes. In Brecht's plays, as well as in his concept of an "Epic Theater," is embodied the "revolutionary" concept that a work of art must struggle "against . . . absorption into the predominant one–dimensionality" (*ODM,* 66). Brecht's work is an "avant-garde" effort "to create an enstrangement which would make the artistic truth again communicable" (*ODM,* 66). What is required, Marcuse declares in a crucial passage, is

> not empathy and feeling but distance and reflection . . . The 'enstrangement effect' . . . is to produce this dissociation in which the world can be recognized as what it is. 'The things of everyday life' are lifted out of the realm of the self–evident. That which is 'natural' must assume the features of the extraordinary. Only in this manner can the laws of cause and effect reveal themselves (*ODM,* 67).

The "trick" here, however, is not to confine this thesis to the realm of artistic endeavor but to apply it to ordinary consciousness where ideology roots itself. The world is a projective "theater" and ordinary awareness has come to be one's "empathetic" and "ideological" manner of participating in it. "The mind is 'peopled,' " writes Castelnuovo–Tedesco; "the figures of the past are not just 'memories' or mere abstractions but current realities as well as remnants of another time. They can be summoned to life and made to appear, three–dimensional, in the mind as on a stage where, like veteran actors, they play once more their classic role."²⁴⁰ To achieve the "distance," the "enstrangement," the "dissociation" (*ODM*, 66–67) Marcuse describes as essential to "recognizing the world as it is" (*ODM*, 67) one must sever the tie to these "veteran actors," empty the "stage" of the internalized objects who impel one toward the "dream" of the prevailing ideology, terminate one's involvement in a "group" that is ultimately a kind of "audience," in other words, leave the "theater."

From the stage of the world men speak; it is not simply pantomime with which we are confronted. What has happened to language, to words, indeed, to the use of words as persuasive symbols, is clearly established in *One–Dimensional Man:*

> How can . . . protest and refusal find the right word when the organs of the established order admit and advertise that peace is really the brink of war, that the ultimate weapons carry their profitable price tags, and that the bomb shelter may spell coziness. In exhibiting its contradictions as the token of its truth, this universe of discourse closes itself against any other discourse which is not on its own terms (*ODM*, 90).

And again, "the fact that a specific noun is almost always coupled with the same 'explicatory' adjectives and attributes [e.g. "free world"] makes the sentence into a hypnotic formula which, endlessly repeated, fixes the meaning in the recipient's mind" (*ODM*, 91). The "authoritarian character of this language" is revealed in a "telescoping and abridgment of syntax which cuts off development of meaning by creating fixed images which impose themselves with an overwhelming and petrified concreteness" (*ODM*, 91). The most effective oppositional weapon here is also "Brechtian"; that is to say, it resides in the ability to put off language altogether, "detach" oneself from the "speech" of the "play," and "dissociate" oneself from those empathizing, internalizing tendencies that derive from the early time—the time which actually culminates in the employment of language itself. As far as its deepest affective signification is concerned, the word is a link to the object. The first "production of sound," Roheim points out, is an emotive response to the presence of the "mother . . . herself." It is "clear that language is used for understanding from person to person and . . . the prototype of all interpersonal relationships is the mother–child situation."[241] Thus, the cessation of ordinary awareness on which hinges the cessation of ordinary political awareness and, hence, of one's "normal" ideological exploitation is inextricably tied to the cessation of ordinary linguistic awareness, and the calculated, bodily transcendence of a verbal universe that has long ceased to be a "place" of relatively uncontaminated "information." Because language no longer "alienates" in the traditional religious sense only, the sense indicated by Huxley's remark that in ordinary consciousness "words are taken for things" and "symbols used as the measure of reality,"[242] because political "repressiveness," and "authoritarianism" (*ODM*, 91) make use of language in its transitional operations, the liberated individual becomes one who can see words precisely as he sees the other symbols of the mind. He is also one who is sufficiently "enstranged" from the object within to put language on and off again at will. When power is transferred from the object to the self, the power of the word expires. "Loss and reclaiming of the object are experienced repetitively through verbalization," writes Leavy; "in fact, the existence of language implies a loss and a restitution, the verbal symbol being a reclaimed object. The 'real' object is lost to consciousness, so the words that signify it may follow in its path."[243] In this way, when a linguist such as Hymes tells us that "speech community is a necessary primary concept in that . . . it postulates the unit of description as a social, rather than a linguistic entity," that in a "sociolinguistic description . . . it is necessary to deal with activities which are in some recognizable way bounded or integral,"[244] he does not rivet simply the sociological aspect of speech but the psychological aspect too. The tie to society, the "social aspect," is ultimately rooted *zu liebe*, in the internalization, identification, and object relation, that commences during the early period and is subsequently projected onto the "social" land-

scape. The "bounded" aspect of speech is a "function" of those
inner boundaries that contain the "good and bad objects" who
"people" the inner world. As for the "integral aspect" of "speech,"
it "magically" ensures the transitional integration of the individual
who strives to answer life's crises through the establishment of the
"dual–unity situation." Greenberg writes that language is, among
other things, "the source of all postlanguage developments," that
"it is not language itself which evolves but rather communication
in general," and finally, that language is capable of begetting "that
which is not language but transcends it, even while it is dependent
upon it."[245] Such considerations are discussed in the next part of
this book where the evolutionary significance of altered awareness
is explored for its social implications. In addition, however, they
remind us 1) that Marcuse's emphasis upon "enstrangement" as a
method of opposing linguistic manipulation engages both the
perceptual and philological realms, and 2) that the transcendence
of language as it appears in the work of the linguist "touches" the
transcendence of language as it appears in those "religious" traditions which aim at the accomplishment of new modes of communication and, through those modes, at the "liberation" of the
individual. From every conceivable angle, then, the radical consciousness from which may spring the radical opposition to society's "one–dimensionality" rests on the achievement of that
"occult" detachment which diminishes the influence of the internalized object. Psychoanalysis as a revolutionary, emancipating
tool is now in a position to remain scientific and, at the same time,
to see the power traditionally associated with the "mystical" realm
work for it.[246]

Part V

CONSIDERATIONS FOR THE FUTURE

Chapter 9

EVOLUTION, PSYCHOANALYSIS, AND THE PROBLEM OF PERCEPTION

1.

What we have termed the transitional mode of awareness marks not merely the prevailing emotive, psychological "style" of the human creature; in a much more fundamental sense, it marks a specific stage in his biological evolution, and in his natural development as a living "system," as a homeostatic form of life, as a "structure" in the current scientific employment of that expression.[247] The preceding sections of this book, taken together, present a certain kind of animal, or organism, lived from within by the internalized object, and an "ordinary consciousness" which is not "ordinary" at all but a complicated network of reception and response. It is a consciousness that is forged in the crises of the early time and designed, above all, to keep open the affective, perceptual channel that leads back to the mothering figure. Accordingly, the recorded history of mankind does not constitute an Oedipal dream, as Freud, Marcuse, and Brown would suggest; it constitutes, rather, a transitional dream where the father "inherits" the split maternal object of the infant. The Oedipal dream of Freud and his followers is, indeed, best regarded as itself a dream—a rationalization unconsciously designed to avoid direct contact with the maternal realm, and internalizations that stand at the very ground of man's existence with the generative roots of consciousness itself. At stake here is not only an accurate understanding of the manner in which the unconscious spins the human plot, but the possibility of discovering an actual method of change—the kind of genuine, concrete, evolutionary change which the Oedipal dead–end simply will not provide. The blunt fact emerges that to achieve the social and individual amelioration described in the work of Freud, Brown, and Marcuse is to alter mankind's organization as a perceiving animal. "Awareness," writes G. S. Klein, "is no unimportant epiphenomenon but has an adaptive import defined by the controlling structures [i.e. by the internalized objects] that affect the deployment of cathexis."[248] Not only must we spy the connection among biological interiorization, defensive internalization, symbolic proclivity, divided inner world, and an ordinary consciousness that has culminated in a transitional approach to "reality," but we must go beyond the spying to the doing, to those physical, bodily practices that can actually disrupt the transitional perception from which springs the "discontent" of our "civilized culture." What follows are several important concepts necessary for the accomplishment of positive evolutionary change.

2.

Reminding the reader that "in evolutionary history, the great majority of steps have been changes within the organism itself," Bateson[249] takes up the danger to the human species which lurks in "man's habit" of "changing the environment rather than changing himself" (*SEM*, 445). As the "power ratio between purposive consciousness and the environment has changed rapidly in the last one hundred years," declares Bateson, "conscious man, as a changer of his environment, is now fully able to wreck himself and that environment—with the very best of conscious intentions" (*SEM,* 445–446). Although the "correctives" (*SEM,* 446) Bateson offers to offset the "danger" are wise and admirable—he speaks of what Buber calls I-Thou relationships, of contact with the natural world, of religion, of love—they only focus, in the last analysis, the overriding need for concrete or "harder" recommendations. For how is the driven human creature to accomplish this turnabout, this "change"? Do not Bateson's words, powerful and timely though they be, constitute but another verbal warning and hope in a long history of "messages"? Surely it is significant, in this context, that the growth and development of those "religious" (*SEM,* 447) feelings which Bateson considers to be essential to the welfare, indeed to the continuance, of the species should be traditionally associated with a method of change that, by severing the tie to the internalized object, and removing a particular kind of affect (transitional anxiety) from the percept, alters physiologically our perception of the world and, in the process, provides the kind of internal refinement (*SEM,* 445) which Bateson regards as evolutionally crucial. Let us look further into the matter by looking further into Bateson's work, for I want to indicate *precisely* the biological and evolutional meaning of the so–called spiritual event.

"Information, in the technical sense," Bateson writes in *Re-Examination of Bateson's Rule,*

> is that which excludes certain alternatives. The machine with a governor does not elect the steady state; it prevents itself from staying in any alternative state; and in all such cybernetic systems, corrective action is brought about by difference. . . . The technical term 'information' may be succinctly defined as any difference which makes a difference in some later event. This definition is fundamental for all analysis of cybernetic systems and organization (*SEM,* 381).

Applying this concept to the problem of "symmetry and metameric regularity as exhibited in the morphology of animals and plants," and referring explicitly to the work of his father who formulated the original "rule," Bateson declares,

> it is difficult today to define precisely what he was after, but, broadly, it is clear that he believed that an entirely new concept of the nature of living things would develop from the study of such phenomena. He held, no doubt correctly, that natural selection could not be the only determinant of the direction of evolutionary change and that the genesis of variation could not be a random matter (*SEM*, 379).

And then, moving to specifics,

> an unfertilized frog's egg is radically symmetrical, with animal and vegetal poles but no differentiation of its equatorial radii. Such an egg develops into a bilaterally symmetrical embryo, but how does it select one meridian to be the plane of bilateral symmetry of that embryo? The answer is known—that, in fact, the frog's egg receives information from the outside. The point of entry of the spermatozoon . . . marks one meridian as different from all others, and that meridian is the future plane of bilateral symmetry (*SEM*, 382).

Hence, "if the step from bilateral symmetry to asymmetry requires additional information, then it follows that in absence of this additional information, the appendage which should have been asymmetrical can only be bilaterally symmetrical. The problem of the bilateral symmetry of reduplicated limbs thus becomes simply a problem of the *loss* of a piece of information. This follows from the general logical rule that every reduction in symmetry requires additional information" (*SEM*, 383–384). Bateson summarizes his "re–examination" as follows:

> it extends the notion of informational control to include the field of morphogenesis and, by discussing what happens in the absence of needed information, brings out the importance of the context into which information is received. Samuel Butler, with uncanny insight, once commented upon the analogy between dreams and parthogenesis. We may say that the monstrous double legs of the

> beetles share in this analogy: they are the projection of the receptive
> context deprived of information which should have come from an
> external source. . . . But every meridian must be ready for the
> activating message, its 'readiness,' being given direction but other-
> wise unrestricted by structure. Readiness, in fact, is precisely not
> structure. . . . This 'readiness' is uncommitted potentiality for
> change, and we note here that this uncommitted potentiality is not
> only always finite in quantity but must be appropriately located in a
> structural matrix, which also must be quantitatively finite at any
> given time (*SEM,* 395–396).

Now, ordinary or symbolical consciousness is *also* a *dream* in
the rich biological sense of Bateson and Butler. The author does
not mean simply, as William James taught us long ago, that our
"normal waking consciousness" restricts the information which
streams toward the organism from the surrounding universe and,
thus, acts as a kind of "filter" that protects us from overstimulation
and allows us to focus our attention; nor does he mean that this
dream is radically enhanced by the further restriction of information which attends our symbolical apprehension of the world, our
tendency to regard the freshly perceived, individual "object" as a
confirmational instance of a general type, usually accorded a
relatively unchanging ideational existence through language (the
"mountain" as opposed to that which is directly perceived, in the
famous Zen aphorism). Instead, he means that the restriction of
information and, hence, the dream is crucially affected, in a way
that bears sharply on the evolutionary issue of change and survival,
at precisely that point where biology and depth psychology meet,
namely the point at which the restrictive aspect of symbolical sight
becomes tinged with the emotive dilemmas that surround the first
and prototypical symbol of human awareness—the maternal figure. The single greatest restriction of information that man imposes on himself as a human being springs directly from his having
positioned, in a psycho–biological defensive gesture, the split
maternal object at the foundation of the symbolizing mind. This is
not said, of course, as if the event were truly voluntary, although in
a certain psycho–dynamic sense it is and must be regarded so if

change is to occur; moreover, one cannot be unappreciative of the evolutionary value in the power to retain images and discover similarities. The neotenous, dependent, anxious human infant can, with his "big brain," respond to the imperfections of mothering by taking his provider inside of him, and does so; his evolutionary potential is put to a defensive use. However, since energy is *habitually* put to this use, and an internalizing, transitional orientation toward "reality" becomes the automatic, indeed, "endemic" mode of humanoid existence, the perception that is biologically specific to man creates not merely a restrictive dream of life but a restrictive dream of life with psychopathological significance, a dream where transitional strivings and capitulations either threaten the survival of mankind or, at the very least, make its days on the planet miserable and full of stress. The transitional dilemma of the human creature is the nightmarish biological and spiritual counterpart of those monstrous beetle legs also created, in Bateson's terminology, through the restriction of information.

The implications for change begin to emerge in earnest and it is the "cybernetic" concept of restriction of information that provides, once again, a clue. By detaching oneself from ordinary awareness, or restricting the symbolical perception that automatically recalls the transitional dilemma and "keeps alive" the regressive, compensatory goals of the early period, one restores his filtering mechanism to its original or pristine condition, frees the mind from its anxious, egotic tendency to *grip* the external world. One no longer "reads" the transitional issue "into" creation, or clutters the biologically defensive screen with materials rooted in the imperfections of infancy and made a part of the perceptual apparatus ("the fall") through the employment of internalization. It is when the human animal "changes himself" (*SEM,* 445) at the perceptual level by gaining the capacity to de–symbolify "reality" and, thus, restrict at will the "input" of a certain class of "data" that he will be in a position to "change his environment" constructively at the level of his societal interactions.

Indeed, in a very real sense, the internalization and splitting of the maternal object constitutes a psychologically asymmetrical response to the adaptive pressures of early life, a response that, left intact, precludes the achievement of integration or symmetry on the part of the "mature" member of the species. It is a kind of inevitable, homeostatic mistake, a distorting mirror of the object–relation, from which derives much that is destructive and tragic in human existence. As for the "readiness" of the "flexible" organism for such an "activating" change, as well as for the reception of that change into a "structured matrix" (*SEM*, 396), they are attested to irrefutably by a 3,000 year history of systematic mystical practice and epistemological investigation.

Bateson writes in another place,

> the Darwinian theory, when purged of Lamarckian ideas, consisted of a genetics in which variation was presumed to be random, combined with a theory of natural selection [that] would impart adaptive direction to the accumulation of changes. But the relation between learning and this theory has been a matter of violent controversy which has raged over the so–called 'inheritance of acquired characteristics.' Darwin's position was acutely challenged by Samuel Butler, who argued that heredity should be compared with—even identified with—memory. Butler proceeded from this premise to argue that the processes of evolutionary change, and especially adaptation, should be regarded as the achievements of a deep cunning in the ongoing flow of life, not as fortuitous bonuses conferred by luck (*SEM*, 253).

He continues:

> but the somatic price of a given change must depend, not absolutely upon the change in question, but upon the range of somatic flexibility available to the organism at the given time. This range, in turn, will depend upon how much of the organism's somatic flexibility is already being used up in adjusting to other mutations or environmental changes. We face an economics of flexibility which, like any other economics, will become determinative for the course of evolution if and only if the organism is operating close to the limits set by this economics (*SEM*, 349).

And finally, in a crucial passage, Bateson declares that the

"Lamarckian premise" may contain a truth for man who possesses, through his ability to control and modify his "condition," a certain and significant "evolutionary flexibility." Indeed, the human animal can "acquire characteristics environmentally" through his own process of "induced selection," characteristics that can actually serve to reduce biological–psychological "stress" and, hence, increase man's potential for survival (*SEM*, 359). "It is precisely my thesis that the simulation of Lamarckian inheritance will have survival value under circumstances of undefined or multiple stress [the stress inherent in ordinary awareness]. . . . Simulated Lamarckian inheritance will have survival value when the population must adjust to a stress which remains constant over successive generations" (*SEM*, 360). The alteration of awareness must be regarded precisely in the light of these remarks, and others like them.[250]

The mode of perception biologically defines the nature of the creature. The alteration of awareness, by severing the tie to the internalized object, not only modifies the organization of the preceptual mode (particularly with reference to stress) but is immediately inherited and steadily increased through the employment of specific, practical methodologies. The alteration of awareness along the lines suggested in the context of this book constitutes an evolutional "simulation of Lamarck" with considerable adaptive value. And there is more: by terminating the "endless" transitional project that marks the current stage of human evolution and that, from the standpoint of energy or "power," coerces the human organism toward the "limits" of its "flexibility" (*SEM*, 349), one reduces not merely the stress that presses on the individual but also the stress that presses on the society, the stress that has resulted in an economic and political "order" which would make the world answer the transitional demand, or the projective, pathological "need" of the anxious humanoid. The "stress of life"[251] comprises, in large measure, the stress of ordinary consciousness because ordinary consciousness predicates the never–ending preoccupation with separation and success; and it is precisely this stress, this consciousness, this mode of perception and behavior, which precipitates those activities that, in Bateson's view, harbor profound evolutionary danger: war, the exploitation of others, the wasteful, irresponsible use and spoilation of the world's resources. In this way, the "restriction" of ordinary awareness constitutes a "Lamarckian event." The alteration of awareness may be viewed as mankind's "cunning" way of discovering an avenue to that precious "inner change" (*SEM*, 445) that will help to ensure not only its survival as a species but its advancement evolutionally as a species as well.

We may view this as the richest biological and psychological meaning of Bateson citing, simply, "religion" (*SEM*, 447) as a possible solution to the current crises and dangers of mankind. Specifically from the psychoanalytical angle we have in this the point at which the psychoanalysis of religion discovers its evolutionary destiny as a diminisher of human suffering and, hence, as an ameliorative instrument.[252] Defensive hostility toward "the occult" on Freud's part, an hostility adhered to by the majority of his followers, blinded psychoanalysis to the meaning of detachment not only as a therapeutic tool, but as a widespread human practice with evolutionary importance. It can be said, in fact, that the orthodox analytical attitude toward religion prevented Freud and his followers from constructing their "road" into the unconscious in a genuinely satisfactory scientific fashion. As a result, they were unable to bring to consciousness, to a level where it could be consciously inherited after the manner of Lamarck, the ameliorative potential of the altered state of mind, or the so-called mystical state. What the individual was doing for thousands of years in a good portion of his "mystical" practice was not striving to "regress" to the "oceanic period" but striving to go beyond the transitional stage of awareness and, in going beyond it, to effectively diminish the degree of stress in his life. As a group, evolutionally, it can be said that those engaged in "mystical" procedures were looking to "induce selection" along Lamarckian lines and, thus, "acquire characteristics environmentally." These characteristics would contribute to evolutionary progress by diminishing divisive (and dangerous) transitional aims. Detachment from the objects of the inner world, which comprises the highest "religious" expression of altered awareness, is, then, the single most immediately advantageous evolutionary step mankind can take at this particular moment in its natural development. It is on this goal that we must concentrate our efforts, and not on technology: "For that way madness lies."

3.

Soleri writes:

> The physical structure is still the skeleton of the spirit, and structure is the bridgetrain on which the spirit travels and grows stronger. The physical energy consumed in the durational journey goes ultimately into the generation of the life energy, which, as knowledge, is not constrained by the physical law of energy conservation but transcends it by creating out of itself more of itself.[253]

He continues, working metaphorically toward the concept of inner pollution, or waste, "If there is any comprehensive definition of pollution it has to be found in the failure of technology to account for a true tuning in on a problem in its totality. That is to say, its failure in fostering the spirit. If the reference 'point' is the spirit then whenever spirit is not incremented, pollution is present in its most comprehensive form: entropy" (A, 4). For "we, the quasie three billions of persons, are consciously and unconsciously working at the invention–conception of an ultra–person or trans–person" who will place the "family" of "man" in a technological and environmental position considerably more enlightened with regard to "spirit" and "waste" than the one in which that "family" currently discovers itself (A, 11).

And then, in a series of statements strikingly relevant to the evolutional and ameliorative implications of Bateson's work as viewed from the perspective of altered awareness, all the problems of population, of energy demand (not energy need, by the way), of conservation of . . . resources, of waste, . . . of pollution, . . . all of them are directly, indissolubly bound to the resourcefulness of our minds in dealing with the coincidence . . . between the quality of life, its complexity and the miniaturized character necessary for its containers; . . . the brain has compressed (miniaturized) the 'universe' in a few pounds–inches of space–matter–energy. Only by way of this miraculous contraction of performances (information, communication) is the brain a concrete process presiding over the other miniaturized 'universe' of the body . . . it is as if step by step evolution would take account of itself and make a complete synopsis (miniaturization) of its achievements in order to have at its finger tips all the available power for the next leap . . . Compression produces reach . . . the utter compression of the brain produces the limitless reach of the mind . . . the omnipresent, omniscient, 'point' is the seat of godliness; . . . [it manifests] the infinite complexity of a being utterly centered upon itself, . . . a point whose next metamorphosis could be the advent of the explosion known as the 'big bang,' initiating a new cosmos, the spiritual universe (A, 12, 23, 45, 57, 65).

As long as the individual's power is invested in transitional goals, which is to say, as long as the individual remains emotively attached to the internalizations of infancy and childhood, the gathering strength, the power, for the "leap" Soleri mentions will be lacking. It is precisely the transitional project, the transitional mode of existence, that breeds the internal "entropy," "waste," and "pollution," and that has its disastrous outward effects on the "human family" as an evolving form of life. The "entropic" stage of human evolution is the waste of power in the service of unconscious objects. It is precisely those methods of altered awareness, of detachment from the early, "immortal" internalizations, that redirect and concentrate the energy of the individual in the direction of the "leap" that Soleri discusses. Indeed, as was made plain earlier, systems of altered awareness are by definition redirectional "technologies" entirely designed to turn the individual's power toward the conflicted inner world, and detach the anxious, stress–filled organism from the insidious, projective game of fulfilling the demand of the internalization by performing certain actions in (and on) the universe "out there."

As one detaches himself from the objects of the inner world, and physiologically prevents or limits the processing of a certain kind of information, he "miniaturizes" his emotive, energic existence, "gathers" himself concentratedly toward the achievement of the "point," "centers" his life on what Soleri calls "the spirit" (*A*, 4) and, thus, terminates a wasteful, "entropic" mode of being. There is a profound individual and social relationship between Soleri's "bang" which announces the "ultra–man," and the "bang" of "Sartori" which announces the awakening of the self. This is the state of containment and centeredness where the world "returns" to its original "suchness" and, hence, to its natural spiritual condition because it is no longer "beheld" through the perceptual "categories" of the early period. Like Freud, Brown, Marcuse, and Bateson, Soleri fails to tell us in his *Archology* what one is actually to *do* in the way of achieving that "point" from which the "transformation" of the individual will spring. The execution of altered awareness, by physically annulling the transitional pathology inherent in the establishment of the ordinary world, provides the person, and ultimately society, with a concrete instrument of "miniaturization," with a "Lamarckian" tool for the accomplishment of "change."

The distinctiveness of man as an animal, Soleri adds, arises largely from the interiorization of the natural environment.

> From life's position . . . the seas and the desert are antithetical. In both of these, life, made of water and voids judiciously sprinkled with other substances, has to fight for its own identity and perpetuity. In the seas, the battle . . . is to keep out the saline fluid not perfectly matching the fluids of life's own composition (they are a 'deviation' from the original broth and the naked proto–life suspended in it). In the desert, the battle is to keep in its own strictly measured and cunningly guarded fluids, an innovation whose occurrence was nothing less than the interiorization of the sea, achieved by every single organism, the actual fantastic invention of a wet, personalized universe for the advent of each individual organism (*A*, 159–161).

The interiorizing physiology developmentally precedes a second great advancement of the evolving creature—the interiorizing mind, the mind that is able, progressively, to forge the symbolic world of language, science, art, and those social or cultural achievements of an ideational or "higher" nature. But this interiorizing mind also makes it possible for an anxious, dependent infant to retain the object of the early period in its traumatizing (and partially projective) ambivalence. The helpless, big–brained baby puts its symbolic power to a defensive purpose that determines perceptually, and, hence, physiologically and emotively, the nature of its entire subsequent experience, the manner in which it will "process" the "data" that stream toward it from the universe. One takes the object in as the sea was taken in; one interiorizes to "adapt." In this way, one produces a distinct, peculiar stage in evolutional history: the transitional stage, the magical stage, the religious stage, the dual–unity stage, the stage of "identification" after the manner in which Freud employs the term in his "revolutionary" *Group Psychology*.

What is the upshot? Namely this: it is now essential to go inward again, to gather oneself together on the inside for a further adaptive "leap" away from the destructive, transitional dream and toward an enlightened tending of the planet and its inhabitants. It is essential to get away from the domination of interiorized "immortals" and toward the use of power for genuinely ameliorative ends that "tune in," as Soleri expresses it, "on the problem in its totality" (*A*, 4). Surely, when he writes that "isolation comes from division, sub–division, not from containment, self–containment" (*A*, 56) Soleri calls to our minds not only the inner division of the transitional mode, the division and internalization of the parental object from which derives the anxious, compulsive tendency to spread oneself out across the vulnerable landscape, but also the "containment" of the altered state of mind, of the detachment that closes those perceptual channels which transform a "neutral" universe into a "fantastic" arena for the rediscovery, or mastery, of the parental figure.

Chapter 10

THE DENIAL OF LIFE

Ernest Becker and the Western Existential Tradition

1.

An examination of Ernest Becker's study, *The Denial of Death,* will conclude this book because it will allow us, 1) to consider a striking alternative to the "program" set down here, 2) to focus upon certain major developments in the "western intellectual tradition," and 3) to summarize and highlight the chief lines of argument upon which the present undertaking is constructed. It is this author's contention that *The Denial of Death* embodies the dead end of a western philosophical and psychological tradition that stretches back to antiquity and the Middle Ages and forward to the world views of existentialism and Freudian psychoanalysis. Accordingly, the book should mark the final rejection and turning away from this tradition, our last and least responsive interest in it, our farewell to it and not our acceptance of it in a disguised, rationalized form. As a book, *The Denial of Death* evinces Becker's attempt to deny certain inescapable "truths" which he discovered in his own experience.

2.

The Denial of Death is characterized, among other things, by its tendency to root itself in ordinary consciousness, by its failure to see in the mode of perception the possibility of ameliorative change. Becker, like Freud and Rank, writes as if ordinary consciousness is reality, as if what is "given" in everyday awareness is itself not subject to modification, as if what we put there is somehow our destiny. Even the "relativity" of a "reality principle" as in Marcuse's *Eros and Civilization* does not go far enough if it fails to make the mode of perception *of* the "reality" an aspect of the "principle," if it does not see that the basis of perception (our ordinary consciousness) is an issue directly bound up with the question of the "real" world. *The Denial of Death* appears to owe nothing to Marcuse, or the entire phenomenological development in 20th-century philosophy. Becker writes "on top" of the problem, very much as Freud does, not recognizing the "top" as an outgrowth of tendencies implanted below in the mode of awareness.

Becker begins by announcing that his intention is to achieve what he calls the "closure of psychoanalysis on religion,"[254] and he tells us that is why he leans so heavily on Rank. Yet religion, to Becker, is not only invariably transitional religion, religion in the old sense, the "breakthrough to faith," the experience of a "higher purpose" or "meaning" when one has set "reason" or "reflection" aside in volitional commitment to the mysterium tremendum, but more, religion, to Becker, is invariably a necessary *illusion* that one *must* believe in to find his way out of that despair that perforce arises when one recognizes his condition as a fallible, mortal creature. This is done as if man's "condition," and, hence, "despair," has nothing to do with the way he perceives himself and his environment. Never is religion in Becker religion in the "mystical" sense of detachment, or the sense of achieving new modes of perception (and, hence, new awareness) at the actual physiological, biological level. Incredible as it may sound, it is Becker's recommendation that one solve his problems by choosing to believe in something that he recognizes to be false; not dubious, or unlikely, or even improbable, but false. Here is a dead end, indeed. How does he discover his way to such a remarkable proposition?

Becker's initial paragraphs deal with what we would term the compensatory, transitional goal of mastery over others, and with what he would term "the need to be a hero." His analysis derives from his discussion of sibling rivalry. "It is not that children are vicious, selfish, or domineering. It is that they so openly express man's tragic destiny [sic]: he must desperately justify himself as an object of primary value in the universe; he must stand out, be a hero, make the biggest possible contribution to world life, show that he counts more than anything or anyone else" (*DD*, 4). And then, in an analysis of money's underlying meaning: "We disguise our struggle by piling up figures in a bank book to reflect privately our sense of heroic worth" (*DD*, 4).

This brings Becker to a general characterization of what we would term the transitional aim of society as a whole:

> [It] is and always has been a symbolic action system, a structure of statuses and roles, customs and rules for behavior, designed to serve as a vehicle for earthly heroism. Each script is somewhat unique, each culture has a different hero system. What the anthropologists call 'cultural relativity' is thus really the relativity of hero systems the world over. But each cultural system is a dramatization of earthly heroics; each system cuts out roles for performances of various degrees of heroism: from the 'high' heroism of a Churchill, Mao, or Buddha, to the 'low' heroism of the coal miner, the peasant, the simple priest; the plain, everyday earthy heroism wrought by gnarled working hands guiding a family through hunger and disease. It doesn't matter whether the cultural hero–system is frankly magical, religious, and primitive or secular, scientific, and civilized. It is still a mythical hero–system in which people serve in order to earn a feeling of primary value (*DD*, 4–5).

Parenthetically, it is remarkable that Becker, in the face of these observations, fails to address himself to economic matters, systems, or the organizational root of "hunger and disease." He also fails to discuss the symbolical aims of the industrial setup, and the egotic, obsessive "need to be a hero" as it expresses itself through "structures" that actually affect the "tragic destiny" of men and women. But what prompts all this "heroism," all this transitional striving?

For Becker, it is the fear of death, the denial of our own mortality and "creatureliness," in other words, man's profound biological anxiety as rooted in the recognition of his inevitable end:

> Animals in order to survive have had to be protected by fear responses . . . As the human infant is in an even more exposed and helpless situation, it is foolish to assume that the fear response of animals would have disappeared in such a weak and highly sensitive species. It is more reasonable to think that it was instead heightened . . . The result was the emergence of man as we know him: a hyperanxious animal (*DD*, 17).

Thus, "the fear of death must be present behind all our normal functioning, in order for the organism to be armed toward self–preservation" (*DD*, 16). A distinction must be made here immediately between what can be called the "animal fear" and "symbolical fear" of death. The question of "self–preservation" has considerably more to do with the former than with the latter.

Certainly the "fear of death" may be discovered everywhere in the human world, as Becker says. But the death that means death to people is, as was demonstrated previously (Chapter Two), always apprehended by them both as a reality and as a symbol. The symbolical fear of death commences when the human organism begins to associate cessation and annihilation with the anxieties he experiences during the course of his development as an infant, his first relationships with other people and events, and particularly with the mother and with the nature of her personality and the quality of her care. As known in ordinary symbolical awareness, the fear of death is integrally concerned with the internalizations of the early time, with the taking in of, what has come to be termed, the "bad object" and the persistent presence of that object at the deep levels of one's character—the levels from which the symbolic capacity derives. Death in the unconscious, notes Rheingold, is a "catastrophic concept" that "originates in certain experiences very early in life." It contains the concepts of "sudden annihilation, torture, painful punishment, desertion" being "overwhelmed by an irresistable force that crushes out life," "rejection, loss of love, powerlessness, and helplessness." To the fully "developed" person, it frequently suggests "the satisfaction of genital longings whether heterosexual or homosexual," "incest," and/or "the return to the womb."[255] The point is, when Becker, himself, observes that death is a "complex symbol" and even underlines those words (*DD*, 19), he invites the realization that the fear of death for humans may have something important to do with the mode of their perception of the problem, i.e. the way they regard it. With the tie to the internalized object severed, and the individual detached from the symbolical universe, the fear of death resumes its identity as precisely an animal fear; it is naturally "there" as a kind of special alertness, a hypersensitivity to danger, and even as a profound, integrated consciousness of aging and mortality. This "process" is registered at all levels of the organism. It is not, however, "loaded" in the way in which it is "loaded" in Becker's book; it is not to be "faced" as a "terrible dilemma" (*DD*, 26–27) but naturally experienced as a biological phenomenon, always present to one's total, animal existence. There is no "denial of death" in this. On the contrary, there is an attempt to desymbolify death and, in doing so, discover and confront its reality as a natural event, to move away from death as a "complex symbol" and toward it as the inevitable biological occurrence that it is. It was when death became mixed up with the proclivity of a symbol–making brain to answer defensively the anxieties of its early experience by internalizing the "bad" features of its environment that the fear of death—in all its unconscious, "sublimated" forms—became such a devastating problem for the evolving human creature. The catastrophic denial, from both the social and evolutionary standpoint, is the denial that there are other modes of consciousness beside the one to which man so neurotically and obsessively clings.

3.

Because he "denies his death," "creatureliness," and "mortality," the individual lives in what Becker calls the Vital Lie:

> Man is literally split in two: he has an awareness of his own splendid uniqueness in that he sticks out of nature with a towering majesty, and yet he goes back into the ground a few feet in order [sic] blindly and dumbly to rot and disappear forever. It is a terrifying dilemma to be in and to have to live with . . . Who wants to face up fully to the creatures we are, clawing and gasping for breath in a universe beyond our ken? I think such events illustrate the meaning of Pascal's chilling reflection: 'Men are so necessarily mad that not to be mad would amount to another form of madness.' Necessarily because the existential dualism makes an impossible situation, an excrutiating dilemma. Mad because . . . everything that man does in his symbolic world is an attempt to deny and overcome his grotesque fate. He literally drives himself into a blind obliviousness with social games, psychological tricks, personal preoccupations so far removed from the reality of his situation that they are forms of madness. 'Character traits,' said Ferenezi, 'are secret psychoses,' . . . masks that people use to bluff the world and themselves (*DD*, 26–27).

Once again, and without dwelling excessively on the point, Becker is describing individuals squarely within ordinary consciousness, and the transitional mode of awareness, living out their symbolical "preoccupations." It is not fated that they stay tied to their infantile internalizations, to their biological fears as they have come to be bound up with their early, negative experiences. The "split" in "man," to which Becker refers, is best regarded as the defensive splitting of infancy and childhood, the defensive splitting that is "inherited" by a dualistic mentation, by an ability to retain information along symbolical lines and, thereby, to forge a subjective position in which one has the illusion of looking out at a terrifying world rather than taking up his natural, biological place *in* it, and that includes its propensity to change and to decay. It is because he cannot discover a way out of this psychological creation of his own that "man" is "tormented."

Becker writes, "what bothers people is really incongruity, life as it is" (*DD,* 34). Thus a philosophical door is shut firmly upon us. Life in the symbolic mode of consiousness, or in the deep, emotive connection to the internalization of the early period, is not what is. There is a "reality," however, presumably some type of objective one, that people are afraid of seeing. In order to see it, they must leave their "symbolic world"—the world where "everything they do" is "an attempt to deny" their "grotesque fate" (*DD,* 26). But is not the world that people will "see" after they have abandoned their symbolic activity also a world that is explicitly perceived through the symbolical channel? After all, Becker has not told us how one perceives a universe that is not vitiated by "symbols" while one remains in the "normal," symbolic mode of awareness. There is not a word in *The Denial of Death* regarding the nature of perception out of the symbolical framework, let alone the methods required to get out of it. Is it not clear that the "grotesque" universe into which Becker stares after he has "faced up" is really the same universe into which he has been staring all along? The "grotesqueness" itself, the "clawing" and the "gasping," is a symbolical "event" derived from the same world from which "men's" ordinary symbolical "preoccupations" are derived. A conclusion opposite to the one Becker reaches when he writes of seeing the world "as it is" would, in fact, be more in keeping with the conditions of his contextual position. When the symbolic games are over they are over, and that includes the symbolic games about "clawing" and "gasping." When the universe is seen "as it is," it is; it is simply there.

Becker's despair and defeatism are found throughout the book. One example occurs just after he has sealed man's philosophical fate by describing what "really is." He writes,

> The child comes upon a world in which he could just as well have
> been born male or female, even dog, cat, or fish—for all that it
> seems to matter as regards power and control, capacity to withstand
> pain, annihilation, and death. The horror of sexual differentiation is
> a horror of 'biological fact' . . . It is a fall out of illusion into
> sobering reality. It is a horror of assuming an immense new burden,
> the burden of the meaning of life and the body, of the fatality of
> one's incompleteness, his helplessness, his finitude (DD, 41).

What must be stressed is that such a depiction, no matter how
accurate it is, does not capture for Becker a stage of awareness with
respect either to the individual or to the species. It captures, rather,
some type of "reality" where the evolution of "man" as a perceiving animal making "realities" through his mode of awareness
comes to a final, irreversible halt. For "it can't be overstressed,"
declares Becker, "that to see the world as it really is [sic] is
devastating and terrifying" (DD, 60). We are returned in this way
to Becker's earlier point that "character traits" are "necessary lies"
and that to exist in the world without them would invite "full and
open psychosis."

What he misses with this point, although he appears to stand
upon the verge of it, is that character traits, being defensive, are
not merely an aspect of ordinary consciousness but constitute a
variety of symbols themselves. They are natural symbols, to
borrow Mary Douglas' expression, in which the body discloses the
manner of its sustenance in the world,[256] as well as its means of
communicating how it chooses to deal with its internal and external environments. Hence, the study of "bodily techniques," the
"character traits" of Ferenczi and Becker, must "take place within
a study of symbolic systems"[257] if those "techniques" are to reveal
their underlying significance. The solution to the problem of
character, and there is a solution despite Becker's gloomy assertions, is to re–enter the realm of one's internalizations, confront
the "reality" of one's separation anxiety (the general catalyst of all
"character traits"), strive to heal one's inner "split" through bodily
methods that relax one's defenses, and return to the world more
securely anchored in the self that existed previously behind the

"armor." The alternative to "character" is not, as Becker says, "psychosis," but detachment from the objects of the inner world. This reveals another aspect of Becker's inadequate psychology: the isolation, or "madness" of psychosis does not consist in a detachment from the object but in an absorption into the bad object, the object that negates and threatens, the object that infuses the "character" with the rejective, malignant "no."[258] It is when one's defenses fail, not when one's defenses go, that "psychosis" occurs. "At times of trauma, loss, disappointment or perplexity," writes Aronson, "the psyche turns toward that set of structures which had been prepared early in the separation–individuation phase." There is a "hypercathexis of . . . early modulating and regulating functions." When the psychotic turns toward his "defensive" world, however, he discovers a negative presence, and it is that which makes grievous mental disorder so "refractory." Aronson continues, "what is cathected is a chamber of horrors, the 'regulatory' and 'soothing' devices a heedless evolution had sculpted into a psychic structure."[259] Thus, detachment in the good sense—in the sense of removing the pathogenic influence by altering the body and hence the awareness into which the internalization made its way—comprises an alternative at the symbolical level to the symbolical dilemma ("character") in which Becker fixes "man." For this reason, as was indicated toward the inception of this chapter, such detachment has explicit communicative, evolutionary meaning. Although death may be a "reality" and even a "fate," the "grotesque" is a symbol, symptom, and stage. Death and the grotesque are not intrinsically related.

4.

Kierkegaard, for Becker, was not merely a thinker far ahead of his time but an anticipator of "modern" theories of mental illness. Kierkegaard recognized that man's deep trouble lay in his effort to "deny reality, overvalue the powers of the symbolic self," and "put aside the facts" of his animal existence (*DD*, 76). "Too much possibility . . . reflects the attempt to exaggerate one half of the human dualism at the expense of the other. In this sense, what we call schizophrenia is an attempt by the symbolic self to deny the limitations of the finite body; in doing so the entire person is pulled off balance and destroyed" (*DD*, 76). And again,

> the person becomes sick by plunging into the limitless; the symbolic self becomes 'fantastic'—as it does in schizophrenia—when it splits away from the body, from a dependable grounding in real experience in the everyday world. The full–blown schizophrenic is abstract, ethereal, unreal; he . . . floats out of his body, dwells in an eternal now, and is not subject to death and destruction (*DD*, 76).

Kierkegaard's solution to this dilemma, or "sickness," was to confront the truth of one's condition in the world. It is the "normal," "cultural" man who is "sick" (*DD*, 86), and he will not get better until he gets worse. It is only after one has "thrown aside" his "cultural lendings" and, like Lear, stood "naked in the storm of life" (*DD*, 86) that the problem of religious faith or "transcendence" receives an opportunity to enter the "existential" picture.

Striking, indeed arresting in all of this, is both Kierkegaard's and Becker's paucity of method. How does one get free of his "normal" defenses, disturbance, character, and the "lendings" of his cultural, psychological development? When Becker writes, following Kierkegaard's cue, that "education for man means facing up to his natural impotence and death," to the task of "unlearning" his "repression," (*DD*, 88), and when he insists that one "destroy the vital lie of character" (*DD*, 88) and "face up to the anxiety of the terror of existence" (*DD*, 89), he only leaves man flailing helplessly in the grip of his emotional life. Kierkegaard did likewise. Becker writes as if the unconscious had no dynamic power, as if one's "defenses" were not rooted in one's very body, one's very senses. Kierkegaard's "program" has, of course, an identical limitation. What exactly does all this "facing up" mean? What does it mean with reference to the manner in which the "sick" organism is to alter its perception of "the data," or "information" it receives from both without and within? What does it mean with reference to the whole weight of one's past life? Such "facing up" can only breed a kind of stoicism, an illusory belief in one's "growth" and "change," in other words, more character. It is astonishing that Becker could offer "facing up" as a solution in a book that deals explicitly with Freud.

5.

Beneath Freud's stoical exterior, says Becker, there was an enormous and persistent fear of death. Indeed, Freud represents for Becker a kind of fascinating contradiction, denying death unconsciously on one hand, yet striving consciously to face it without flinching on the other. Freud is tempted to indulge his religious inclinations as defense against the dread of cessation, yet attacks and exposes "religion" and "the occult" as infantile, illusory refusals to "face up." The group psychology of Freud, which demonstrates man's capacity for transference relations, man's urge to "escape reality" by "identifying" with something greater and higher than himself, constitutes Freud's greatest contribution to understanding man. It discloses man's fundamental predicament, his contradiction—his underlying sense of his own helplessness and mortality and need to deny this by wedding himself to what is, or seems to be, all–powerful and timeless. Becker writes,

> [Freud] was haunted by death anxiety all his life and admitted that not a day went by that he did not think about it . . . He especially feared dying before his mother because he was afraid at the thought that she might have to hear of his death . . . What are we to make of . . . this? I think it is a fairly routine and superficial way of handling the problem of death . . . Instead of experiencing the stark terror of losing oneself as a disappearing object, one clings to the image of someone else (*DD*, 102–103).

In such "displacement" and "clinging" we have an expression of what Becker calls the transference and what we would call the transitional mode of behavior.

> [Man] is not just a naturally and lustily destructive animal who lays waste around him because he feels omnipotent and impregnable. Rather, he is a trembling animal who pulls the world down around his shoulders as he clutches for protection and support and tries to affirm in a cowardly way his feeble powers. The qualities of the leader . . . and the problems of people fit together in a natural symbiosis . . . the powers of the leader stem from what he can do for the people, beyond the magic he himself possesses. People project their problems onto him, which gives him his role and stature. Leaders need followers as much as they are needed by them: the leader projects onto his followers his own inability to stand alone (*DD*, 139).

And then, "transference is not a matter of unusual cowardice but rather of the basic problems of organismic life, problems of power and control" (*DD*, 143). It is of "life itself" that one is afraid; the "human condition is just too much; . . . it is overwhelming" (*DD*, 145). Now, it is precisely here, in the face of this "dilemma," in the face of this need for transference relations, that one reaches the heart of Becker's discussion, the sections devoted to Rank.

Rank differed from Freud in many respects, writes Becker, but chiefly in his attitude toward religion. Where Freud viewed religion as regression, superstition, escape, neurosis, Rank saw in it a necessary dimension of mankind's effort to cope with its basic, impossible predicament. "The only way out of human conflict is full renunciation, to give one's life as a gift to the highest powers . . . Man is a 'theological being' and not a biological one . . . The neurotic opts out of life because he is having trouble maintaining his illusions about it" (*DD*, 173, 175, 189). In this way, "the question for the science of mental health must become an absolutely new and revolutionary one, yet one that reflects the essence of the human condition: On what level of illusion does one live?" (*DD*, 189). At this juncture, one could ask, can Becker be serious? Is mankind to "face up" to the "truth" of its "condition" on the one hand and, on the other, ignore that "truth" by choosing to live out an "illusion," by believing in something one knows to be false? When Becker writes, "it begins to look as though modern man cannot find his heroism in everyday life any more . . . He needs revolutions and wars. . . . That is the price modern man pays for the eclipse of the sacred dimension" (*DD*, 190), it begins to look as though he *is* asking the reader to do this. Let us resolve the issue by looking further into Becker's discussion.

First, there is the categorical statement, derived from Rank and set forth by Becker as a key to the new, "revolutionary" psychiatry: "With the truth one cannot live" (*DD*, 188). Second, and equally remarkable, is the following:

> Neurosis is the contriving of private obsessional ritual to replace the socially agreed one now lost by the demise of traditional society. The customs and myths of traditional society provided a whole interpretation of the meaning of life, ready–made for the individual; all he had to do was accept living it as true. The modern neurotic *must do just this* if he is to be 'cured': *he must welcome a living illusion* (*DD*, 199, my emphasis).

Again, we have Becker declaring, "We said earlier that the question of human life is: on what level of illusion does one live. This question poses an absolutely new question for the science of mental health, namely: What is the *best* illusion under which to live?" (*DD*, 202) And finally, in what must surely be the most confused sentence Becker ever wrote, "What is the ideal for mental health, then? A lived, compelling illusion that does not lie about life, death, and reality" (*DD*, 204). Such remarks ultimately reveal the pathetic dead end of a western philosophical, psychological tradition that has death, defeat, and absurdity at its core and that refuses simply to "face up" to *its* "condition," to live it out, and to stop looking for an escape from the very trap it has fashioned. Becker attacks the "illusions" of "man" for 200 pages and then offers "man" as a solution to the "despair" bred of his "real" condition that he choose to believe in what he knows to be an illusion, in fact, decide coolly which illusion is "best" for him, and then take it up.

When Becker asserts that Kierkegaard and Rank "join" in this psychological "closure" (*DD*, 174) he not only misleads the reader, but misunderstands the problem. Kierkegaard's answer to the "sickness" of "man" is a non–rational one and depends on the person's ability to actually give up reason and achieve a kind of mystical transcendence, a transcendence that becomes a "solution." One does not choose faith in the sense that Becker asks us to choose the "best illusion," or in the sense that he recommends "illusion" as a "therapy" for the disturbed. Kierkegaard was writing about salvation, the feeling that one has been saved, the "real thing," and not about an "illusion" that serves a useful purpose, either for oneself or for others. There is simply *no* connection at all between Kierkegaard and Rank except in the subject matter they treat, with the modern "theologian," Rank, offering the rational version the living faith to which Kierkegaard turned in the traditional Christian manner of Augustine, Teresa, and St. John. Indeed, Kierkegaard's preoccupation with the inadequacy of reason, the mentation of the "ordinary" man, and the transcendental "leap" marks his peculiar, groping attempt to urge the individual toward an alteration of awareness, a new, living consciousness, a sensorial breakthrough. Lacking familiarity with the psychoanalytic and phenomenological problems which surround the development of ordinary awareness at the neurophysiological level, however, Kierkegaard was unable to offer mankind concrete methodological recommendations for change, the kind of recommendations which, at the intuitive level, have come to be an aspect of religious transformation in the east. Becker and Rank, by contrast, come to their conclusions through the intellect alone; their entire project, in fact, comprises the triumph of reason, a triumph that is finally a defeat in that it fails to deal with the problem of genuine religious faith and, therefore, furthers the elevation of the ego—the symbol, and the transitional mode of existence. Surely Becker is not suggesting that all men "get saved" in the old religious sense; he's not preaching, he's reasoning. Yet, to repeat, that is precisely what Kierkegaard is suggesting. What makes Kierkegaard so special is the unique direction from which he comes to the old conclusion, matters of methodology excepted. What Becker is suggesting comes through his very words and makes itself clear enough:

"Mental health is a problem of ideal illusion" (*DD*, 205). "Ideally," it is "a freely chosen dependency" (*DD*, 206).

Of course there is nothing mentioned in Becker as to how one goes about making his "chosen" illusions work other than 1) "facing up," the serious methodological limitations of which we have already mentioned, and 2) following the "therapeutic" advice that one must choose. Thus, one must give up the "truth" he has gained by "facing up" to the "truth," for "with the truth one cannot live" (*DD*, 188). The despair of *The Denial of Death* originates in this sad, paradoxical muddle. For surely Becker realized, at some level, that his "plan" was either ridiculous or authoritarian, with the "doctors" pinning the "illusions" onto the "neurotics." Surely, *Becker* was not able to believe in "illusions." In a hugely ironic way, *The Denial of Death* only affirms Freud's trenchant analysis of "religion" in *The Future of an Illusion* ("illusion" being, of course, a key term in Becker's discussion). One can easily imagine Freud saying, "Well, here it is, the old illusion again, but now, of all things, we have a psychoanalytic writer recommending it to us! We're supposed to choose it, like pragmatists."

It is no surprise, in the face of all this, that Becker's writing becomes truly passionate when he is describing the absurd world "as it really is." Through those passages Becker's deepest convictions emerge: "The tragedy of man's dualism, his ludicrous situation, becomes too real. The anus and its incomprehensible, repulsive product represents not only physical determinism and boundness, but the fate as well of all that is physical: decay and death" (*DD*, 31). In another section: "We are witness to the new cult of sensuality . . . Its aim is to deny one's lack of control over events, his powerlessness, his vagueness as a person in a mechanical world spinning into decay and death" (*DD*, 84). No "illusions" are going to obscure Becker's vision, that world which is "spinning into decay and death." Finally,

> What are we to make of a creation in which the routine activity is for organisms to be tearing others apart with teeth of all types—biting, grinding flesh, plant stalks, bones between molars, pushing the pulp

greedily down the gullet with delight, incorporating its essence into one's own organization, and then excreting with foul stench and gasses the residue. Everyone reaching out to incorporate others who are edible to him. The mosquitos bloating themselves on blood, the maggots, the killer–bees. . . . the soberest conclusion that we could make about what has actually been taking place on the planet for about three billion years is that it is being turned into a vast pit of fertilizer (*DD*, 282–283).

This is, without doubt, the most fervent passage in Becker's book; it attests to the "knowledge" beneath the "illusion"; it comes after the passage about choosing the best "story" in which to believe. For those who are not going to be "saved" in Kierkegaard's sense (in the old, genuine sense of actual conversion) this is what is left—the choice between the fertilizer pit and the "illusion" one likes "best" (or that somebody else thinks is "best"). Is Becker attempting to "save" mankind paternally by suggesting that it is all right to indulge in "illusions" while he carries the weight of "reality?"

6.

When Becker writes that "to live is to play" (*DD*, 201), and stresses the need of individuals to rediscover their sense of adventure, creation, and mystery, he fails to recognize that ordinary consciousness itself impedes such development by breeding the transitional view of the world, by sustaining the emotive attachments to symbol and "character," by reactivating an underlying anxiety over separation, and in short, by preserving those very "truths" with which "we cannot live" (*DD*, 188). Creative play in the highest sense, as was affirmed in the chapter on Marcuse, springs directly from the ability to put off one's world of symbols, sever the emotive, perceptual tie to the inner world, and relinquish one's ordinary, "workaday" awareness. What Becker takes to be a problem of "life" (*DD*, 145) is ultimately a problem of perception. How does one perceive the world in the deepest, widest emotive and ideational sense? Although "illusions" will not work because they are not real, and "salvation" in the old sense may mark a graver disturbance than the "sickness" of the "ordinary" man, the alteration of consciousness can prove beneficial in that it actually modifies the perceptual apparatus and, hence, the projective orientation toward the world. It cannot be overemphasized that Becker's "illusion," a term with perceptual overtones, offers no method whatsoever for affecting "changes" within man. We are told implicitly to remain in the same mode of symbolical sight, with the same tense body (which is a function of that mode) and, at the same time, to "get an illusion," that will help us to "get better." To put the entire matter in another, perhaps more striking way, there is nothing in *The Denial of Death* that allows us to find a solution to the problem of the transference relation. This is a problem with obvious perceptual significance. Not only does Becker take the transference to be an inescapable and universal mode of contact with the universe—an assumption that is analytically and philosophically unwarranted—he offers us in "illusion" a solution to the "dilemma" that derives its chief power from the preservation of the transference relationship itself. Indeed, the "best" illusion is the "best" manipulation of the person's transference proclivities, either by himself through "facing up" or by the current "mental healers." Can anyone be secure with such a scheme? Instead of *changing* individuals, particularly where their passions are concerned, we merely redirect them in the precarious belief that we know "best."

Contemporary men and women are not facing the old choices of character, psychosis, illusion, and salvation—the choices that emerge from Becker's work. They have within reach a method of detachment that can mitigate the transference or transitional mode of awareness, which can put them in control of the symbolical world rather than the other way around, and which, most of all, can contribute to their growth and evolution as members of the remarkable human species. Becker's book ultimately depicts not the denial of death but the denial of life—new, evolving, communicating life, that is no longer in the service of the "immortal" internalizations, or "processing the data" in the old, transitional way. And indeed, to have a method, an actual, understandable, physical method of disrupting the powerful union between symbolic capacity and separation anxiety, to have a method through which to escape the transitional bias of our present–day organization as animals, can only be regarded as the greatest possible luck. We must put that method to the greatest possible use. In their *Sacrifice* Hubert and Mauss write that the sacrificial action, which comprises the essence of transitional religion, is designed ultimately to nourish "the eternal life of the species."[260] When we recall that the sacrifical victim is projectively a version of the internalized object, and further, that altered awareness, a non–transitional "religious" condition, is firmly based in an organismic detachment from the internalized object of infancy, we see the direction from which religion and evolution meet. It is precisely in giving up the emotive tie to the inner world that the transcendence of ordinary religion is accomplished. From an evolutionary angle, religion does not consist in transference "illusions" but in the attainment of man's highest perceptual and spiritual potentials, potentials which, in their social application, harbor the possibility of diminishing the dangerous, pathogenic inequities to which Marx so tellingly referred as the "old crap." The alteration of awareness, although it may not be able to ensure the "eternal life" of the species, may well be able to make more feasible the species' continued existence.

As perceivers, we must strive to understand as completely as we can the psychodynamic forces that have produced our ordinary consciousness. Additionally, we must work to fully understand the methods by which deleterious, pathogenic materials can be removed from the perceptual life of the organism as a whole, not merely from the "mind," as if it dwelt apart from the body. What psychoanalysis has long relegated to the periphery of its concern, namely mysticism, the occult, the desire and the need to alter one's awareness, must be brought to the center. Such developments can provide enormous advantages to the inhabitants of a troubled world.

NOTES

[1]Roheim, Geza. *The Origin and Function of Culture*. New York: Anchor Books, 1971, pp. 122, 131.

[2]Lidz, Ruth W. and Lidz, Theodore. "Male Menstruation: A Ritual Alternative to Oedipal Transition." *International Journal of Psychoanalysis*, Vol. 58, 1977, p. 28.

[3]Roheim develops this concept at length in *Gates of the Dream*, New York: International Universities Press, 1970. Pages 595 and following provide a useful summary.

[4]Freud, Sigmund. *Civilization and Its Discontents*. Trans. Joan Riviere. London: The Hogarth Press, 1975, p. 9. Further references to this work will appear in the text with abbreviation *CD* and page number.

[5]For a particularly vivid exemplification of the key role of separation anxiety in infancy and childhood, and its relation to the mothering figure, see Bettleheim, Bruno. *The Uses of Enchantment*. New York: Vintage Books, 1977, pp. 145, 159.

[6]Freud, Sigmund. *The Future of an Illusion*. Trans. W. D. Robson–Scott. New York: Anchor Books, 1953, p. 4. Further references to this work will appear in the text with abbreviation *FI* and page number.

[7]Piaget, Jean. *Six Psychological Studies*. Trans. Anita Tenzer. New York: Vintage Books, 1967, p. 9.

[8]Ornstein, Robert E. *The Psychology of Consciousness*. San Francisco: W. H. Freeman and Co., 1972, pp. 42–43.

[9]At times in reading Freud, one senses his ability to see psychological issues tied

to the development of ordinary awareness; one senses, in fact, his closeness to the whole matter. For example, in "The Unconscious" (1915) he notes that ideas themselves are not simply perceptions but "libidinal cathexes" (*Collected Papers*. Trans. Joan Riviere. London: The Hogarth Press, 1971, Vol. IV, p. 111). In *Beyond the Pleasure Principle* (1920) he speculates on the projective nature of temporal apprehension, something to which we will turn our attention later (Trans. James Strachey. New York: Bantam Books, 1959, pp. 54–55). Yet the link is never made between 1) the idea; 2) the development of the time sense; 3) the relationship of projection to internalization; and, 4) the specific psychological issues arising from the mother–infant interaction, the interaction that transpires *as* the ability to have ideas and *as* the time sense develop.

[10]Brown, Norman O. *Life Against Death*. New York: Vintage Books, 1959, p. xiii. Further references to this work will appear in the text with the abbreviation *LAD* and page number.

[11]Gruen, Arno. "The Discontinuity in the Ontogeny of Self." *The Psychoanalytic Review*, Vol. 61, 1974–1975, pp. 561–562.

[12]Marshall, Perry H. "Developmental and Restitutive Aspects of 'Imaging.' " Presented to the *Seattle Psychoanalytic Society*, December, 1976.

[13]Marcuse, Herbert. *Eros and Civilization*. New York: Vintage Books, 1955, p. 7. Further references to this work will appear in the text with the abbreviation *EC* followed by the page number.

[14]For the Freud of *Moses and Monotheism* matriarchy is a secondary development sandwiched, as it were, between the early and late patriarchal stages. Marcuse takes issue with this on page 59 of *Eros and Civilization*. In this respect, both Brown and Marcuse are closer to Reich than Freud. For Reich, patriarchy was the evil of evils, and a return to matriarchy the answer to just about everything. See Reich, Wilhelm. *The Mass Psychology of Fascism*. Trans. Theodore P. Wolfe. New York: Orgone Institute Press, 1946, pp. 73 ff.

[15]Becker, Ernest. *The Denial of Death*. New York: The Free Press, 1973, pp. 131–132.

[16]Freud, Sigmund. *Group Psychology and the Analysis of the Ego* (1921). The Standard Edition, Vol. 18, 1955, p. 70. Further references to this work will appear in the text with the abbreviation *GP* followed by page number.

[17]See Slater, Philip E. *Microcosm: Structural, Psychological, and Religious Evolution in Groups*. New York: John Wiley and Sons, 1966.

[18]Freud, Sigmund. "The Defence Neuro–Psychoses." *Collected Papers*. Ed. Joan Riviere. New York: Basic Books, Inc., 1959, Vol. I, p. 63.

[19]Ibid.

[20]Freud, Sigmund. "Organic and Hysterical Paralyses." *Collected Papers. Ed. cit.*, Vol. I, p. 49.

[21]Freud, Sigmund. "The Defence Neuro–Psychoses." *Collected Papers. Ed. cit.*, Vol. I, p. 63.

[22]Mushatt, Cecil. "Mind–Body–Environment: Toward Understanding the Impact of Loss on Psyche and Soma." *The Psychoanalytic Quarterly,* Vol. 44, 1975, p. 85.

[22a]Ibid., p. 86.

[23]Freud, Sigmund. "The Defence Neuro–Psychoses." *Collected Papers,* Vol. I, p. 163.

[24]Rank, Otto. *The Trauma of Birth.* London: Kegan, Paul, 1929, p. 57.

[25]Grof, Stanislav. *Realms of the Human Unconscious.* New York: E. P. Dutton and Co., Inc., 1976, pp. 56–60, 95–96, 117.

[26]Leboyer, Frederick. *Birth Without Violence.* New York: Alfred A. Knopf, 1975, p. 15.

[27]Ibid., pp. 17–18.

[28]Ibid., p. 18.

[29]Ibid., pp. 24–28.

[30]Ibid., p. 19.

[31]Freud, Sigmund. "An Outline of Psychoanalysis." *The Standard Edition. Ed. James Strachey,* Vol. 23, 1964, p. 205.

[32]Rheingold, Joseph C. *The Fear of Being a Woman.* New York: Grune and Stratton, Inc., 1964, p. 30.

[33]Ibid., p. 31.

[34]Ibid., p. 162.

[35]Searles, Harold F. *Collected Papers on Schizophrenia and Related Subjects.* New York: International Universities Press, 1965, pp. 224–225.

[36]Rheingold, Joseph C. *The Fear of Being a Woman.* New York: Grune and Stratton, Inc., 1964, p. 148.

[37]Neumann, Erich. *The Great Mother.* Princeton, N.J.: Princeton University Press, 1970, pp. 148–149.

[38]Mushatt, pp. 86–88.

[39]Ibid., p. 89. My emphasis.

[40]Ibid., p. 90.

[41]Ibid., p. 91.

[42]Ibid., p. 93.

[43]Gruen, Arno. "The Discontinuity in the Ontogeny of Self." *The Psychoanalytic Review,* Vol. 61, 1974–1975, p. 560.

[44]Ibid., p. 561.

[45]Ibid.

[46]Ibid., p. 562.

[47]Winnicott, D. W. "The Location of Cultural Experience." *The International Journal of Psychoanalysis,* Vol. 48, 1966, p. 371.

[48]Bleich, David. "New Considerations of the Infantile Acquisition of Language and Symbolic Thought." Presented to the *Psychological Center for the Study of the Arts,* State University of New York, Buffalo, 1970, pp. 8–9.

[49]Ibid., p. 9.

[50]Ibid., p. 10.

[51]Gruen, p. 563.

[52]Siomopoulos, Gregory. "Poetry as Effective Communication." *Psychoanalytic Quarterly,* Vol. 46, 1977, p. 508.

[53]Roheim, Geza. *"Magic and Schizophrenia.* Bloomington: Indiana University Press, 1962, p. 203.

[54]Ibid., p. 169.

[55]Roth, David and Blatt, Sidney J. "Spatial Representations and Psychopathology." *Journal of the American Psychoanalytic Association,* Vol. 22, 1974, p. 871.

[56]Bachelard, Gaston. *The Poetics of Space.* Boston: The Beacon Press, 1969, p. 5.

[57]James, William. *The Principles of Psychology.* New York: Henry Holt and Co., 1890, Vol. I, p. 620.

[58]See Flavell, J. H. *The Developmental Psychology of Jean Piaget.* Princeton: Van Nostrand, 1963, pp. 317–318.

[59]See Dupont, M. A. "A Provisional Contribution to the Psychoanalytical Study of Time." *International Journal of Psycho–Analysis,* Vol. 55, 1974, p. 483.

[60]Ibid.

[61]See Hartocollis, Peter. "Origins of Time." *The Psychoanalytic Quarterly,* Vol. 43, 1974, p. 248.

[62]Ibid., p. 250.

[63]Ibid., pp. 252–253.

[64]Dorpat, T. L. "Internalization of the Patient–Analyst Relationship in Patients with Narcissistic Disorders." *International Journal of Psycho–Analysis,* Vol. 55, 1974, p. 185.

[65]Hartocollis, p. 254.

[66]Piaget, Jean. *Six Psychological Studies.* Trans. Anita Tenzer. New York: Vintage Books, 1968, pp. 13–17.

[67]Ibid., p. 17. Piaget insists here on the connection between ideational maturation and "affect."

[68]Lee, Dorothy. "Codifications of Reality: Lineal and Nonlineal." *The Nature of Human Consciousness.* Ed. Ornstein, Robert E. San Francisco: W. H. Freeman and Co., 1973, p. 128.

[69]Ibid., p. 131.

[70]Ibid., pp. 133–134.

[71]Ibid., pp. 138–141.

[72]Ibid., p. 141.

[73]Ibid., p. 142.

[74]Aronson, Gerald. "Defense and Deficit Models: Their Influence on the Therapy

of Schizophrenia." *International Journal of Psycho–Analysis,* Vol. 58, 1977, pp. 11–16.

[75]See Horton, Paul C. "The Mystical Experience." Journal of the *American Psychoanalytic Association,* Vol. 22, 1974, pp. 372–379. See also Prince, Raymond, and Savage, Charles. "Mystical States and the Concept of Regression." *The Highest State of Consciousness.* Ed. White, John. New York: Anchor Books, 1972, pp. 114–134; Podvoll, E. "Psychosis and the Mystic Path." *Psychoanalytic Review,* Vol. 66 (1980), pp. 571–590.

[76]James, William. *The Varieties of Religious Experience.* New York: The New American Library, 1958, p. 304.

[77]Ibid., pp. 304, 311.

[78]Ibid., p. 312.

[79]Ibid., p. 296.

[80]See Ellis, Havelock. "Mescal: A New Artificial Paradise." *The Drug Experience.* Ed. David Ebin. New York: The Grove Press, 1961, pp. 225–236. Mayhew, Christopher. "Peyote." *The Drug Experience. Ed. Cit.,* pp. 293–306.

[81]Huxley, Aldous. *The Doors of Perception.* London: Penguin Books, 1974, pp. 16–17.

[82]Ibid., pp. 17–18.

[83]Ibid., pp. 20–21.

[84]Ibid., pp. 25–26.

[85]Ibid., p. 23.

[86]Kleitman, Nathanial. "Patterns of Dreaming." *Altered States of Awareness,* Ed. Timothy J. Teyler. San Francisco: W. H. Freeman and Co., 1972, p. 49.

[87]Neisser, Ulric. "The Processes of Vision." In *The Nature of Human Consciousness,* Ed. Cit., p. 205.

[88]Castaneda, Carlos. *Tales of Power.* New York: Simon and Schuster, 1974, p. 205.

[89]Quoted in Laura Huxley's *This Timeless Moment.* New York: Ballantine Books, 1971, p. 132.

[90]See Eisendrath, C. R. *The Unifying Moment: The Psychological Philosophy of William James and Alfred North Whitehead.* Cambridge, Mass.: Harvard University Press, 1971, pp. 143, 264.

[91]See Bonaparte, Marie. "Time and the Unconscious." *International Journal of Psycho–Analysis,* Vol. 21, 1940, p. 467. The quotation of Freud appears as a footnote in this paper and was written specifically for it.

[92]Deikman, Arthur J. "Deautomatization and the Mystic Experience." In *The Nature of Human Consciousness. Ed. Cit.,* pp. 227–228.

[93]Eccles, John C. "The Physiology of Imagination." *Altered States of Awareness. Ed. Cit.,* p. 39.

[94]Jacobson, Edith. *The Self and the Object World* (1954). *The Psychoanalytic Study of the Child.* New York: International Universities Press, Vol. 9, p. 91.

[95]Suzuki, Shunryu. *Zen Mind, Beginner's Mind.* New York: John Weatherhill, Inc., 1973, pp. 128–129.

[96]See note 91.

[97]See Horton. (note 75)

[98]See Laura Huxley. *This Timeless Moment. Ed. Cit.,* p. 126. The phrase I am using in my text is Aldous Huxley's, as quoted by his wife.

[99]Huxley, Aldous. *The Perennial Philosophy.* New York: Harper and Row, 1970, p. 134.

[100]Mushatt, p. 85.

[101]Gruen, p. 561.

[102]Mushatt, p. 86.

[103]Ornstein, Robert E. and Naranjo, Claudio. *On the Psychology of Meditation.* New York: The Viking Press, 1972, p. 169. The quotation is from Ornstein's section of the book.

[104]Deikman, p. 225.

[105]See Heron, Woodburn. "The Pathology of Boredom." *Altered States of Awareness,* Ed. Cit., p. 76.

[106]Dicara, Leo V. "Learning in the Autonomic Nervous System." In *Altered States of Awareness,* p. 76.

[107]Ibid., p. 79.

[108]Ibid., p. 74.

[109]Kohler, Ivo. "Experiments with Goggles." In *Altered States of Awareness. Ed. Cit.,* p. 108.

[110]Ibid.

[111]Bertalanffy, Ludwig von. *Problems of Life.* New York: Wiley, 1952, p. 134.

[112]Slotkin, J. S. "Menomini Peyotism." In *The Drug Experience, Ed. Cit.,* pp. 237–269.

[113]Shah, Indries. "Mysteries in the West." In *The Nature of Human Consciousness,* p. 280.

[114]All the examples cited in this paragraph are from Lecture XVI.

[115]James, William. *The Varieties of Religious Experience. Ed. Cit.,* p. 53.

[116]See Huxley, Aldous. *The Perennial Philosophy. Ed. Cit.,* p. 290.

[117]Ibid., p. 165.

[118]Kapleau, Philip. "Zen Meditation." *The Nature of Human Consciousness,* Ed. Cit., p. 238.

[119]Ibid.

[120]Suzuki, Shunryu. *Zen Mind, Beginner's Mind.* Ed. Cit., p. 128.

[121]Wallace, Robert K. and Benson, Herbert. "The Physiology of Meditation." In *Altered States of Consciousness. Ed. Cit.,* p. 131.

[122]See Horton. (note 75)

[123]See Huxley, Aldous. *The Perennial Philosophy,* p. 213.

[124]Eliade, Mircea. *Myths, Dreams, and Mysteries.* New York: Harper and Row, 1960, p. 98.

[125]Mendel, Gerard. "Theory of Power." Trans. Diamanti, Joyce. *The Psychoanalytic Study of Society,* New York: International Universities Press, 1975, Vol. VI, pp. 235–318.

[126]Reich, Wilhelm. *The Mass Psychology of Fascism.* Trans. Theodore P. Wolfe. New York: Orgone Institute Press, 1946, p. 13.

[127]Gesell, Silvio. *The Natural Economic Order* (1916). London: Peter Owen Ltd., 1958, p. 32.

[128]Ibid., p. 266.

[129]See Horton, Paul C. "The Mystical Experience." *The Journal of the American Psychoanalytic Association,* Vol. XXII, 1974, pp. 372–379.

[130]Winnicott, D. W. *The Maturational Processes and the Facilitating Environment.* New York: International Universities Press, 1965, pp. 110–114, 180–181. See also Winnicott's essay, "The Location of Cultural Experience." *International Journal of Psychoanalysis,* Vol. XLVIII, 1966, pp. 368–372.

[131]I am quoting Vivian Fromberg's report of Phyllis Greenacre's paper, "The Transitional Object and the Fetish: Special Reference to the Role of Illusion." *The Psychoanalytic Quarterly,* XL, 1971, pp. 384–385.

[132]Roheim, Geza. *Magic and Schizophrenia.* Bloomington: Indiana University Press, 1955, p. 109.

[133]*The Upanishads.* Trans. Mascaro, Juan. London: Penguin Books, Ltd., 1965, p. 50.

[134]See Brown, Norman O. *Life Against Death.* New York: Vintage Books, 1959, p. 246.

[135]Desmonde, William H. "On the Anal Origin of Money," In *The Psychoanalysis of Money.* Ed. Borneman, Ernest. New York: Urizen Books, 1976, p. 125.

[136]Ibid., p. 126.

[137]Ibid., pp. 129–130.

[138]Roheim, Geza. "Primal Forms and the Origin of Property." In Borneman, Op. Cit., p. 153.

[139]Ibid., p. 154.

[140]Ibid., p. 163.

[141]Posinsky, S. H. "Yurok Shell Money and 'Pains.' " In Borneman, *Op. Cit.,* pp. 188–189.

[142]Ibid., p. 189.

[143]Ibid., p. 190.

[144]Ibid., p. 195.

[145]Reich, Wilhelm. *Character–Analysis*. New York: Orgone Institute Press, 1949, pp. 90–91.

[146]Roheim, Geza. *Psychoanalysis and Anthropology*. New York: International Universities Press, 1969, pp. 264–265.

[147]Ibid., pp. 181–182.

[148]Ibid., p. 228.

[149]Ibid., p. 237.

[150]Ibid., p. 268.

[151]Ibid.

[152]Ibid., p. 275.

[153]Ibid.

[154]Bergler, Edmund. *Money and Emotional Conflicts*. New York: International Universities Press, 1959, p. 6.

[155]Ibid.

[156]Ibid., p. 19.

[157]Hubert, Henrique, and Mauss, Marcel. *Sacrifice: Its Nature and Function* (1898). Chicago: University of Chicago Press, 1964, p. 9. Subsequent references will appear in the text with the abbreviation *S* followed by page number.

[158]For a more recent discussion of sacrifical behavior see Bakan, David. *Disease, Pain, and Sacrifice*. Chicago: University of Chicago Press, 1968.

[159]Stanislav Grof is particularly convincing on this point. See his *Realms of the Human Unconscious*. New York: E. P. Dutton and Co., 1976, Chaps. 3 and 4.

[160]Schafer, Roy. *Aspects of Internalization*. New York: International Universities Press, 1968, Chap. 8.

[161]Einzig, Paul. *Primitive Money*. Oxford, England: Pergamon Press, 1951, pp. 72, 75. Subsequent references will appear in the text with the abbreviated form *PM* followed by page number.

[162]Weber, Max. *The Protestant Ethic and the Spirit of Capitalism*. Trans. Parsons, Talcott. New York: Charles Scribners, 1958, p. 53.

[163]Laum, Bernhard. *Heiliges Geld*. Tübingen: J. C. B. Mohr, 1924. See especially pp. 322, 373–374, 384.

[164]Huxley, Aldous. *The Perennial Philosophy*. New York: Harper and Row, 1970, p. 134.

[165]Reich, Wilhelm. *The Function of Orgasm*. Trans. Theodore P. Wolfe. New York: Bantam Books, 1967, Chap. 6.

[166]Lenin, V. I. "Three Sources and Three Component Parts of Marxism." In *Karl Marx and Frederick Engels: Selected Works*. New York: International Publishers, 1968, p. 25.

[167]Marx, Karl. *Kapital*. Ed. Engels, Frederick. Chicago: Charles H. Kerr, 1906,

Vol. 3, p. 106. Subsequent references will appear in the text with the abbreviation *Kap* followed by volume and page number.

[168]Marx, Karl. "Reflections of a Youth." In *The Writings of the Young Marx*. Trans. Easton, Loyd, D. and Guddatt, Kurt H. New York: Doubleday and Co., 1967, p. 39.

[169]Lax, Ruth F. "The Role of Internalization in the Development of Certain Aspects of Female Masochism." *International Journal of Psychoanalysis*, Vol. LVIII, 1977, p. 293.

[170]Ibid., p. 289.

[171]Smith, Sydney. "The Golden Fantasy: A Regressive Reaction to Separation Anxiety." *International Journal of Psychoanalysis*, Vol. LVIII, 1977, p. 313.

[172]Birnbaum, Norman. "Beyond Marx in the Sociology of Religion?" In *Beyond the Classics? Essays in the Scientific Study of Religion*. Ed. Glock, Charles Y. and Hammond, Philip E. New York: Harper and Row, 1973, p. 19.

[173]See Hartocollis, Peter. "Origins of Time." *The Psychoanalytic Quarterly*, Vol. XLIII, 1974, p. 248.

[174]See Dylan Thomas' poem, *The Force That Through the Green Fuse Drives the Flower*.

[175]Marx, Karl. *Grundrisse: Foundations of the Critique of Political Economy*. Trans. Martin Nicolaus. London: Penguin Books, 1973, p. 202.

[176]Marx, Karl. "Money and Alienated Man." In *The Writings of the Young Marx*, Ed. Cit. p. 266.

[177]Marx, Karl. Ibid.

[178]Marx, Karl. "Feuerbachian Criticism of Hegel." In *The Writings of the Young Marx*, p. 281.

[179]Marx, Karl. "Economic and Philosophic Manuscripts." In *The Writings of the Young Marx*, p. 295.

[180]Ibid., pp. 289–290.

[181]Ibid., p. 291.

[182]See Grof, p. 76.

[183]Schafer, Chap. 8.

[184]Weber, Max. *The Protestant Ethic and the Spirit of Capitalism*. Ed. cit.

[185]Marx, Karl. "An Exchange of Letters." In *The Writings of the Young Marx*, p. 214.

[186]Marx, Karl. "The Centralization Question." In *The Writings of the Young Marx*, p. 135.

[187]Ibid.

[188]Ibid.

[189]Marx, Karl. "Critique of Hegel's Philosophy of Law." In *The Writings of the Young Marx*, p. 251.

[190]Idem. "Economic and Philosophic Manuscripts," p. 305.

[191]Martin Buber discusses this issue, although from a very different perspective, in *Paths in Utopia*. Boston: Beacon Press, 1958, Chap. 8.

[192]Marx, Karl. "Critique of Hegel's Philosophy of Law." In *The Writings of the Young Marx*, p. 250.

[193]James, William. *The Varieties of Religious Experience*. New York: Mentor Books, 1958, p. 298.

[194]Marx, Karl. "Economic and Philosophic Manuscripts," In *The Writings of the Young Marx*, pp. 289–295.

[195]Galbraith, John. *The New Industrial State*. New York: Mentor Books, 1972, p. 25. Subsequent references will appear in the text with the abbreviation *NIS* followed by page number.

[196]Harrington, Michael. *Socialism*. New York: Bantam Books, 1974, p. 37.

[197]Pederson–Krag, Geraldine. "A Psychoanalytic Approach to Mass Production." *The Psychoanalytic Quarterly*, Vol. XXI, 1951, p. 445.

[198]Ibid.

[199]Ibid.

[200]Ibid., pp. 445–446.

[201]Ibid., p. 446.

[202]Ibid., p. 445.

[203]Freud, Sigmund. *Civilization and Its Discontents* (1930). Trans. Riviere, Joan. London: The Hogarth Press, 1975, pp. 55–56. Subsequent references will appear in the text with the abbreviated form *CD* followed by the page number.

[204]Lichtenstein, Heinz. "Identity and Sexuality." *Journal of the American Psychoanalytic Association*, Vol. IX (1961), pp. 179–260.

[205]See Freud, Sigmund. "Notes Upon a Case of Obsessional Neurosis" (1909). *Collected Papers*. Trans. Strachey, Alix and Strachey, James. New York: Basic Books, 1959, Vol. III, pp. 296–363. See also Faber, M. D. and Dilnot, A. F. "On a Line of Iago's." *The American Imago*, Vol. XXV (1968), pp. 86–90.

[206]We see here again the limitations of Reich's thought, which suggests that our civilization might become desirable were individuals to achieve a "liberation" of their "sexual response." Our discussion makes clear the dependency of that response on the "systems" of the mind, in particular, ordinary consciousness. Because Reich's analytical "methods" leave the individual within his symbolical awareness, they cannot bring about genuine, lasting amelioration. See *The Function of Orgasm*. Trans. Wolfe, Theodore P. New York: Bantam Books, 1967.

[207]La Barre, Weston. *The Ghost Dance*. New York: Doubleday and Co., 1970, p. 19.

[208]Swan, Jim. "Mater and Nannie: Freud's Two Mothers and the Discovery of the Oedipus Complex." *The American Imago*, Vol. XXXI (1974), p. 33.

[209]Spitz, Rene A. *The First Year of Life*. New York: International Universities Press, 1965, pp. 51–52, my emphasis.

[210]Becker, Ernest. *The Denial of Death*. New York: The Free Press, 1973, p. 132.

[211]Brown, Norman O. *Life Against Death*. New York: Vintage Books, 1959, p. 45. Subsequent references will appear in the text with the abbreviated form *LAD* followed by page number.

[212]I assume, of course, that the infant has reached the level of projective defense. In many instances of a borderline nature structural difficulties arise precisely because the infant fails to attain defensive "mechanisms." See Stolorow, Robert D. and Lachman, Frank K. "The Developmental Prestages of Defense." *The Psychoanalytic Quarterly*, Vol. XLVII (1978), pp. 73–102.

[213]See Schafer, Roy. *Aspects of Internalization*. New York: International University Press, 1968. Schafer's bibliography will serve as a guide to further reading.

[214]Kernberg, Otto. *Object Relations Theory and Clinical Psychanalysis*. New York: Jason Aaronson, 1976, p. 61.

[215]See Faber, M. D. "Analytic Prolegomena to the Study of Western Tragedy." *Hartford Studies in Literature*, Vol. V (1973), pp. 31–60.

[216]See Faber, M. D. " 'Oedipus Rex:' A Psychoanalytic Interpretation." *The Psychoanalytic Review*, Vol. LXII (1975), pp. 239–268.

[217]Brown, Norman O. *Love's Body*. New York: Vintage Books, 1966, p. 144. I go into greater detail on this book in note 219 below.

[218]Merleau–Ponty, M. *Phenomenology of Perception*. Trans. Smith, Colin. New York: Humanities Press, 1962, p. 291, my emphasis.

[219]Before passing on to Marcuse I shall offer a few remarks on *Love's Body* (see note 217 above), the book that appeared seven years after Brown's completion of his major work, *Life Against Death*. Although Brown is considerably more aware in *Love's Body* than he is in the earlier volume of the significance of "introjection" in the foundation of the self (pp. 143–145), and in the development of cultural "alienation" as rooted in the attitude toward "property" (p. 145), he relies almost entirely for his "inspiration" on the work of Melanie Klein. Although he talks of her "followers" (p. 143), they really are not present in the book with the exceptions of Heimann and Bion. As in *Life Against Death* the discussion, as a whole, is overwhelmingly centered on *Freud and his followers*. This explains, perhaps, why *Love's Body* is replete with theoretical presentations which do not jibe with the emphasis upon the early time, as it comes through the work of Klein. For example, the superego, as in Brown's earlier effort, is still fundamentally *paternal* (p. 144); there is no concentration on its maternal roots and, hence, on the relation of anxiety to guilt. Similarly, Brown's presentation of the psychodynamic issues that swirl around the existence of the state is predominantly patriarchal, echoing the writings of Freud, particularly *Moses and Monotheism* and *Totem and Taboo* (pp. 10–21). The psycho-

dynamics of familial organization are also presented from a Freudian perspective with the accent on the brothers, *male* sibling rivals, the "dreaded primal *father*—the "male horde" (pp. 9–10, 17, *et. passim*). It is as if Brown's failure to *explore* the Kleinean development, to trace it into and through the work of followers such as Spitz, Jacobson, Fairbairn, and Winnicott, prevents him from seeing the *extension* of early psychodynamic problems into corresponding spheres of cultural life. The *infant's* world is Kleinean in *Love's Body;* the *social* world is still largely Freudian, with, once again, the curious exception of "property." This theoretical mixture makes for a confusing view of the "human experience." Clearly then, those "pre–Oedipal" factors mentioned in *Life Against Death* are still not explored in *Love's Body* for their widest cultural and interpersonal significances. Most of all, Brown's later book consists presentationally of fragments, gems of Brown's mind which contain, each one, the kernel of what he takes to be a central idea in the understanding of human beings. *Love's Body,* for this reason, never achieves a coherent, consistent, explicitly articulated theoretical position. It is not supposed to, perhaps. This may explain its prophetic, biblical quality, a quality foreshadowed in the final pages of *Life Against Death*. Brown is inclined to continue here his discussion of "Dionysius," of the "mad god" who breaks down the "boundaries" that separate and alienate men from each other and from themselves (p. 161); yet, as in the previous volume, he has nothing concrete to offer us in the way of accomplishing the "breakdown." The following is a good example of the pathetic methodological approach of the book as a whole: "The unconscious to be made conscious; a secret disclosed; a veil to be rent, a seal to be broke open; the seal that Freud called repression. Not a gradual process, but a sudden breakthrough. A reversal of meaning; the symbolism suddenly understood. The key to the cipher; the sudden sight of the real Israel, the true bread, the real lamb" (p. 217). What thrilling words, but what are we to do in the way of actually fulfilling their "hope?" Brown is content to point out the promised land but not the actual, bodily methodological *way* to it. For all these reasons, *Love's Body* does not mark a significant development beyond *Life Against Death*. The best of Norman O. Brown, and that is very good indeed, can be found in the earlier work.

[220]Marcuse, Herbert. *Eros and Civilization*. New York: Vintage Books, 1955, pp. 22–23. Subsequent references will appear in the text with the abbreviated form *EC* followed by page number.

[221]As a glance at the dictionary will disclose there are at least two definitions of the term "Nirvana," one usually "regressive" and the other denoting the transcendence of ordinary consciousness. Fritjof Capra writes, "in the state of *Nirvana* the false notions of a separate self have for ever disappeared and the oneness of all life has become a constant sensation. *Nirvana* is the

equivalent of *Moksha* in Hindu philosophy and, being a state of conscious-
ness beyond all intellectual concepts, it defies further description. To reach
Nirvana is to attain awakening." See *The Tao of Physics*. London: The
Chaucer Press, 1975, p. 102.

[222]See Part Two of this book, particularly the information related to notes 61
through 63.

[223]See Amar, Andre. "A Psychoanalytic Study of Money." In the *Psychoanalysis
of Money*. Ed. Borneman, Ernest. New York: Urizen Books, 1976, pp.
277–291.

[224]As most "religious" phenomena evince transitional aims, the genuinely social
impulse is not to be discovered in the ordinary religious world either.
Weston La Barre makes plain the reactive nature of ordinary as opposed to
non–ordinary religion. As we usually conceive of it, religion comprises a
psychological response to crisis. For all its claims, it does not decathect the
ego. The social impulse is maximized in the truncation of the tie to the
internalized object. See La Barre's *The Ghost Dance, Op. cit.*

[225]Winnicott, D. W. "The Location of Cultural Experience." *International Journal of Psychoanalysis*, Vol. XLVIII (1966), p. 368.

[226]Ibid., pp. 369–371.

[227]Ibid., p. 371.

[228]See Richard E. Haymaker, *From Pampas to Hedgerows and Downs: A Study of
W. H. Hudson*. New York: Bookman Associates, 1964, p. 285.

[229]Huxley, Aldous. *The Doors of Perception*. London: Penguin Books, 1956, pp.
26, 38, my emphasis.

[230]See Prall, Robert C. "The Role of the Father in the Preoedipal Years." *Journal
of the American Psychoanalytic Association*, Vol. XXVI (1978), pp.
143–161.

[231]Swan, Jim. *Op. cit.*

[232]See Neumann, Erich. *The Great Mother*. New York: The Bollingen Foundation, 1963.

[233]See Section One of Part Four, above. See also note 204, above.

[234]Etchegoyen, Ricardo H. "Some Thoughts on Transference Perversion." *International Journal of Psychoanalysis*, Vol. LIX (1978), p. 45.

[235]See Part One of this volume; also Becker, Ernest. Chap. 7.

[236]Marcuse, Herbert. *One–Dimensional Man*. Boston: Beacon Press, 1969, p.
222. Subsequent citations will appear in the text with the abbreviated form
ODM followed by page number.

[237]See Schafer. Chap. 8.

[238]Edelman, Murray. *The Symbolical Uses of Politics*. Urbana: University of
Illinois Press, 1964, pp. 5–6.

[239]It is, of course, of genuine psychological significance that the view of the
universe traditionally associated with altered awareness should echo strik-

ingly the most crucial developments of modern physical theory. See Capra, Fritjof.

[240]Castelnuovo–Tedesco, Pietro. "Reminiscence and Internal Objects." *International Journal of Psychoanalysis,* Vol. LIX (1978), p. 24.

[241]Roheim, Geza. *Psychoanalysis and Anthropology.* New York: International Universities Press, 1969, p. 441.

[242]Huxley, Aldous. *The Perennial Philosophy.* New York: Harper and Row, 1944, p. 134.

[243]Leavy, Stanley A. "The Significance of Jaques Lacan." *The Psychoanalytic Quarterly,* Vol. XLVI (1977), p. 216.

[244]Hymes, Dell. *Foundations in Sociolinguistics.* Philadelphia: University of Pennsylvania Press, 1974, pp. 47, 52.

[245]Greenberg, Joseph H. *Language, Culture, and Communication.* Stanford: Stanford University Press, 1971, p. 91.

[246]In his *Essay on Liberation* (Boston: Beacon Press, 1969) Marcuse takes up the matter of consciousness as it bears on the problem of revolution. He suggests on page 37 that the "dissolution of ordinary and orderly perception," of "the ego shaped by the established society," may have a role to play in the developments of the future. "The revolution must be a revolution in perception." Such words strikingly support the thesis of this book. However, as Marcuse fails to analyze consciousness and perception in terms of their affective roots, in terms of their origins in early object relations, his suggestions fail to achieve full theoretical stature. They simply do not lead to a concrete methodology. In the last analysis, they are *passing* suggestions.

[247]See Piaget, Jean. *Structuralism.* New York: Harper and Row, 1970. See also Bertalanffy, Ludwig von. *General Systems Theory.* New York: George Braziller, 1968.

[248]Klein, G. S. *Perceptions, Motives, and Personality.* New York: Alfred A. Knopf, 1970, p. 248.

[249]Bateson, Gregory. *Steps to an Ecology of Mind.* New York: Ballantine Books, 1972, p. 445. Subsequent references will appear in the text with the abbreviated form *SEM* followed by page number.

[250]George Gaylord Simpson writes in *The Meaning of Evolution, New Haven:* Yale University Press, 1948, p. 329: "Man has the power to modify and within certain rather rigid limits to determine the direction of his own evolution. This power is increasing rapidly."

[251]See Seyle, Hans. *The Stress of Life.* New York: McGraw–Hill, 1956.

[252]The emphasis on alteration of awareness as a restriction of information with psychoanalytic import reflects a recent shift in psychoanalytic theory toward an information and systems approach. See Peterfreund, Emanuel. *Information, Systems, and Psychoanalysis.* New York: International Universities Press, 1971.

[253]Soleri, Paolo. *Matter Becoming Spirit: The Arcology of Paolo Soleri.* New York: The Anchor Press, 1973, p. 4. Subsequent references will appear in the text with the abbreviated form *A* followed by page number.

[254]Becker, Ernest. *The Denial of Death.* New York: The Free Press, 1973, p. xiv. Subsequent references will appear in the text with the abbreviated form *DD* followed by page number.

[255]Rheingold, Joseph C. *The Mother, Anxiety, and Death.* Boston: Little, Brown and Co., 1967, p. 19.

[256]Douglas, Mary. *Natural Symbols: Explorations in Cosmology.* London: Barrie and Rockcliff, 1970, p. 65.

[257]Ibid.

[258]Lichtenstein, Heinz. *The Malignant No.* Presented to the Western New York Branch of the American Psychoanalytic Association, Buffalo, March 1, 1967.

[259]Aronson, Gerald. "Defence and Deficit Models," *The International Journal of Psychoanalysis,* Vol. LVIII (1977), p. 15.

[260]Hubert, Henri and Mauss, Marcel. *Sacrifice: Its Nature and Function* (1898). Trans. Halls, W. D. Chicago: University of Chicago Press, 1964, p. 97.

INDEX

Separation anxiety, 48
Sexuality, transitional, 173
Shah, Indries, 94
Sibling rivalry, Becker on, 255
Sin
    alienation of, 123
    guilt as, 181–182
Slotkin, J. S., 94
Smith, Sydney, 135
Social advancement, Marx on, 228
Society, Becker and, 255
Soleri, Paolo, 249–252
Sperling, M., 53
Spitz, Rene A., 36, 53, 184
Stress, 19, 247–248
Sublimation, internalizaton and, 192
Sufis, the, 94
Sullivan, H. S., 53
Sunset and Evening Star
    (O'Casey), 57–58
Super-ego, the, 174, 175, 182–184
    guilt and, 179
Surrogate parental structures, 171
Suzuki, Shunryu, 88, 97
Swan, Jim, 183–184, 223
Symbol formation, 52–60, 62–67
Symbolic Use of Politics
    (Edelman), 232
Symbols, culture and, 62
Symonds, John Addington, 80

Taboos, money and, 117–118
Teresa, St., 266
Thanatos, 27
    Eros and, 185, 203, 204
Thomas, Dylan, 138
Time
    as duration, 86–87
    energy and, 69, 70, 71
    James on, 85, 86
    power and, 209–213

Transcendental meditation, 94–95
Transference
    Becker on, 263–264, 269
    Brown on, 193–195
Transformation, 129
    individual, Brown and, 251
Transitional object, mother-infant
    relationship and, 105
Transitional religion, 270
Transitional sexuality, 173
Traumatic anxiety, 48–76
    birth and, 48, 50–52, 57, 67–68
    causality and, 72–76
    childhood and, 52–60, 63, 68–72
    the conversion process and, 48–60
    Freud and, 48–49, 53
    infancy and, 52–60, 63
    sensuality and, 58–60
Trobriander tribe, 74–75

Unconscious, the, 40
    Freud and, 126
Unity of self, 121
Upanishads, 107

Varieties of Religious Experience,
    The (James), 95–96
Vital Lie, the, 258–261

Wallace, Robert K., 98
War, Freud on, 26
Weber, Max, 107, 116, 117, 150
Winnicott, D. W., 36, 64, 66,
    104–105, 217, 218

Yoga, 25, 81
Yuroks, the, 109–110

Zazen posture, 96
Zen Buddhism, 94, 97, 244